UNDERSTANDING SOCIAL PROBLEMS, POLICIES, AND PROGRAMS

SOCIAL PROBLEMS AND SOCIAL ISSUES
Leon Ginsberg, Editor

Understanding Social Problems, Policies, and Programs
by Leon Ginsberg

UNDERSTANDING SOCIAL PROBLEMS, POLICIES, AND PROGRAMS

by
Leon Ginsberg

UNIVERSITY OF SOUTH CAROLINA PRESS

Copyright © 1994 University of South Carolina
Published in Columbia, South Carolina, by the
University of South Carolina Press
Manufactured in the United States of America

Library of Congress Cataloging-in-Publication Data

Ginsberg, Leon H.
    Understanding social problems, policies, and programs / by Leon H.
Ginsberg.
       p. cm.
    Includes bibliographical references and index.
    ISBN 0-87249-998-7 (pbk. : alk. paper)
    1. Public welfare administration—United States. 2. United
States—Social policy. 3. Social problems—United States.
I. Title.
HV95.G518   1994
361.973—dc20   94-12556

CONTENTS

PREFACE

Among the human services professions social work is unique in the degree of its emphasis on social policy. Among the four traditional areas of the social work curriculum, social welfare policy and services, which this text shortens in name to "social policy," is unique because it is not shared with the curricula of related disciplines. Clinical services, which, in social work, fall under the curriculum area of social work practice, are central to several other professions such as counseling, clinical psychology, and school guidance. Human behavior and the social environment, a required area of study for social workers, is basically drawn from content developed by other disciplines such as biology, economics, psychology, and sociology. Social research, the final required area of social work study, is always a part of the curriculum for those who study in the social and behavioral sciences as well as other fields.

Although there are subdisciplines in some of the other human services fields which deal with social policies, in none of them is social policy content so central to the overall curriculum as it is in social work. Social work, which has a different sort of history than other fields that view their mission as that of helping people cope with or overcome personal or social problems, has historically focused on social policy.

The roots of social work are in social reform. References are made in ancient religious works to serving the needy and providing for the welfare of the aging, widows, the disabled, children, and other groups of people who cannot fully care for themselves. The provision of those services is a rudimentary form of social work. The religious injunctions requiring people to help the less fortunate are the earliest examples of social policies. The more formal, written history of the profession, which can be traced to early-seventeenth-century England, includes examples of the provision of assistance to the disadvantaged as well as the struggles of churches and governments to develop social policies that would achieve social welfare objectives without creating a dependent welfare class.

Although the current primary focus in educating social workers is on helping them learn how to serve communities, individuals, families, and groups, in a variety of circumstances and in a variety of ways social policy precedes any social work practice. For that matter, it may be argued that all human services, including education, mental health, health services, and crime prevention and control, are based upon societal decisions that

vii

such services are needed and worthy of financial support. Without such policies there is an absence of legal and social mechanisms for the services to be provided (a process that social work calls "sanction") and no financing for those services. Large numbers of clinical psychologists provide their services within socially sanctioned and supported agencies such as schools, mental hospitals and centers, and clinics. Most physicians earn substantial portions of their incomes from programs that result from social policy, such as Medicaid and Medicare, but also from employer-provided health insurance. Hospitals have comparable sources of income.

Before one can speak about educating or employing teachers, there must be social policies established that provide for the financing of public education and the preparation of students. Before social welfare services are provided, the potential providers must begin with the creation and implementation of social policies that allow such provisions.

The historical social reform nature of social work has long led to the recognition of the primacy of the development of policies. Not only are the professional social work organizations involved in the development and advocacy of such policies, the profession considers it an obligation of each practitioner to engage in social policy development and advocacy.

Throughout the history of organized social work the threads of social reform and policy development have been pervasive. For those viewing social work from the outside, however, the social policy orientation can be confusing. Nevertheless, it is of major importance because social work programs are involved with so many external analysts and controllers of their operations. Each agency—local, state, or federal, public or voluntary—is scrutinized and often governed by a board of directors, legislative committee, or executive branch structure that may have only a modest understanding of social workers and social programs. Similarly, viewing the profession from the opposite direction, new students of social work often wonder why they are exposed to social policy courses when their reasons for enrolling have to do with "helping people," not studying the intricacies of policies and programs.

This book is designed to help two divergent audiences—the board, committee, and executive branch leaders of social work and the students who aspire to membership in the social work profession—understand the social policy dimensions of the discipline. A third audience is, of course, teachers of social policy, who are likely to be those who communicate social policy concepts to leaders and students.

There are already several books designed for those with interests in social work's approaches to social policy in print, many of them quite

viii

good. Most could be used in tandem with this brief guide to the overall concepts of social policy. This book is designed to help students of social policy understand the array of social policy concepts, rather than specific elements of those policies. It can be used as a stand-alone text for a beginning social policy course, especially if it is supplemented with articles and reference books such as *The Encyclopedia of Social work* as well as *The Social Work Dictionary* and *Social Work Almanac,* all of which are published by the largest of the discipline's professional organizations, the National Association of Social Workers. This book, coupled with exploration of those references for detailed information on programs and policies, as well as the definitions, degrees, and levels of services, ought to help any student of the subject better understand social policy.

The original audience for these ideas consisted of doctoral students in the University of South Carolina College of Social Work. The doctoral program in the college is designed to prepare social work teachers for baccalaureate and master's programs. For years before I taught Theoretical Analysis of Social Policy, the one doctoral course on the subject, I had taught or supervised the teaching of social policy courses for bachelor of social work and master of social work (MSW) students in the United States, Colombia, and Mexico. I had also served on accreditation site visit teams to many schools in the United States and Canada; had been a member of the Commission on Accreditation of the Council on Social Work Education, which accredits social work programs; and had worked as a social policymaker and consultant in state and federal programs. Perhaps because of that extensive exposure and involvement in social policy theory from a number of directions, I realized that the task of educating social policy teachers, who might find themselves on faculties anywhere in the world, was more difficult than it seemed. That is because there is so little unanimity on what fundamental social policy content ought to be. Each course, each of the several texts, each of the thousands of social policy teachers, seemed to have their own approaches to or emphases of the subject matter. The accreditation guidelines are specific enough to help programs determine the content they must include in their teaching, yet they permit (as most educators would agree they should) wide latitude in the design and emphases of the courses.

Therefore, I found it necessary to help those potential social policy teachers understand the broad range of meanings given to social policy and the variety of approaches used in the field to teach the subject matter. If I focused on historical, descriptive, and social problems approaches to the subject, which are the emphases of the College of Social Work's introductory course, I would not well serve a student who might find employment as a faculty member in a program that emphasizes social policy analysis or the practice of social policy development and implementation. Or if I spent the semester teaching how to convey social policy ideas by tracing and coping with a specific social problem, as some instructors in some colleges and universities do, my students would be baffled when they were required to teach a didactic course that focused heavily on social program descriptions.

I resolved the problem by recognizing and categorizing the hundreds of social policy teaching examples to which I had been exposed. I thought that all of the social policy courses I had encountered were organized around one or a combination of several of the six components I had identified. The six components are: historical, social problems and social issues, public policy, descriptive, analytic, and policy practice. So the framework for my teaching rested on these six components, with lectures, readings, book reports, class presentations, and term papers all organized around them. The students, I thought, needed to understand all six, if the course was to be useful to them.

The course was taught first in 1987. I have now taught it seven times, and, so far as I can determine, the six components effectively encompass the current understandings of social policy, the books, and the courses I encounter in accreditation consultations and reviews. Several doctoral students have assumed positions as teachers of social policy. All we lacked was access in book form to the model of social policy curriculum which is the basis for the kind of course described.

This is that book. For the spring semester of 1993 the University of South Carolina granted me sabbatical leave to put my ideas into a more formal version than my notes and course syllabi. Although this book is not designed to parallel the many fine social policy texts already in print, it should help students and instructors better understand one or more of those texts. The content is also sufficiently complete to make it useful as a stand-alone text, especially for foundation level—baccalaureate or first-year MSW—courses on social welfare policy and services. With some additional material from classroom lectures, additional readings, research papers, or the use of key reference works, the book could serve as a worthwhile and complete introduction to the subject. It is designed to meet the accreditation requirements of the Commission on Accreditation for the content area and to provide students with sufficient foundation knowledge to understand advanced courses in social policy as well as the social policy underpinnings of other content areas. Readers of the book, whether they are students or board members or other kinds of supervisors of social work programs, should capture a fundamental understanding of the nature and various perceptions of social policy as they are presently taught in social work and social work education.

The book does not present any special ideological points of view about social policy. That is, it is not especially oriented to incremental, radical, conservative, or liberal ideologies—although social policy, by its nature, implies some belief that government ought to be involved in serving the needs of citizens. For example, how to solve the complex problem of financing health care, which was the most critical social policy issue facing the United States at the time this book was written, is not addressed. Instead, the book is designed to help readers identify and analyze the issues surrounding the development of such a complicated social policy.

The book also avoids specific religious orientations, which are important components for many of the social work education programs that are associated with religious denominations. Communicating the social policy components of those religious mandates is an important function for such programs, and this text does not interfere with the capacity of a program to add such orientations to the mix of information provided in social policy courses.

There are ideological differences among existing social policy texts as well as varying degrees of commitment to one or more of the orientations discussed here. Some texts are more historical than others, some are almost exclusively analytical, others focus on social issues and problems, and still others are largely descriptive. Most texts combine two or more of the components offered here, which is also true of most social policy courses. The only specific point of view advocated here is that there are several orientations for understanding and teaching about social policy. This book infers that all those orientations are legitimate and, in many cases, essential to a sound understanding of the subject matter. The book leaves the addition of ideology and specific values to the courses and instructors for whom it is intended. It should be noted here that the term "social policy" is often used in this volume as a shorthand designation for the total subject matter of this book—social problems, policies, and programs.

My thanks go to several of my MSW and Ph.D. students in social policy courses who helped me formulate the ideas that are presented here as well as to my colleagues at the University of South Carolina and my former colleagues at West Virginia University and the University of Oklahoma. I also learned a good deal about teaching social policy from the faculty and students of two universities in Colombia, South America, at the Escuela de Trabajo Social at Universidad Autonomo de Mexico, and at social work schools in Romania, where social work had been outlawed—as it had been in many Soviet Union nations, perhaps because of its inclusion of social policy—under the former regime and restored during the 1990s. The 1992 University of South Carolina doctoral students in social policy—Dorothy Callahan, Liz Cramer, Steve Hardin, Deborah Rice, and Jean Sullivan—were especially helpful when they learned I was working on this book. They contributed oral and written reports that were organized around these orientations. Some of their work is cited in the chapters to which their ideas made a contribution.

This book owes a special debt to David P. Fauri, Ph.D., Professor, School of Social Work, Virginia Commonwealth University, and Barbara J. Ettner, M.Ed. and doctoral candidate, School of Social Work, Virginia Commonwealth University, for their annotated bibliography of policy journals, which is found in the appendix.

Understanding Social Problems, Policies, and Programs

Chapter 1

SOCIAL POLICY IN SOCIAL WORK
AND THE OTHER HUMAN SERVICE PROFESSIONS

This book is about social policy, which is one of the required curriculum areas for people who study social work and other human services fields in colleges and universities. The other areas of study in the human services are usually professional practice, which defines what social workers and others in the human services do in their efforts to help people; human behavior and the social environment, which teaches about the ways in which families, individuals, groups, communities, and societies develop and behave; and research, which covers the methods that are used to better understand and evaluate human services and social welfare programs.

Social welfare is, of course, the total system of programs, services, and policies which provides for human well-being. Social security retirement benefits for older adults, medical care for people with disabilities, and protection against abuse or neglect for children are examples of social welfare, which some call "social services." Social work is the largest profession that works within the social welfare system. The creation of the social work profession a century ago, its growth over the years, and its occasional declines are all products of social policy. So are all the developments of the other human services professions such as gerontology, nursing, rehabilitation counseling, and other specialized disciplines that deal with the problems and needs of people. Policies are the source of all social welfare. Services only develop when there are social policies that create, finance, and provide for administering them. Therefore, all human services workers are educated, employed, and paid because of social policies. Without social policy there would be no programs of social welfare or social services, and there would be no workers to carry out those policies.

The curriculum areas described earlier—social work practice, social research, human behavior and the social environment, and social welfare policy and services—are all part of the education of the helping professions. Psychology, counseling, nursing, medicine, education, physical therapy, speech therapy, physical education, and virtually all of the other professions that help people overcome their personal, physical, or social

1

problems or needs include those areas in their curricula. Social work, however, is somewhat different because it requires more extensive education about social policy than some other human services fields. That is because social work has always believed that human problems are not simply problems of individual humans. Instead, social work believes that human problems can often best be solved through social policies. Conversely, social workers have found that many human problems result from the lack of social policies that could prevent those problems. In other cases, social workers believe, some social policies *cause* human problems. Increasingly, all of the human services fields are adopting that point of view and are finding, in the practice of their work, that attention to social policy is crucial to effectively resolving human problems.

HOW SOCIAL POLICY AFFECTS LIFE

The worst social policy and the starkest example of how influential social policies are is that associated with the socioeconomic system of slavery. Slavery was actually an American social policy, prior to the Civil War, which allowed some people to own other people. White slave owners could buy and sell black people. They could punish them in any way they wanted. They could have sexual intercourse with them and force them to bear children. They could kill them, if they chose to do so. They could keep them from learning to read or write. President Abraham Lincoln, during the Civil War, and Congress and the northern states, after the war, implemented some new social policies—freeing the slaves; making them citizens; guaranteeing all people, including former slaves, equal rights; and providing the former slaves the right to vote. Those new policies were contained in presidential proclamations, federal laws, and amendments to the Constitution. The treatment of some human beings as property and the changes of that treatment, redefining black people as American citizens, were both consequences of social policies.

Until 1920, when the Nineteenth Amendment to the U.S. Constitution was passed, most American women were not permitted to vote, a fact that is unthinkable in the 1990s. Both the denial of the vote to women and the extension of suffrage to them were social policies.

The Holocaust of World War II, in the 1930s and 1940s, when it was the official policy of the Nazi regimes in Germany and many other European nations to seize, relocate, and kill Jews, Gypsies, homosexuals, people with mental disabilities, and other groups, was a social policy.

2

So is the "ethnic cleansing" taking place in the former nation of Yugoslavia in the 1990s, in which many Muslims have been arrested, raped, and murdered.

Almost everything that affects people is a social policy. Social policies determine, in part at least, the ways we marry and divorce, the ways parents may treat their children, the ways we work, the rules under which we employ others in jobs, and our educations. Social policies define what is and is not a crime, how we receive medical care, and the kinds of help we receive when we are unemployed, disabled, or too old to work. Almost anything that influences our lives can be found in social policies.

SOCIAL WORK AND SOCIAL POLICY

Social work's counseling or casework services are somewhat similar to those we find in many of the other helping professions. Our understandings of the ways in which people behave are actually taken from other helping professions and social sciences. Our social research is often indistinguishable from that employed in other helping professions and the social and behavioral sciences. In fact, the methods we use were typically developed by and are now borrowed by social work from other fields, especially psychology and sociology. Our *Code of Ethics,* when it deals with the ways we treat clients, is, in most respects, similar to those of the other helping disciplines.

It is our extensive involvement with social policy that actually distinguishes social work as a profession. It is what makes it different from related approaches to helping people.

A Definition

Social policy textbooks define *social policy* in various ways, some (DiNitto 1992) emphasizing policies that are developed through government—public policies—and others extending the definition to include policies made by professional organizations such as the National Association of Social Workers and voluntary agencies such as United Way and family service societies. For us the best definition is taken from the *Social Work Dictionary* (2d ed.); according to this widely used and comprehensive source, *social policy* is:

> The activities and principles of a society that guide the way it intervenes in and regulates relationships between individuals, groups,

3

communities, and social institutions. These principles and activities are the result of the society's values and customs and largely determine the distribution of resources and level of well-being of its people. Thus, social policy includes plans and programs in education, health care, crime and corrections, economic security, and social welfare made by government, voluntary organizations, and the people in general. It also includes social perspectives that result in society's rewards and constraints. (Barker 1991, 220)

The examples of slavery and the Holocaust have to do with the well-being of people. The issue of suffrage deals with society's rewards and constraints. Rules about work and family life are concerned with the ways society regulates relations among people. Clearly, almost anything that has an impact on our lives is a product of one or a group of social policies.

Social Work Ethics and Social Policy

Social work's long-standing professional interest in social policy has been underscored in a number of ways, other than, most obviously, the ways it educates its new practitioners. Today social workers are obligated *to do something* about social policy. In the 1990 statement of its *Code of Ethics* the National Association of Social Workers says:

The Social Worker's Ethical Responsiblity to Society
Promoting the General Welfare—The social worker should promote the general welfare of society.

1. The social worker should act to prevent and eliminate discrimination against any person or group on the basis of race, color, sex, sexual orientation, age, religion, national origin, marital status, political belief, mental or physical handicap, or any other preference or personal characteristic, condition, or status.
2. The social worker should act to insure that all persons have access to the resources, services, and opportunities which they require.
3. The social worker should act to expand choice and opportunity for all persons, with special regard to the disadvantaged or oppressed groups and persons.

4

4. The social worker should promote conditions that encourage respect for the diversity of cultures which constitute American society.
5. The social worker should provide appropriate professional services in public emergencies.
6. The social worker should advocate changes in policy and legislation to improve social conditions and to promote social justice.
7. The social worker should encourage informed participation by the public in shaping social policies and institutions.
    (National Association of Social Workers [NASW] 1990, 9)

The statement makes it clear that social workers need to learn about social policies not only when they are students; we are also obligated to practice—to do something about—social policy throughout our careers.

Of course, social workers have different routes to being involved in social policies. Some of us are administrators or have other policy jobs in voluntary and government agencies and can propose policies, implement policies, or even develop and promulgate social policies that effect the well-being of people. Other social workers carry out their social policy mandates by involving themselves in social action organizations and political campaigns. Others contribute to social policy by writing and speaking to legislators and administrators in order to influence them to support policies to improve people's lives. Still others of us support social policies by being active in our professional organizations or by simply carrying out policies that make a difference in the lives of people.

No matter what our specific roles, social workers have always known that helping people involves much more than talking to clients or meeting with groups or even providing assistance and other services to those who need them. Helping people requires helpful policies. In the long run a social policy can make much more difference in the lives of those we serve than all of the counseling, economic, or protective services we might provide them. Social policies can change the bases of their lives, prevent future problems, and continue to help them cope with their problems, long after they might have encountered those problems or received the services or a human services agency or professional.

An agency may help a client find a job; a social policy may guarantee that person employment for as long as he or she can work. A human services worker may help a client find ways to pay medical bills; a social policy may guarantee the client medical care. An agency may provide a family with a Christmas basket, but a social policy may provide that family with enough money to support itself and buy its own holiday baskets in the future.

SOCIAL POLICY AND THE PRACTICE OF SOCIAL WORK

In addition to knowing about and working toward improvements in social policy as a professional, ethical obligation, social workers also *use* social policy in their professional work. At times social work students believe that practicing, or "doing," social work is, for most social workers, a process of talking to people about their personal or family problems. Others believe social work practice involves meeting with groups of clients and helping them solve one another's difficulties or helping a community identify and take steps to resolve its social needs. While these examples are clearly parts of the roles of most social workers, many also perform their duties by understanding, explaining, and applying social policies.

For example, parents who visit with a human services worker to help them cope with a troubled child need and receive casework or counseling services of some kind from that worker. The counseling is designed to help them cope with their feelings about the troubled child, develop some strategies for dealing with the child, or even obtain additional help such as group treatment, recreational involvement, or tutoring for the child. The worker, however, would also call upon a fund of knowledge about social policies that might assist the family. If, for example, the child has handicaps or limitations, he or she might be eligible for a program of financial assistance called Supplemental Security Income (SSI) or special health care through the Crippled Children's Program; or transportation to special education classes; or a court action that could "emancipate" a minor child, which in effect helps a child who cannot be kept under control at home to become a legal adult, despite his or her young age. In many cases the contribution of the worker is based upon knowing about and helping clients use social policies that provide necessary services.

Social programs are the real source of help for clients. In the example above the worker and the client would have never come together had it not been for a social policy that provided a program in which parents with such problems have access to human services workers who can help

6

them. It was social policy that made the whole interchange possible. Little happens in the human services unless there is social policy to authorize, sanction, and pay for it. So, as was suggested earlier, the practice of the human services professions is a product of social policy, and social policy is fundamental to everything else that goes on in human services work.

OTHER DISCIPLINES AND SOCIAL POLICY

None of what has been suggested so far means that social work is the only human services discipline that deals with social policy. All human services workers need to understand and use social policy, and all are, to an extent, products of and implementers of social policy. Professional ethics are also taught to students, sometimes with greater emphasis than social work devotes to the subject. In the other disciplines, however, there is usually less attention to and a less central role for social policy in educational programs. In some cases social policy is an elective subject rather than a required part of the curriculum, as it is in social work at both the baccalaureate (BSW) and master's (MSW) levels.

Some fields are even more emphatic about the importance of social policy. For example, students of political science, especially those who study in the related field of public administration, may be required to take a number of social policy courses. Some colleges and universities have whole programs, with undergraduate majors and graduate degrees, in policy or public policy, which, of course, include social policy. Political science and public administration are not, however, primarily human service fields, although many students of both often have careers in the human services. Therefore, social work, among the human services professions, is the field that most directly includes and emphasizes social policy in its curriculum.

THE COMPONENTS OF SOCIAL POLICY

Even with the knowledge that social policy is central to social work teaching and practice and even with the clear definition provided by Barker (1991), it is still true that social policy is often a confusing subject for some social workers. Chances are good that they had never heard of social policy before entering a social work major or an MSW program. It is a term not normally discussed in high school or in other

7

undergraduate courses. In fact, it is a term that is not usually heard in the normal course of conversations or even featured in newspapers and magazines. Social policy discussions, unless they are concrete and personal, are not what people pursue at home, at parties, or in classrooms. Many people may have an opinion, say, on the marital relations of the president and his wife, but few will have more than the broadest attitudes about presidential policies. Remarks such as "Get those bums off welfare," "Don't raise my taxes," or "We ought to bomb ____ off the earth" are often as close as we get to real policy discussions. Therefore, objective, well-informed analyses of policy issues, books and films about policy, and term paper assignments on social policies may be relatively new or uncommon experiences for students.

Even seasoned human services workers may not know very much or think very much about social policies. I recall a visit with a distinguished hospital social work director many years ago. He had recently interviewed a job applicant and asked what the applicant would like to emphasize if employed at the hospital. The applicant expressed a strong interest in policy. Policy, the applicant hoped, would be the emphasis of her professional career. The social work director told me: "Policy! We don't need policies! We have bookshelves full of policies, and more of them is the last thing we need!" Of course, the applicant was not proposing the writing of more policies. But the hospital social work director's understanding of the term was quite different than the applicant's.

Neither, however, was wrong. *Social policy* has many meanings, and, in the absence of background in the subject, it is a confusing term for many students and practitioners. It is even a confusing term for many social work professors, a group for whom this book was originally designed. Part of the reason for the confusion about the meaning of *social policy* is that the term actually means many things. Educators and authors in the social policy field define the subject in different ways. The textbooks in the social policy field are also quite varied and emphasize different aspects of the term.

As a way of describing the field of social policy and the various approaches taken to it, it is worthwhile to analyze and define these approaches and what they seek to emphasize. Several years of study of the field, review of the textbooks and articles that have been written about it, and consideration of the ways that numerous baccalaureate and graduate social work programs teach the subject suggest that there are six components of social policy as it is studied and taught in the field of social work. These components are the organizing themes of this book.

Sources of the Components

The components of social policy teaching and scholarship come from a number of different sources. Primary among them are the curriculum requirements of the social work accrediting bodies. Accreditation has long been a critical part of social work education, and, historically, social work education programs have aspired to offer degrees that were accredited. According to G. A. Lloyd (1987), formal social work education began at the end of the nineteenth century and has continued throughout the twentieth. In the 1930s professional standards were developed, and graduate social work education programs joined together in the American Association of Schools of Social Work (AASSW). For several reasons, the most important being that most people did not enter social work until they had finished their undergraduate studies, social work education was long considered a postgraduate field, despite the fact that undergraduate programs had been offered for many years and finally became eligible for accreditation some twenty years ago. There was even a competing organization to the American Association of Schools of Social Work, the National Association of Schools of Social Work (NASSW), which began in 1942. The conflict between the two organizations was over whether social work, at the graduate level, should be a one- or a two-year program, with the AASSW favoring two years and the NASSW one year. The conflict was resolved with the development of the Council on Social Work Education (CSWE) in 1952, which has continued since then to be the sole organization representing and accrediting social work education. It has accredited master's programs since it began, and in 1974 it began accrediting baccalaureate social work degrees, many of which had existed as long or longer than the master's programs (Lloyd 1987). There are close to fifty doctoral education programs in social work in the United States (Ginsberg 1992).

Throughout these procedures for setting standards for social work education, curriculum materials on social policy have always been required. They have been part of the necessary educational components since education for social work practice began. The ideas about social work curriculum were clarified and refined in 1959 in the thirteen-volume

9

Social Work Curriculum Study, which was led by Werner Boehm (1959) and involved many of the leading social work educators of the time. Based upon that study, the Council on Social Work Education promulgated, in 1962, a curriculum policy statement (Lloyd 1987). The statement has been updated every few years since then, most recently in 1992, when separate statements were provided for baccalaureate and master's education.

The curriculum statements on social policy have changed over the three decades since they began. In some statements, perhaps responding to the activism of the 1960s, it was expected that programs would prepare students to become active participants in social policy development. In later statements such commitments to action were dropped, but the learning content has remained similar. Students have been consistently required to learn about the history of social work, which often includes learning about some of the figures that have influenced its development, about the making of public policy and the political process, as well as how to analyze and evaluate social policies and programs.

The 1992 *Curriculum Policy Statement,* published by Council on Social Work Education (CSWE), has a variety of requirements for content on social policy. For example, in its statement about the purpose of master's social work education, the *Statement* says that graduates should be able to "analyze the impact of social policies on client systems, workers, and agencies and demonstrate skills for influencing policy formulation and change" (CSWE 1992, 5).

In its description of the foundation content (which is required for both baccalaureate and beginning master's programs) on Social Welfare Policy and Services, the *Statement* says:

> The foundation social welfare policy and services content must include the history, mission, and philosophy of the social work profession. Content must be presented about the history and current patterns of provision of social welfare services, the role of social policy in helping or deterring people in the maintenance or attainment of optimal health and well-being, and the effect of policy on social work practice. Students must be taught to analyze current social policy within the context of historical and contemporary factors that shape policy. Content must be presented about the political and organizational processes used to influence policy, the process of policy formulation, and the frameworks for analyzing social policies in light of the principles of social and economic justice. (CSWE 1992, 9)

10

Scholarship by social work writers and researchers as well as scholarship from other fields, such as public policy and political science, has also made a mark on social policy content. Several books, written by social workers, have been influential in defining the field of social policy and the knowledge that students are expected to acquire during their studies. Some of those scholars and researchers are oriented to understanding the history of the social work profession, others the systematic analysis of social programs and services, and still others have written about the practice of social policy, an orientation that has consistently involved large numbers of human services professionals, many of them social workers.

Religion has traditionally been an important source of social policy. The original mandates to help the needy and the ethical bases for providing social services are found in sacred books, such as the Bible, as well as in the oral traditions and holy documents and teachings of various religions.

Government, itself, has also been influential in defining the social policy information that social workers need. Legislation, government regulations, pronouncements of government officials, and the administration of public programs have all influenced what must be learned, especially in terms of teaching about public policy. During the presidential terms of Ronald Reagan and George Bush (Ginsberg 1987, 1990) and the leadership term of Prime Minister Margaret Thatcher of Great Britain, governments tried to change some of their approaches to social policy from the government providing services to encouraging the distribution of services through "nongovernmental organizations," which have traditionally been called private, or voluntary, agencies in the United States.

Because so many of the social services are voluntary, or private, the policy-making activities of nongovernmental organizations have a major impact on social policy. For example, the local United Ways are the largest fund-raising and allocating organizations in the voluntary social services sector. Their decisions about social services funds are significant, affecting social policy within their own communities. Similarly, social welfare planning councils, or community councils, which operate in many larger communities, have a similar impact on the policy-making process.

Social welfare agencies, themselves, define social policies, often in relation to public policies. When the federal and state governments, in the 1980s, changed the emphasis of their strategies to delivering many services through nongovernmental, voluntary agencies, these agencies

11

began following policies of seeking contracts with governments as a way of developing their services. Agency executive directors became, in many cases, "presidents," and a corporate-like management style permeated their organizations.

Individual social workers also make policy. D. Pierce (1984) describes a "personal social policy." In the course of their normal duties practicing social workers daily make social policies, whether they intend to do so or not. Everything from the most specific, such as the behavior required of children in a youth club affiliated with a YMCA or a Jewish Community Center, to decisions about whether or not to remove a child from the child's parents is a policy, and, although there may be broad policy guidelines covering such issues as well as supervisors who are available for consultation and guidance, many decisions are made by the worker on the spot. Over time these decisions, if they work, are repeated by the individual worker and often replicated by colleagues; thus, they become social policies. The practice of social work, in other words, creates social policy. And, as we will learn, it is the job of some social workers to actually *practice* social policy—to develop, write, and promulgate policies.

The Six Components of Social Policy

Systems theorists tell us that everything is made up of smaller and smaller building blocks, down to such tiny things as electrons, genes, and viruses. A social policy paradigm with ten thousand components would simply not provide a comfortable route for learning about the subject. I highlight six components of social policy; they are interrelated rather than mutually exclusive. That is, each contains some elements of all the others. Each, in turn, could easily be subdivided into smaller parts; another observer could assert, for example, that there are really four or eighteen to twenty-six key components of social policy. Nevertheless, after seven years of work defining the field of social policy, I find these six components are distinct and broad enough to provide an effective range of study, and teaching, as well as broad enough to offer students and teachers a useful model, or paradigm.

Historical. Social policy can be understood in terms of its historical roots and developments. As mentioned, all social work students are required to learn about the history of the organized profession. History is the branch of knowledge that records and/or analyzes past events.

12

Chapter 2 discusses the historical component of social policy, the early development of social welfare services and the modern era, from Social Security to the present.

Social Problems/Social Issues. Another way to study social policy is by studying social problems, or social issues, a subject that is well-developed in sociology and, to an extent, in other social sciences. As has already been suggested, social policy is viewed by many as a consequence of social problems. When society determines that a problem is large enough to be considered a problem for large numbers of people, it becomes a social problem. For example, the personal misfortune of having nowhere to live became the social problem of homelessness; the personal misfortune of having a poor or unsafe family life became the social problem of child neglect or maltreatment; and the personal lack of income or resources became the social problem of poverty. Chapter 3 examines the social problems/social issues component of social policy.

Public Policy. One of the most critical of the six components in this model is public policy. Chapters 4 and 5 deal with public policy in detail. The component includes all of the policy decisions made by public, or governmental, bodies such as legislatures and courts; executives such as governors or the president; executive branch agencies, such as state departments of social services or the U.S. Department of Health and Human Services; and independent agencies, which are not executive, legislative, or judicial bodies but do perform some of the same functions.

Descriptive. Part of learning about social policy is simply learning about the programs and services that constitute social welfare. Those programs and services are results of social policy. One classic way of discussing social policy is in the form of a triad: *problem, policy, provision.* In other words, many observers believe that social problems lead to the development of social policies, the ultimate outcomes of which are provisions of social services. Understanding the myriad provisions—mental health services, financial assistance, job training, day care, and everything else that social agencies and social workers provide—which arise from social policy is necessary for understanding social policy. And, of course, being able to help others means, among other things, knowing what services are available to people who face problems.

Analytical. Understanding social policy requires much more than simply knowing what those policies entail. To be an effective professional in the human services one must also know what those policies consist of—who is helped by them most and who is helped by them least, how they are financed, and what alternatives may exist. Chapter 6 covers the analytical approach, the subject of many social policy textbooks.

Policy Practice. Some social workers and other human services professionals practice social policy. That is, they promulgate social policies; write policies for agencies; translate statutes passed by legislative bodies into regulations that agencies and their employees implement; interpret and consult about policies for those who deliver services to clients; and draft legislation for state legislatures and the U.S. Congress. Chapter 9 explains the practice component of social policy.

CONCLUSION

This chapter has offered definitions of social policy and explained why social policy is central to human services professions. It has examined the ways social policy affects people's lives and pointed out its special place in the field of social work as well as its roles in some of the other human services professions. The chapter also introduces the six components of social policy that constitute the basic outline for this book and upon which the subsequent chapters are based.

DISCUSSION QUESTIONS

1. Describe some of the ways in which social policy affects the lives of all people. Provide examples from social services programs you have studied, from your employment in social welfare, or from your field placement or internship.
2. This chapter suggests that social policy is more central to the study and practice of social work than to the other human services professions. Do you agree? If so, explain why you agree or, if you disagree, explain that position.
3. Based upon your experience or other readings, do you agree with Barker's definition of social policy? If so, explain why you agree. If not, explain how you might want to change it.
4. Do you believe that social policy ought to have a greater or lesser role within the social work curriculum you have experienced? Explain your answer.

REFERENCES

Barker, R. (1991). *The social work dictionary,* 2d ed. Silver Spring, MD: NASW Press.

Boehm, W. M. (1959). *Social work curriculum study.* 13 vols. New York: Council on Social Work Education.

Council on Social Work Education (CSWE) (1992). *Curriculum policy statements for master's and bachelor's degree programs in social work.* Alexandria, VA: CSWE.

DiNitto, D. M. (1991). *Social welfare: Politics and public policy,* 3d ed. Englewood Cliffs, NJ: Prentice-Hall.

Ginsberg, L. (1987). Economic, political, and social context. In A. Minahan et al. (Eds.), *Encyclopedia of social work,* 18th ed., xxxiii–xli. Silver Spring, MD: NASW Press.

Ginsberg, L. (1990). Introduction. In L. Ginsberg et al. (Eds.), *Encyclopedia of social work,* 18th ed. 1990 supp., 1–11. Silver Spring, MD: NASW Press.

Ginsberg, L. (1992). *Social work almanac.* Washington, DC: NASW Press.

Lloyd, G. A. (1987). Social work education. In A. Minahan et al. (Eds.), *Encyclopedia of social work,* 18th ed., 695–705. Silver Spring, MD: NASW Press.

National Association of Social Workers (1990). *Code of ethics.* Silver Spring, MD: NASW Press.

Pierce, D. (1984). *Policy for the social work practitioner.* New York: Longman.

Chapter 2

THE HISTORICAL COMPONENT: MILESTONES IN SOCIAL POLICY

Although not as well known as other social institutions such as education and religion, social services have a long history. Historians who specialize in the study of social policy history note that as long as there have been civilizations there have also been social welfare services to help people deal with their needs or problems. The earliest forms provided mutual help; that is, when a family was in need, because, for example, its crops failed or because of illness or death, other families came to its assistance with food, shelter, and other resources. It is probably true that in modern society mutual help is still the most pervasive form of assistance. Often when parents are temporarily or permanently unable to care for children, neighbors and family members will pitch in to help. Families share food, pass around clothing, help one another with transportation, and make loans or provide cash assistance to those who cannot handle their own requirements.

Any study of social policy history will demonstrate that the roots of all current programs and services, such as those discussed in chapters 6 and 7 and elsewhere in this book, can be found in the earliest recorded history. There is nothing really new about most of our social policies. Whatever they are, many have probably been attempted or proposed earlier in some form.

This chapter is not intended to comprehensively cover the total history of social welfare services or social policy. Instead, its purpose is to highlight the fundamental facts about the history of social welfare and social policy and to demonstrate some of the ways in which current social policies, as well as proposed social policies, are rooted in the past. The goal is to help the reader place social policy in historical context—to learn about the sources of some of the fundamental programs and also how new programs might be better designed and administered with the knowledge available from earlier efforts.

Those who want to embark on a more serious study of social policy history or the histories of social welfare or social work should consult one of the many excellent social welfare histories, such as those by B. S. Jansson (1993), P. J. Day (1989), and J. Axinn and H. Levin

(1992). Each has a different emphasis, but each also outlines the fundamental concepts that are important for understanding how social policy has developed throughout history. Another excellent historical analysis of the treatment of poverty is M. B. Katz's *The Undeserving Poor* (1989).

PERSISTENT THEMES IN SOCIAL POLICY

Studying the history of social policy is a reliable way to confirm the fundamental and persistent themes of social policy, according to this book's point of view. These themes are:

1. Human societies have tended to provide those in need of help with resources that will help them physically survive.
2. Societies resist helping people more than they need to be helped in order to physically survive.
3. Those who receive society's help are expected to use no more help than they need.
4. Those who receive social help are ideally expected to contribute to the society if they are able to do so—through public service work or through training and rehabilitation activities that will reduce or eliminate their need for help.
5. In some way societies categorize those who seek aid, finding "worthy" and "unworthy" groups, although social workers and other human services professionals believe that this is a false dichotomy. The worthy are typically those who "cannot help themselves," and the unworthy are those for whom having unmet needs is considered to be "their own fault" (see Katz 1989).
6. Assistance benefits should never be as great as or greater than the income of the community or society's lowest-paid workers.
7. The primary responsibility for assistance ought to belong to oneself and one's own efforts. Secondarily, it may fall to family members or neighbors or, if those sources cannot provide help, to an organized charity, church, or other nongovernmental institution. Beyond these sources, responsibility lies with the government.

In these discussions of social work history, as well as those in subsequent chapters, it should be possible to see these fundamental principles at work. Chapter 6 focuses on economic social policy for those whose primary problem is a lack of money, food, housing, and other necessities. Chapter 7 focuses on the services designed to help people with other

17

kinds of needs such as those faced by maltreated children, the aging, and those with physical and mental disabilities.

The division of social programs into economic and noneconomic programs and services is relatively common in the modern social welfare field. In some situations separate agencies are responsible for the two kinds of help. Generally, there is different legislation covering the two kinds of help. The reality is, however, that many of those needing financial assistance and other concrete forms of help also face the kinds of problems addressed by personal, noneconomic social services, and vice versa. Although there is often a distinction made between financial assistance and personal social services, the problems that cause them to be needed are often interrelated.

Social Policy before Nations

Social policy predates the development of the nation-state. Before there were governments there were churches, communities, tribes, and feudal lords. Religious groups, in particular, have always provided some forms of social welfare; although they recognize different doctrines, all of them require their adherents to help the disadvantaged and have done so historically (Leiby 1987). Religious involvement in social welfare, which continues in the 1990s, has traditionally been central to the history of social welfare. Feudal lords, many of whom attributed their power to God, provided some forms of social assistance to those who were dependent upon them.

Day (1989) provides an excellent discussion of the ways in which social welfare developed in a variety of cultures and regions. She covers ancient as well as modern social welfare development and shows that China, Greece, and early Roman society, among others, developed social welfare policies. She also describes the Jewish and Christian contributions to such policies as well as later British programs, which are often emphasized in the study of social welfare history.

Among the early biblical injunctions to provide social assistance are those found in Deuteronomy 24:19–22. God orders his people to refrain from going over their fields, olive trees, and vineyards a second time after harvesting their produce because these second harvests should be given to aliens, orphans, and widows. He promises his blessings to those who follow the injunction. The order to help the disadvantaged is a reminder to the Jews that they were once slaves in Egypt and had been in need, then, themselves.

Religious groups have also governed other elements of family and community life, which have, in turn, affected the social welfare of people. Day (1989), for example, points out that Christianity, a religion that spread throughout the world, supported monogamy and viewed divorce negatively. That Christian social policy was important in securing and extending the well-being and rights of women, by providing a social context in which women would not bear the sole responsibility of caring for and raising children. The traditional Islamic law that men could have as many as four wives provided a clear structure to social relations at the family level in the face of an unbalanced population, in which there were more women than men.

The Elizabethan Poor Law of 1601

The most important of the laws governing social policy in all of history, especially after the rise of the nation-state, was the English Elizabethan Poor Law of 1601. That law, which was officially called an Act for the Relief of the Poor, is produced completely and in its original form in Axinn and Levin (1992) and contains or implies the seven themes listed previously.

According to Leiby, the 1601 Poor Law:

1. Defined the duty of the parish (which was the local government, comparable to today's counties) to provide relief to the poor.
2. Established overseers of the poor to relieve poverty. These were among the earliest social workers.
3. Gave the overseers the power to raise funds and use them in their poverty relief.
4. Affirmed that government relief was a last resort, after family and friends assisted the poor.
5. Defined helpless (or worthy) people, whose problems included illness, the feebleness of old age, being orphaned, and disability.
6. Established workhouses and other solutions, such as deporting to the colonies "sturdy beggars," often as indentured servants, who asked for help but who appeared capable of providing for themselves. (Leiby 1987)

According to Leiby (1987), the Statute of Charitable Trusts and Uses, which was also enacted in 1601, made possible and established the rules for the creation of charitable trusts and benefits by the wealthy or groups of people with the desire to be helpful and the resources to provide the help.

The Elizabethan Poor Law, compared to earlier statutes, represented humanitarian reforms. Day describes, for example, the punitive 1536 "Act for Punishment of Sturdy Vagabonds and Beggars," which outlawed begging and giving to beggars and penalized violators with "branding, enslavement, and execution" (1989, 112).

American and European social policy, today, contains many of these same programs, principles, and services. Although the programs and services have, of course, changed substantially, the basic concepts have had an amazing constancy.

Laws were passed in England to uphold the principles of that country's social policy; the Workhouse Test Act, for example, which forced the unemployed to work for any relief they received (Alexander 1987), was passed in 1697 by the English Parliament. There were some policies in England, and elsewhere, which have not persisted. For example, the Law of Settlement and Removal of 1662 prevented those who needed help from moving from parish to parish to find that help (Alexander 1987). That law and similar policies were designed to make certain that people received no more than they were entitled to receive by preventing them from collecting twice, in two different parishes. The law also helped maintain a labor pool in the parish so that employers could readily employ workers.

Although in our day assistance agencies try to follow careful procedures to prevent clients from collecting from more than one agency or receiving more than they are entitled to receive, aggressive efforts to prevent free movement from place to place have largely been abandoned. In fact, states are no longer permitted to impose residency requirements as conditions for receiving assistance.

Colonial Social Policy

Social policy in the American colonies was based, as might be expected, on the English laws, and during that time there was no central American government. Each colony passed and enforced its own laws. The first of the colonial poor laws was passed in Rhode Island in 1647 (Alexander 1987).

In the colonies as well as in England a variety of methods were used to provide assistance to those in need who could not otherwise benefit from mutual assistance. Orphaned or abandoned children, for example, were often "farmed out" to the lowest bidder—sent to families where they could work for a very low fee; the receiving family would charge the parish for providing them with basic necessities. That practice is something of a forerunner of our system of foster care for children, although foster children cannot be required to work. In the 1536 act, idle children could be taken from their parents and indentured (Day 1989). It is important to remember that these kinds of laws governing children were established before universal, compulsory education and, in fact, before children were viewed as special kinds of humans, with needs that were different than adults', an attitude that persisted until late in the last century. The creation of child labor laws, for example, was a relatively late social policy development in the United States and elsewhere.

Workhouses and poorhouses, which were used to provide lodging and food to those who could not live on their own, in return for productive work such as sewing military uniforms or farming surrounding property, were another form of social assistance during the colonial period.

An innovation that has continued to dominate public social assistance was the provision of "outdoor" relief—that is, giving assistance directly to the person, or family, in need, within his or her own home, rather than in an institution. Assistance was also provided in two general forms—cash and kind—which have continued for the centuries during which social policy has been recorded. Cash is simply money, which the person or family can use as they choose in meeting their needs. Kind is assistance in the form of goods or services such as housing, food, clothing, and medical care. Cash and kind remain the method of assistance in such diverse programs as financial aid, public housing, food stamps, and Medicaid, the medical welfare program of the United States.

CRISES

One of the understandings of social policy that arises from the study of history is that human success or need often results not from the good or evil nature of the persons in need but are, instead, a consequence of social, economic, and natural forces, which change human circumstances, sometimes in astounding ways. For example, the Bubonic Plague, or Black Death, in the fourteenth century in Europe caused extensive suffering and need among great populations and created a social policy crisis. Similarly, the end of feudalism there, with its dislocation of the serfs, who had long relied on their feudal lords for support and been tied to them, and the Protestant Reformation, which ended the employment and support of many Roman Catholic people, created the need for help on a broad scale. In colonial America, Indian massacres and smallpox epidemics, among others, also caused otherwise self-sufficient people to become needy. More current phenomena, such as the Great Depression of the 1930s, as well as other economic dislocations, wars, droughts, famines, and epidemics such as AIDS are examples of the ways in which forces far beyond the control of individuals and families cause individuals and families to experience need.

There is still dispute in social policy debates, however, about the degree of responsibility individuals or families and larger social forces have for handling social problems and needs. How a society thinks about that issue is a significant factor in how that society will cope with its citizens' needs and how it will develop social policy.

Local Responsibility

It is critical to understanding social policy history in the United States to be aware that services were originally local rather than national. Local responsibility for services was reasonable in a time when life was local, economies were largely agricultural, and before there were such national innovations as stock exchanges and commodity markets or even provisions for the interchange of funds among localities. Communication and transportation of all kinds—mail, roads, vehicles—were limited. Larger units of government had limited responsibilites and powers, and matters had to be settled on a local level. A major phenomenon in the development of American social policy is the passing of primary social policy responsibility from local governments to increasingly higher levels of government. In the second half of the twentieth century the federal government became the unit with the largest influence over American social policy.

The Role of Voluntary Efforts

In early America, according to B. S. Jansson (1993), there was a rapidly developed and strong tradition of private philanthropy, which preceded the American Revolution and continued after the nation was founded. He describes an early series of efforts to develop firefighting services, educational programs, and orphanages, sometimes with private funds and sometimes with partnerships between private donors and governments. Jansson (1993) emphasizes the importance of religious bodies in the development of American social welfare. Churches were among the few voluntary organizations that developed in early times. Protestant churches also incorporated ideas about the religious mandate to share one's blessings with the less fortunate.

Residential Approaches

Throughout the history of social welfare in America, however, there has been a belief that disadvantaged people should not be coddled—that they should be helped only minimally lest they become dependent upon charity. The workhouse concept, the major form of "indoor relief," was a popular way of dealing with the needy. According to Jansson (1993), the Virginia Colony's legislative body decided in 1688 that every county should have a workhouse. New York also created a number of these facilities in the early and middle eighteenth century. Throughout the early years of U.S. history workhouses dotted the landscape. In later years the same facilities became "county farms," "poor farms," and other kinds of institutions for the poor, elderly, or disabled, which were in some ways forerunners of our kind of residential services for the aged. J. W. Landon (1985) says that these kinds of facilities were the primary means of dealing with poverty in early America. They were overcrowded, and the living conditions were poor. Of course, in a society that believed poverty resulted from the individual's character flaws (Colby 1990), a punitive environment was a reasonable choice. Again, one of the significant developments throughout social welfare history has been the change from institutional care of the disadvantaged—including the poor, the disabled, the elderly, and children who could not live with their own families—to assistance to people in their own homes or to smaller, more homelike group facilities.

The Early Federal Role

Social assistance programs for the disadvantaged, as mentioned, began essentially as local services. The federal government, despite the clause in the preamble of the U.S. Constitution "to promote the general welfare," was not viewed as the level of government that ought to be

23

involved directly or even indirectly in helping individual citizens. The role of the federal government was historically limited to matters such as international relations, operating the money system and the national banks, and resolving disputes between states.

That principle was most dramatically clarified by a presidential veto dealing with congressional legislation to provide help to persons with mental illness. A reformer of services to that group, Dorothea Dix, traveled the nation seeking financial support for decent housing and treatment and for the construction of state asylums. She and her supporters persuaded Congress to provide public land for the "insane," which Congress did, in the amount of ten million acres. Their legislation added care for the blind and deaf to services for mentally ill individuals (Axinn and Levin 1992), yet President Franklin Pierce, one of the least known American presidents, vetoed the legislation in 1854. In his veto message he acknowledged the responsibility of citizens to discharge a high and holy duty of providing for those who "are subject to want and disuse of body or mind." He concluded, however, that providing such help was not the job of the federal government: "I can not find any authority in the Constitution for making the Federal Government the great almoner of public charity throughout the United States" (qtd. in Axinn and Levin 1992, 47).

Both before and after the Pierce veto of the land grants pursued by Dix, charitable services were the province of private charities and state and local governments, not the U.S. government.

War Veterans. Of course, there were federal programs for persons who were in need and who were clearly the responsibility of the federal government. After each war, beginning with the Revolutionary War, for example, financial assistance was provided to veterans and their widows and orphans (Axinn and Levin 1992).

Native Americans. In one of the least humane periods in American government the United States government also developed, and continues to develop, social policies regarding Native Americans, those who were on the continent before the European settlers. At the time the national government was created, and for many years thereafter, U.S. presidents, themselves white males, upheld the idea that white European Americans should control all of North America. When Native Americans resisted and defended their territories, the national government responded with legislation, armed action, raids, and murders (Day 1989); by the second half of the nineteenth century the Native American population had been severely reduced and those who remained were largely without power.

In the early nineteenth century, in 1824, the federal government established the Bureau of Indian Affairs, which was originally under the jurisdiction of the War Department but later moved to the Department of the Interior. The bureau has never been, specifically, a social welfare agency, but it has always carried out social policies regarding Indians. It is another example of the federal government's direct service relationships with some individuals. It was not until one hundred years after the establishment of the Bureau of Indian Affairs that Native Americans were made citizens of the United States, with passage of the Indian Citizenship Act in 1924 (Blanchard 1987).

The Civil War and Former Slaves.   Federal policies were necessary after the Civil War in order to deal with the large number of freed slaves from the southern states whose state governments had been defeated by the federal government and were, therefore, unlikely to be of assistance. The United States established the Freedmen's Bureau, which existed from 1865 to 1872, to assist the former slaves economically, although, according to J. Leiby (1987), the policy itself was better than the execution of the policy. The federal bureau was quickly dissolved, and care of the former slaves was made a function of the local authorities within a few years.

With the exceptions of war veterans, Native Americans, immigrants upon their arrival to the nation, and former slaves, the U.S. Government remained clear of direct helping relationships with individual citizens for most of its history, until the twentieth century. Social policy was the province of state and local governments and charities, which received their funds from contributions by private donors.

The Great Depression.   A worldwide economic crisis was the impetus for the development of new, national social policies and the greatest changes in the relationship of the U.S. government with its citizens. That crisis was the Great Depression, which began in 1929, under the presidency of Herbert Hoover, a Republican who was known for having organized a food relief program in Europe to help those who were unable to care for themselves at the end of World War I. There were several causes of the Great Depression, but the dramatic incident with which it began was the crash of the stock market. Its results were widespread unemployment, instant poverty for many who had been prospering, and very low prices but few who could purchase even low-priced goods (Jansson 1993). By the time all the effects of the Depression were known a large proportion of the American population was unable to provide for itself financially. It is difficult for middle- and upper-class Americans today to understand the atmosphere of that era, a time when many people suffered—or had close friends, neighbors, or relatives who suffered—from the crippling economic realities of the time.

Simply put, the effects of the Depression were so pervasive that human need became a common, no longer an isolated, experience. The poor could no longer be blamed for their poverty; there were simply too many poor. Even among the hardest-working, best-prepared people in the nation there were those who were unable to support themselves. Old means of providing assistance—such as charities, workhouses, and local relief programs financed primarily by donations—as well as the relative isolation of the federal government from its citizens, in terms of addressing social needs, became untenable. Nevertheless, President Hoover continued the policies of Pierce and agreed with the former president's ideology and interpretation of the Constitution on this matter—that social policy issues were the responsibility of local governments and private charities (Jansson 1993).

Local governments, which relied upon local taxes, were, in fact, finding it difficult to survive. Those who were required to pay the taxes had few or no funds with which to pay. Many local governments could not support police forces and certainly could not add thousands of impoverished citizens to their assistance rolls. Private charities, which relied upon funds from benefactors with sufficient means to make generous donations, could not sustain, in many cases, and certainly could not expand their services to incorporate large numbers of newly disadvantaged people. The benefactors were as likely to have experienced financial reversals and unemployment as those they once supported.

In short, the entire social and economic structure of the United States was near collapse. The old rules could no longer prevail because new circumstances made them irrelevant.

Franklin Delano Roosevelt

In 1932 Franklin Delano Roosevelt, FDR, of New York was elected president. He defeated Hoover under circumstances common to other elections, in which an incumbent is not returned to office. Essentially, when there are economic difficulties U.S. voters tend to defeat incumbent presidents, a situation that Jimmy Carter, in 1980, and George Bush, in 1992, found to be true.

Roosevelt was an exceptionally interesting president for those connected with the human services. He was, for example, the only president

26

who had a physical disability; he could not walk, as a consequence of polio, and used a wheelchair to get around. He was also the only president to be elected more than twice. Others, before FDR, had voluntarily limited themselves to two terms. After Roosevelt the Constitution was amended so that no president would be allowed to run for more than two terms. But Roosevelt was elected three more times after his initial election in 1932—in 1936, 1940, and 1944. He died in office in 1945.

But Franklin Roosevelt is remembered by social workers for more than those personal and political characteristics. He is best remembered for making major changes in the role and functions of the United States government.

The New Deal. Roosevelt called his legislative program the New Deal. Several of its elements were economic in emphasis and are, therefore, beyond the direct scope of this chapter. His major programs were directed toward the goals of restoring the U.S. economy, controlling the buying and selling of stocks and bonds, preventing future depressions, and providing the U.S. government with the authority to respond to economic crises such as the Great Depression. His main tools followed the teachings of the economist John Maynard Keynes, whose ideas about economic policy are discussed in chapter 5. Several of his programs, however, had major social welfare connotations.

The New Deal Social Welfare Programs. Primary examples of the ways in which the New Deal established social welfare programs that dealt directly with individual citizens as means for reducing individual or family economic need were two programs, the Works Progress Administration (WPA) and the Civilian Conservation Corps (CCC). These had been preceded by other efforts such as the Federal Emergency Relief Administration (FERA), which also helped create jobs as well as providing other forms of assistance for promoting economic recovery. The FERA was headed by Roosevelt's top assistant in his social programs, Harry Hopkins, who is widely regarded as one of the most important figures in the historical development of social work.

The WPA was created by Roosevelt's executive order in 1935 and continued until 1943. It eventually provided jobs for eight million people. It provided for the creation of work in many fields, such as construction of public buildings and roads, as well as providing employment for artists and scholars who, for example, painted murals in public buildings and conducted research on social issues (Axinn and Levin 1992). WPA workers received compensation that was greater than they would have received under relief programs. The WPA is the forerunner of many other work

27

programs that followed it and which continue into the current era, such as the Manpower Development and Training Act of 1961, the Comprehensive Employment and Training Act (CETA) of 1973, the Job Training Partnership Act of 1982, and many others. The WPA marked the formal beginning of the federal government's interest and activity in job training, work experience, and employment for those who cannot obtain employment on their own (Jansson 1987).

Under the program called the Civilian Conservation Corps, which was enacted by Congress in 1933, young, unmarried men ages seventeen to twenty-three were employed and housed in national parks and forests to carry out conservation work. They were provided with food and lodging as well as education and were paid small salaries, which they could send to their families, if necessary. The program continued until 1941 (Alexander 1987).

The Social Security Act of 1935.   For human services workers, and perhaps for the domestic history of the United States, the most important of the New Deal innovations was the Social Security Act of 1935. It was and remains one of the most complex pieces of legislation ever passed in the nation. It established the fundamental social services policy of the United States and continues to govern most of the human services provided to the nation's citizens. Although it preserved a major role for the states in the operation of some of its provisions, it established for all time that the U.S. government could have a direct, helping relationship with its citizens. B. S. Jansson (1993) calls the Social Security Act the Magna Carta of American welfare. He has good reason for his conclusion. The act touches or has the potential to touch the lives of all Americans.

Over the thirty-five years I have spent as an active social worker I came to know some of the original architects of the Social Security Act—persons such as Eveline Burns, Wilbur Cohen, and Ernest Witte. The days when the act was developed must have been exhilarating for those then-young social reformers. Their goal, and Roosevelt's, was not only to provide aid for people who were suffering from economic disadvantage but to prevent permanently such disadvantage in the future. The basic idea was to finance a system for the permanent security of the American people through an insurance program in which employed people would make contributions while they worked and receive benefits when they no longer worked. It was designed as a massive, low-cost insurance program that could end once and for all poverty. It also provided for those who were in temporary economic need and had provisions for the

28

survivors of employed people who were covered by Social Security.

The Social Security Act is periodically changed by amendments, some of which are far-reaching and others relatively technical. The fundamental nature of the act has remained constant, however, for the almost sixty years that it has been part of American social policy.

Provisions of the Social Security Act. Financing of most of the Social Security Act insurance provisions comes from contributions paid by employees and their employers or by self-employed people alone. Virtually all working people in the United States are now covered, although there were many exceptions when the original act was passed. The amounts of the contributions have changed often over the years to reflect inflation and increased benefits.

The major provisions of the Social Security Act are:

1. Old-Age and Survivors' Insurance. This program provides for pensions for employees when they retire and payments to their surviving spouses and minor children, should they die.
2. Disability Insurance. This program was added in the 1956 amendments and provides for payments to workers who are physically or mentally disabled and to eligible family members.
3. Medicare. This program was added in 1965 and provides health care insurance for people sixty-five years old and older as well as some younger people who have specific disabling health problems. A related component is Medicaid, another state and federally financed program that provides medical coverage for low-income people who are not old enough for Medicare as well as for Medicare recipients whose medical needs are more costly that Medicare provides (Ozawa 1987; Ginsberg 1983).
4. Unemployment Compensation. This program provides cash benefits to people who have lost their jobs and is paid for by a tax on employers. It provides benefits for up to six months in amounts that vary from state to state. In times of great economic problems such as recessions, the period of time is often extended (Day 1989).
5. Aid to Families with Dependent Children (AFDC). This program was developed for families whose work histories and contributions would not yield sufficiently large social insurance payments with which to meet their needs. It was, and continues to be, a partnership program of the state and federal governments. It is paid for through general tax revenues. The payment levels, eligible

family sizes, and other details are determined by the individual states under federal guidelines.

6. Supplemental Security Income (SSI). This is a program that, like AFDC, is financed by general tax revenues, although in this case they are all federal funds, for low-income, elderly, physically or mentally disabled, or blind people.

   Originally, the programs and services of SSI, which was created in 1972, were three federal-state programs for those now served by SSI, which were similar to the AFDC program. SSI placed the administration of the programs with the federal government, through the Social Security Administration, which also administers the social insurance programs and sets national payment standards (Ginsberg 1983).

7. The Maternal and Child Welfare Act was also part of Social Security. It established child welfare services in the states for dependent, neglected, homeless, and potentially delinquent children as well as vocational training and rehabilitation programs for physically and otherwise disabled children. It also provided funds for programs to promote the health of children and mothers through prenatal and birthing services for mothers (Day 1989).

Clearly, the Social Security Act became the primary source of social and economic assistance in the United States. It provides extensive services that go beyond those enumerated here, although for the most part it follows the persistent themes of social policy described in this chapter.

For example, those who receive services such as retirement benefits and Medicare are people who in all but a small number of cases contributed financially to the Social Security Trust Fund, in which the payments are deposited. The beneficiaries are expected to help themselves through a mechanism established by government. The principle that those who receive assistance should generally be victims of forces that they cannot control is demonstrated by numerous provisions of many of the programs described here. For example, recipients of unemployment insurance must have been employed and must have lost their jobs through no fault of their own; those who voluntarily quit their jobs or who are fired are ineligible. Similarly, children are not expected to meet their own needs, and, therefore, the Aid to Families with Dependent Children and the Maternal and Child Health Act provide for the young. The SSI services and the aid programs that were its forerunners are for older adults and persons with disabilities.

There are also features of the assistance provisions of the Social Security Act that require recipients to help themselves. The unemployed must be searching for work, for example, or must be involved in work training programs. More recent changes in the requirements of the AFDC program require that many recipients search for work or be involved in an education or training activity. And the programs generally pay less than the lowest-paying job, which is another of the themes of social policy which has been discussed.

Rediscovering and Treating Poverty and the Civil Rights Movement— the Kennedy and Johnson Presidencies

The most notable and active era for social policy development, after the New Deal, was in the 1960s, through programs and legislation introduced and supported by President John F. Kennedy and his successor, after he was assassinated, President Lyndon Johnson. President Kennedy called his program the New Frontier, and President Johnson called his the Great Society. The 1960s was a decade of major social ferment. Two separate but interrelated issues and phenomena marked the era.

Civil Rights. Perhaps most significant in the development of the civil rights movement of the 1960s were events that occurred in the 1950s. Among these were the Supreme Court decision in a case called *Brown v. Board of Education,* in 1954, which required the ending of the South's longstanding policies that separated African American and white schoolchildren, an example of the ways in which courts actually make social policy. Until that decision, states were permitted to have "separate but equal" educational facilities for pupils. The effect of the *Brown v. Board of Education* decision was to decree that separate schools could inherently not be equal schools. That decision was followed by many others requiring states to allow African Americans to enter formerly white-only colleges and universities and led to legislation guaranteeing such things as equal opportunity in employment and the end to discrimination in public places.

Another event of the 1950s that led to the civil rights changes of the 1960s was the Montgomery, Alabama, bus boycott in 1954 led by Reverend Martin Luther King, Jr., who was assassinated in 1968 and whose birthday is now honored by a national holiday in January. King's boycott and the many other protests, demonstrations, and vigils that followed it were a major part of the impetus for the civil rights executive orders and legislation that followed.

31

It is difficult to explain the impact of the civil rights movement of the 1960s to those who did not live through the times that preceded it, especially in the South. That is because the changes are largely the elimination of some acts rather than the development of new programs or structures. Until the 1960s public facilities such as hotels, restaurants, theaters, and buses maintained strictly separate accommodations for African Americans and whites. Public parks had separate water fountains and bathrooms, one marked White and another marked Colored. Likewise, buses posted statements that said the front was reserved for whites, and the back for African Americans, then commonly called "coloreds." Theaters had seats in the balcony for African Americans, main auditoriums were reserved for whites. In some places white and African American professionals were forbidden to hold meetings or have meals together, even in private facilities. White and African American athletes could not, of course, be on the same teams, and they were also forbidden from competing together in sporting events. Some major southern colleges and universities, which now have large numbers of African American athletes, had none, and their sports teams were furthermore forbidden from playing against teams that did. Housing was sold and rented in a discriminatory fashion. African Americans were not permitted to live in white neighborhoods, and African Americans and whites were not legally permitted to marry one another in many states.

African Americans protested, lobbied for legislation, sought relief in the courts, and, before the Kennedy-Johnson presidential era was over, had overturned virtually all of the legally sanctioned discriminatory practices that had been the pattern in the South and, in some ways, in the North as well, for all of the twentieth century.

Leaders such as Thurgood Marshall, who was the National Association for the Advancement of Colored People (NAACP) attorney who designed the legal battles that led to the court decisions and, ultimately, much of the legislation that reduced discrimination against African Americans, made major social changes for the American population. He was appointed to the U.S. Supreme Court by President Lyndon Johnson and remained a justice until 1991.

The civil rights movement led to federal laws guaranteeing African Americans the right to vote and ending discrimination in education and employment and in "public accommodations" such as restaurants, theaters, and transportation. Of course, federal laws could not deal with all of the individual issues associated with the discriminatory practices in the United States. Many state and local governments passed laws, how-

32

ever, which applied the civil rights requirements of the federal laws to their own governments.

Among the many changes that resulted from the civil rights movement have been the election of large numbers of African Americans to public office, often in places where they might previously have had difficulty voting; affirmative action policies that require employers with histories of discrimination to balance their work forces to include minority workers; and an increased influence of African Americans in the total fabric of American social and economic life.

Ultimately, the civil rights movement also led to changes in the treatment of other population groups including Latinos, Native Americans, gay men and lesbians, and people with disabilities.

The Antipoverty Movement. In 1962 Michael Harrington published his landmark book, *The Other America,* which influenced presidents Kennedy and Johnson, legislators, social scientists, and social workers. Harrington documented what Kennedy had discovered during his 1960 campaign for the presidency—that, although the United States was thought to be a prosperous nation that had eliminated poverty with the Social Security Act, there were still large numbers of Americans who did not share that wealth. Kennedy was particularly moved by the poverty he saw in West Virginia, a state that was pivotal in his winning the Democratic presidential nomination. Kennedy made an issue of poverty in his campaign, along with other reform issues.

Early in Kennedy's presidency he established the Peace Corps, a program that has continued into the 1990s and which enrolls Americans in a two-year period of service in nations that seek Peace Corps help, mainly for help with development projects. Kennedy was also instrumental in arranging for the distribution of surplus food, purchased by the federal government as a means of maintaining farm prices, to low-income people. He also helped to establish the Appalachian Regional Commission, which was designed to provide economic development, education, and other services to help that historically disadvantaged region overcome its poverty.

Other kinds of social policy changes were made in the 1960s, many of them in areas that have long been of concern to social workers. For example, states were required to employ more professionally educated social workers to help people overcome the basic causes of their poverty, rather than simply giving them assistance that, the Kennedy administration believed, would tend to perpetuate their dependence on government. Restrictive rules governing recipients of AFDC were liberalized so

33

that families could work and retain a larger part of their earnings. Food stamps were introduced as an alternative to distributing surplus foods. Causes and cures for juvenile delinquency were studied, and some programs were attempted.

Poverty in the United States was not viewed as an ethnic minority problem. In fact, Harrington (1962) and others have continually reminded the nation that most of the American poor are white. However, minorities of color such as African Americans, Latinos, and Native Americans are disproportionately poorer than white Americans. That is, the percentages of minority populations who are poor is much greater than the percentage of whites who are. Therefore, it was assumed that real discrimination could not be overcome so long as minorities were denied social and economic justice or opportunity, even if their legal rights were protected. It was a time of great social unrest among minorities, especially African Americans, whose neighborhoods were the scenes of riots in many large American cities during the 1960s.

It was also a time of mass social action of other kinds, such as the development of the National Welfare Rights Organization, which protested against financial aid programs they considered to be punitive and lobbied for reforms. In general, following the demands for civil rights in the 1960s, there was great social concern and action about poverty and minority rights.

In that context Kennedy outlined, and after he was assassinated Johnson worked with Congress to pass into law and implement, the Economic Opportunity Act of 1965, a comprehensive attack on poverty. The act established the Office of Economic Opportunity and put into place a variety of programs and services. Among them were: Head Start, a program for preschool children; the Job Corps, a residential and job training program comparable, in some ways, to the Civilian Conservation Corps; work-study programs for students; and community action programs, which provide funds to local communities to make it possible for them to work on problems they identify themselves. Many of these programs continue to operate. In addition, there were accelerated efforts to place the unemployed and the underemployed in jobs, to develop training programs, and to create new aid programs for colleges and public schools. The federal government created Volunteers in Service to America (VISTA), which functioned in impoverished areas of the United States in a manner similar to the Peace Corps overseas.

Many minorities were involved as participants in these programs and as staff members who helped operate them. While problems still remain, the combination of the civil rights reforms and the antipoverty efforts has made major changes in the socioeconomic status of minorities in the United States.

There were many other social policy changes associated with the Lyndon Johnson presidency, some of which were inspired by the Kennedy presidency. The Social Security Act was amended in 1965 to add Medicare for older adults and Medicaid for low-income families and individuals, two of the most costly and important social programs in American social policy.

From Nixon to Carter

From 1961 until 1981 social policy remained relatively constant. There were some additions to social services, including reforms in services to children. There were also some reductions in budgets and some efforts to reverse social policies that had been previously implemented. Although there were efforts at major social policy reform under presidents Nixon, who introduced a sweeping welfare reform program called the Family Assistance Plan, and Carter, who introduced a similar plan called the Better Jobs and Incomes Program, through the presidencies of Richard Nixon, Gerald Ford, and Jimmy Carter the nation did not substantially alter its social policies. Neither Nixon's nor Carter's plan was passed by Congress. Economic conditions that were less satisfactory than they had been in the 1960s made some reductions in social programs attractive to some government officials. So did the lengthy, divisive, and expensive Vietnam War.

One of the reasons that the Nixon and Carter reforms failed to gain congressional approval was because they were projected to cost more than the existing programs. (Another was the opposition of the National Welfare Rights Organization, which thought the reform plans were not as generous as they should be.) Under President Nixon the federal government created the Supplemental Security Insurance program.

The Reagan Years

In the 1980 presidential election Ronald Reagan, former governor of California, defeated the incumbent, Jimmy Carter. Reagan had campaigned for, and ultimately implemented, policies that reduced social programs. His basic position was to remove the federal government from

35

direct service relationships with citizens, which was the classic position of his political party, the Republican party. Throughout the Reagan presidency, from 1981 through 1988, and, to a lesser extent under his vice president and successor, President George Bush, social programs were viewed largely as inappropriate for the federal government. The enunciated social policy was that the best solution to human problems was a strong economy—in which jobs would be plentiful and lucrative and in which investments would be profitable (Ginsberg 1987, 1990). There were several reactions and consequences to that policy. For one, Congress insisted on minimizing the reductions in social programs proposed by the presidents and, on its own initiative, added to them. Congress even passed, and President Reagan signed into law, a welfare reform plan, the Family Support Act of 1988, which was somewhat similar to those proposed in the 1970s by presidents Nixon and Carter.

Although political leaders such as presidents Reagan and Bush might have preferred otherwise, the American commitment to social assistance programs has continued to be maintained and to grow since the major social policy developments of the New Deal. In 1992 the nation elected a new president, Bill Clinton. When he took office he undertook the establishment of youth services programs, health care reforms, and a number of other initiatives that resembled programs from John F. Kennedy's presidency. Among proponents of social policy and social provisions there was general enthusiasm for the new president.

CONCLUSION

The history of assistance programs for the socially and economically disadvantaged is lengthy. It can be traced to earliest times. That history shows that societies are generally unwilling to see their members go without adequate food, clothing, and shelter and that they typically take steps to prevent or otherwise address such problems.

Certain principles of assistance have long persisted among civilized societies. They provide that assistance ought to be adequate but not so generous that it discourages work; whenever possible, societies insist that those who receive help contribute something to the society, through work or training for work. The abiding social policy principles also suggest that societies divide their needy persons into those who appear to be able to help themselves and those who appear to be unable to do so.

DISCUSSION QUESTIONS

1. How fair is the concept that no one should receive assistance that is greater than the lowest-paid worker's earnings? Could family size or special conditions such as age or disability raise questions about the concept?

2. What are some of the primary similarities and differences between the social assistance programs of the New Deal and the programs of the Kennedy and Johnson presidencies?

3. Discuss the ways in which the civil rights movement and the movements for improved social programs were related.

4. Describe what you believe are the underlying differences in the concepts of social policy between Presidents Johnson and Reagan.

REFERENCES

Alexander, C. A. (1987). History of social work and social welfare: Significant dates. In A. Minahan et al. (Eds.), *Encyclopedia of social work,* 18th ed., 777–88. Silver Spring, MD: NASW Press.

Axinn, J., & Levin, H. (1992). *Social welfare: A history of the American response to need,* 3d ed. New York: Longman.

Blanchard, E. L. (1987). American Indians and Alaska Natives. In A. Minahan et al. (Eds.), *Encyclopedia of social work,* 18th ed., 142–50. Silver Spring, MD: NASW Press.

Brown v. Board of Education of Topeka, Kansas. (1954). 74 SC 686.

Colby, I. (1990). American social welfare: Miles to go before I sleep.... In D. Elliott, N. S. Mayadas, and T. D. Watts (Eds.), *The world of social welfare: Social welfare and services in an international context,* 13–34. Springfield, IL: Charles C. Thomas.

Day, P. J. (1989). *A new history of social welfare.* Englewood Cliffs, N.J.: Prentice-Hall.

Ginsberg, L. (1983). *The practice of social work in public welfare.* New York: Free Press.

Ginsberg, L. (1987). Economic, political and social context. In A. Minahan, et al. (Eds.), *Encyclopedia of social work,* 18th ed., xxxiii–xli. Silver Spring, MD: NASW Press.

Ginsberg, L. (1990). Introduction. In L. Ginsberg et al. (Eds.), *Supplement to the Encyclopedia of social work,* 18th ed., 1–11. Silver Spring, MD: NASW Press.

Ginsberg, L. (1992). *Social work almanac.* Washington, DC: NASW Press.

Harrington, M. (1962). *The other America.* New York: Macmillan.

Jansson, B. S. (1993). *The reluctant welfare state: A history of American social welfare policies,* 2d ed. Pacific Grove, CA: Brooks-Cole.

Jansson, D. S. (1987). Federal social legislation since 1961. In A. Minahan et al. (Eds.), *Encyclopedia of social work,* 18th ed., 593–600. Silver Spring, MD: NASW Press.

Katz, M. B. (1989). *The undeserving poor: From the war on poverty to the war on welfare.* New York: Pantheon.

Landon, J. W. (1985). *The development of social welfare.* New York: Human Sciences.

Leiby, J. (1987). History of social welfare. In A. Minahan et al. (Eds.), *Encyclopedia of social work,* 18th ed., 755–77. Silver Spring, MD: NASW Press.

Ozawa, M. (1987). Social security. In A. Minahan et al. (Eds.), *Encyclopedia of social work,* 18th ed., 644–54. Silver Spring, MD: NASW Press.

Chapter 3

THE SOCIAL PROBLEMS
AND SOCIAL ISSUES COMPONENT

Social problems are the targets of social policy. It is impossible to talk about social policy history, analysis, or provisions without referring to the social problems those policies are designed to address. Throughout this book social problems are identified as the sources of social policy and programs. Were it not for the problems, and the perception that those problems need to be resolved, there would be no interest in a society's developing these policies and programs.

Some of the scholarship and courses about social policy focus, in large measure, on social problems. In addition to social work courses on social welfare policy and services, courses on social problems are offered in many other fields, especially sociology. Like others of the components discussed in this book, the social problems field is, in some ways, a discipline unto itself, with its own specialized scholarship and literature.

This chapter covers the social problems component of social policy. It suggests some conceptualizations of problems and provides methods for distinguishing social problems from more isolated, personal problems. It also includes examples of current social problems as well as analyses of how they came to be identified as such.

WHAT IS A SOCIAL PROBLEM?

Although the term has been used frequently in this book, as if the author and the readers fully understood the term's meaning, there is actually a need to clarify just what is and what is not a social problem. Several authors have provided definitions of the term. R. W. Maris (1988, 6), a sociologist, says: "*Social problems* can be defined as general patterns of human behavior or social conditions that are perceived to be threats to society by significant numbers of the population, powerful groups, or charismatic individuals and that could be resolved or remedied." R. L. Barker (1991, 220) says that social problems involve "conditions between people leading to social responses that violate some people's values and norms and cause emotional or economic suffering."

It is noteworthy that Barker's definition includes social responses, which is another term for social policy, while Maris's definition does not. Barker is a social worker, whose 1991 *Dictionary of Social Work* was reviewed and, in some cases, modified by social workers before it was published, appears to take the position that a problem is not really a social problem until society decides to do something about it. Maris suggests that a problem may exist whether or not it is responded to. Maris agrees, however, that social problems ordinarily, at least potentially, have solutions. It would be difficult to say, for example, that earthquakes and other natural forces are social problems; they are not because they cannot be controlled or stopped. Aspects of the consequences of earthquakes, however, could be defined as social problems. Lack of preparedness to deal with earthquakes in earthquake-prone areas could be defined as a social problem. It meets Maris's and Barker's definitions, and there are possible solutions. Similarly, when people continue to be allowed to build residences along faults, this may also be defined as a social problem.

Among the most important theoreticians of social problems was the sociologist C. Wright Mills (1959), who helped make the distinction, implicit in both Maris's and Barker's definitions, between the private troubles of the individual and the social problems of the broader public and the society. Private troubles—those that impact relatively few people—may be tragic, yet they only constitute social problems when they affect large numbers and when society, as represented by government, sees the troubles as a threat to many people or to the whole society. Threats may be perceived to exist when the consequences of the problem are costly, when others fear they will be injured because of the problem, or when people believe that they might be victims of the problems. There are many humorous and ironic aphorisms that illustrate the differences between private troubles and social problems. One is: "How do you tell the difference between an economic recession and an economic depression?" The answer, which has been attributed to President Harry Truman (in England and Anderson 1992, 3-D4), is: "It's a recession when your neighbor loses his job; it's a depression when you lose your own."

When AIDS, or acquired immunodeficiency syndrome, the disease affecting an alarming number of human beings worldwide, appeared to be a condition that affected small numbers of gay men and intravenous drug users, it was thought of as a private trouble. When it became clear that AIDS affected a wide range of people, including heterosexuals, and that it was quickly spreading, governments and those they represent began to perceive it as a social problem.

40

There are varying reactions to social problems. What appears to be a solution to a problem to one group of observers is viewed as yet another problem to others. For example, some social workers will say that the major social problem in the United States is poverty, and they may cite the low levels of payments in the Aid to Families with Dependent Children program as yet a more specific related problem. Others may say the opposite—that AFDC payments are too large and that they encourage people to avoid work and to subsist on the public's support rather than through their own efforts.

For some a major social problem is the unwillingness of elected officials to use the death penalty for major crimes. For others the existence of the death penalty is the real social problem.

When President Bill Clinton, in 1993, proposed a social policy to deal with what he perceived as a problem—discrimination against gay men and lesbian women in the military—others said that the real problem was the possibility that the president would revise the discriminatory policies. As we will see, values affect perceptions of social problems. What does and does not constitute a social problem depends upon the values of the observer. Societies define issues as social problems when there is widespread concern about those problems among the citizenry. A classic community organization scholar, Murray G. Ross (1967), helped generations of social workers understand that communities only coalesced around problems or needs that they, themselves, have considered significant, not necessarily problems that external experts have identified as social problems. It is the shared belief that the problem represents a serious threat to a community or the larger society which provides people with the will to do something about it.

An interesting means for studying social problems is used by the Fordham Institute for Innovation in Social Policy. Among its efforts is the publication each year of its "Index of Social Health," which translates sixteen social problems into one figure, based upon progress or decline in the statistics governing those problems. The 1992 index, for example, was 41.9, compared to an index of 75.3 in 1970 (Miringoff 1992). The institute studies indicators such as infant mortality, poverty among the aging, unemployment, and child abuse, among others.

THE CAUSES OF SOCIAL PROBLEMS

What causes social problems? This is a persistent concern of human services workers and policy analysts, who theorize that they cannot solve or prevent social problems unless they understand their causes. Those who write about social problems have developed schemes for classifying and theorizing about their causes.

L. Cramer (1992) analyzed the work of J. G. Manis (1976), who wrote about four conceptualizations, or causes, of social problems and a fifth that synthesizes the others. They are:

Pathology—the understanding of social problems as the consequences of the personal inadequacies of those who are involved in the problem. Therefore, crime, drug abuse, pregnancy among unmarried adolescents, and other serious problems would be the result of the diseased behavior of those who are subject to the problem. This model suggests that the problems reside in the individuals and that their solution requires changes within the individuals.

Social disorganization—the idea that, when problems arise, it is because of a breakdown in the norms of the group, or society, in which they occur. The poverty and other social problems faced by ethnic minority group members in the United States come, this conceptualization asserts, from the breakdown of authority and social norms among the members of that group. Problems such as drug abuse, gang violence, and crime are viewed as results of the general weakening of the family as a source of guidance and support, as well as the decline of other social organziations and institutions.

The value-conflict concept—the concept that problems have to do with issues of right and wrong, essentially matters of belief and values. Should those who violate the law be punished or rehabilitated? Are "treatment" programs examples of "coddling" those who violate the law? Is abortion a form of murder, as some assert, or is it the logical and moral right of a woman to have control over her own body? Should schools focus primarily on vocational preparation, or should the emphasis be on understanding the arts, sciences, and humanities? Or, as we see being questioned more and more in various parts of the world, which religion, if any, represents the absolute Truth?

Deviance—this concept, somewhat comparable to pathology, reflects ideas about deviant behavior, that is, behavior that deviates from accepted social norms. Deviance is any social behavior that departs from that which is regarded as normal or socially acceptable in a society or a social context (Jary and Jary 1991).

In her research and analysis on the Manis approach Cramer said the pathology and deviance models, or paradigms, were difficult to distinguish. *The Social Work Dictionary* (Barker 1991, 169) defines *pathology* as "the study of the nature of physical or mental diseases, including causes, symptoms, effects on the subject, and the circumstances in which the disease occurs. The term is also used more broadly in referring to physical or behavioral deviations from that norm that can or do result in disease or dysfunction." The same source defines *deviance* as "the act of differing sharply from normal behavior or maintaining standards of conduct, norms, and values that are in marked contrast to accepted standards" (62).

Clearly, some social problems are the result of deviance from social norms; this is especially true of crime. Sometimes deviance is a consequence of pathology, yet, as Maris (1988) states, many social problems are not related to pathology or deviance. Age and ethnic discrimination, involuntary unemployment, low income, inadequate services for people with disabilities, and economically based homelessness are all examples of such problems.

PUBLIC OPINION

Public opinion is what synthesizes the four concepts described above and is what M. G. Ross (1967) described. A social problem is what the society, which means the majority of the people or the opinion leaders who can sway a majority, believes is a social problem. Society's beliefs, norms, and values determine what is and is not a social problem, and these are all based, in some way or another, on public opinion. The opinion leaders may be political figures, the media, or businesses, any of which can mobilize public opinion to define an issue as a social problem. Maris (1988) suggests in his definition that charismatic individuals may also influence the perception that an issue is a legitimate social problem. Television personalities, leading members of the clergy, and leaders of mass organizations may influence what society believes is a social problem.

Segregation of African Americans in the South, following slavery, was, by Manis's (1976) criteria, one of the most profound social problems in American history. It may have taken the protests of a few charismatic individuals such as Rosa Parks, who refused to take a seat in the back of a bus in Montgomery, Alabama, in 1956; Martin Luther King, Jr., who mobilized the movement that arose from Ms. Parks's refusal; and Malcolm X (Branch 1988) to solidify the discontent of African Americans and those whites who opposed segregation and make it a widely accepted social problem that required resolution.

43

The Self-Fulfilling Prophecy

A special form of public opinion is the "self-fulfilling prophecy," a phenomenon described by students of society, in which people expect something from another individual, or a group or a social phenomenon (Merton 1957), and, when large numbers of people believe something is true, it will become true because they believe it. Of course, the prophecy cannot apply to purely physical phenomena; public opinion does not cause floods. If, however, people believe that the economy is failing, they might take a variety of actions because of that belief, such as removing their money from banks, ceasing to make purchases, avoiding the expansion of their businesses, any of which weaken the economy and are potential causes of economic failure. Stock market crashes happen in the same way. If people believe the market is going to decline, they sell their stocks, converting them to cash, and, in doing so, they cause a market decline. Believing that the market will rise has comparable consequences: people buy stocks so they will earn profits, and they attempt to do so before the prices rise too much. Their purchases, which constitute competition for stocks, cause an increase in the market. The self-fulfilling prophecy, here represented as an economic phenomenon, is a major factor in all things social, including the identification of social problems.

TECHNICAL IDENTIFICATION OF SOCIAL PROBLEMS

Cramer describes another approach to social problem identification proposed by Manis (1976), which is called the knowledge-values paradigm. He suggests that there should be means for objectively identifying problems that could be scientifically determined to be detrimental to human well-being. The seriousness of a problem could also be assessed, Manis suggested, by applying several criteria to the problem:

1. Magnitude—amount or extent of the problem
2. Severity—level of actual harm caused by the problem
3. Primacy—level of the consequences.

(Manis 1976, 133)

R. W. Maris (1988, 7), in his definitions of social problems, agrees with some of these principles. He suggests, for example, that cancer is considered a social problem because of its magnitude, severity, and pri-

44

macy, in that cancer causes nearly a half-million deaths each year, while allergies, which are pervasive, cause only five to ten thousand deaths annually.

Values and, therefore, perceptions of social problems change over time. In the 1960s, President John F. Kennedy suggested that a great social problem was the lack of meat in the diets of low-income Americans. By the 1990s too much meat (because of the fat and cholesterol) in the American diet is considered a social problem. Lack of exercise is also currently perceived as a social problem, but it was not widely considered a social problem during the 1960s.

METHODS FOR STUDYING SOCIAL PROBLEMS

Maris (1988) also suggests a series of methods for studying social problems, believing that to do this requires the study of actual data. He proposes four methodological approaches, or sources (99):

1. Records, Documents, and Official Statistics (99)
2. Case Studies and Participation in Small Groups (101)
3. Surveys (102)
4. Experiments (104).

Human services workers use all of these methods for identifying and assessing social problems, especially those who work in the social policy practice area. One of the most popular and widely used means for doing so is the "needs assessment," an approach that may involve any one or a combination of Maris's approaches. By conducting such assessments, community planners, administrators, and many other kinds of human services workers determine the course of action they or their agencies may most wisely take.

PROMINENT SOCIAL PROBLEMS

If one were to categorize and rank the problems that human services workers deal with, they might be:

Economic disadvantage. The lack of sufficient income is the basis for most of the social policy expenditures and social programs in the United States. Social Security (or OASDI), food stamps, AFDC, child support enforcement, unemployment compensation, worker's compensation, public housing, school lunch programs, Head Start, and many others of the social provisions in this nation arise out of the economic problems of some people (in the case of means-tested programs) and the potential of economic disadvantage for others, in the case of some entitlements, especially those that are preventive in nature. Addressing the problems of economic disadvantage is also fairly straightforward—to provide people with resources they need and lack. Although many critics of such programs assert that it does no good to "throw money at the problem," many recipients of aid would disagree. Providing money is the initial step in solving economic problems, followed by longer-range solutions, such as employment or job training, for those who are able to use them.

Physical illness. Health problems are probably the second most serious social problem, although they, too, are often really problems of economic disadvantage. Treating illnesses is a technical, professional matter in the province of healing professionals such as practicing nurses and physicians. However, the social problem of physical illness relates to the delivery of and access to health care services and the financing of those services. Of course, some physical illnesses are also social problems because they are communicable and/or affect large numbers of people (such as cancer), reduce the labor force (as influenza periodically does), or cause early deaths, which often cause economic hardships within families. Many human service workers are engaged in providing assistance to people who are affected by ill health.

While this book was being written, there were extensive public discussions of the best means for controlling health care costs and providing access to health care for citizens. One of the proposals in early 1993 was to place controls on physician fees and also hold down the awards made in medical malpractice suits (Pear 1993). Many analysts believed these were two of the most significant factors in the increases of health care costs.

Mental Illness. Mental illnesses have some of the same dimensions as physical illnesses, in addition to threatening institutions or weakening the economic viability of the nation, as some special kinds of mental illness, such as alcohol or drug abuse, may do. Mental health programs are typically the largest employers of social work professionals.

Crime and delinquency. The social consequences of violence, theft, and other misbehavior are great. Social programs designed to deal with crime prevention, apprehension and treatment of offenders, and services in imprisonment, parole, and probation are among the most important tasks of human services workers.

46

Maltreatment. The abuse and neglect of the aging population and of children are among the most severe and pervasive social problems in the United States. Large numbers of social and other human services workers are engaged in dealing with that abuse and neglect.

Lack of services to special population groups. Special help for the aging, children, adolescents, and other disadvantaged groups is the focus of many human services workers. Help for developmentally disabled and physically handicapped people are among the major assignments of human services workers.

Lack of resources for programs. Human services workers deal with raising funds for the financing of social programs. The lack of such funds may be viewed as a social problem.

AN EXAMPLE OF THE EMERGENCE OF A SOCIAL PROBLEM

C. A. Rittenhouse (1991) studied a specific issue that had been identified as a private trouble but which is now perceived by many to be a social problem. The problem is known as PMS, premenstrual syndrome, which is relatively newly named but has a long history in folklore and conventional wisdom. PMS is the cause of what some observers believe is problematic behavior, based on the stress during the days immediately before menstruation that some women are believed to experience. L. Cramer (1992, 5–6) says that "one of the deep mythic themes about women's menstrual cycles is that women's cycles in some way affect women's ability to handle roles and responsibilities, particularly in the public sphere."

Some believe that the fundamental reason for denying women executive and other managerial roles in the economy is the perception that menstrual cycles make women's behavior unpredictable and erratic. Therefore, it is possible that women have been denied major roles in society because of the deep mythic belief that they are unsuited for such roles and that this is related to their menstrual cycles.

Rittenhouse (1991) suggests that PMS became a widely discussed social problem, rather than the private trouble of some women, because the mythology and cultural beliefs about the roles of menstrual cycles in women's behavior began to be questioned. Dramatic events also helped propel what had been considered a private trouble into a social problem— for example, trials of two women in England who, when tried for murder, used PMS as part of their defense (Cramer 1992).

Dramatic events, which are brought to public attention by the media, have been critical in a variety of cases in which so-called private troubles have become social problems. In December 1993, for example, an Illinois couple was charged with crimes such as neglect when they went to Mexico on vacation and left their children, aged nine and four, home alone. At nearly the same time, a ten-year-old child in New York was kidnapped and held in a tiny cell for several days, and in this case there were some indications of sexual abuse. These two cases received extensive coverage in the media and became popular subjects of public concern. Were they of sufficient concern to cause child maltreatment and neglect to receive greater attention as social problems, in the public mind? Perhaps not. It is likely that most of those who became aware of these cases—and many people did become aware of them—viewed them as fairly singular dramatic events or examples, not as part of a widespread pattern, which they probably are.

In England, in February 1993, a two-year-old child, James Bulger, was murdered by two ten-year-old children (Schmidt, Feb. 1993). The story made news all over the world, despite the fact that such incidents of children murdering other children occur frequently in many nations, including the United States. It is likely that the story was of special significance because of England's reputation for tranquility and its relatively small number of murders each year as well as because of the young age of the victim and the perpetrators.

The two ten-year-olds, whose identities were made known to the public after they were convicted, were Jon Venables and Robert Thompson. The abduction and murder took place in Liverpool, when Thompson and Venables found Bulger in a shopping mall, persuaded him to join them, and took him to a railroad track where they murdered him with rocks and beatings.

The two boys were found guilty of the murder by a jury, after they were eleven years old, and were given indeterminate sentences. They would first serve in secure children's institutions and, when they became legally old enough, would be transferred to secure juvenile facilities. It is also likely that they will serve time in adult prisons, since predictions are that they will stay incarcerated until they are at least young adults (Schmidt, Nov. 1993).

Child protective services workers are all able to describe cases of child sexual abuse, the restriction of children with chains and in locked rooms, as well as cases of children who are routinely left alone while their parents participate in recreation or work. Perhaps the cases that achieved such broad public recognition seemed different or striking because the families appeared to have middle-class socioeconomic status, and thus the means to avoid neglecting or harming children. The parents who left the two children alone did so to vacation alone in an attractive Mexican resort. (They later relinquished the children for adoption.) Had they been of lower socioeconomic status, say parents who left their children alone while they spent their time in a local tavern, it is doubtful that the case would have achieved such notoriety. Such events, which occur every day, may reach public attention if, while the parents or guardians are away, there is a fire or other catastrophe in which the children die. There are, however, sufficient numbers of child neglect cases—nearly 400,000 per year according to the National Center on Child Abuse and Neglect (1993)—to clearly make this a social problem, to be addressed through federal, state, and local social policies and programs.

HUMAN SERVICES WORKERS AND SOCIAL PROBLEMS

One of the roles of human services workers is to identify and bring to public attention the social problems that they encounter in their daily work. In many ways human services workers are the "early warning system" for social problems. Social workers and their counterparts are among the first to see the development of widespread, disabling problems. This has been true for a number of widely accepted and publicly addressed social problems.

For example, physicians and nurses were among the first to identify the problem of physical child abuse. They began seeing children in emergency situations who were described by their parents as accident victims. The medical personnel, in their diagnoses, began identifying patterns of broken bones and contusions which were shared among large numbers of families. Out of their observations they identified "the battered child syndrome," which was a forerunner of the more generally defined category of child physical abuse. Their observations helped child protective services workers and medical personnel learn to discern whether the child was the victim of an accident or actually a victim of abuse by his or her caretakers.

A more recent example is the elevation to the level of a social problem of a phenomenon called the "Munchaussen Syndrome by Proxy" (Mercer & Perdue 1993). That syndrome, which has been portrayed on television and in other popular media as well as in the professional literature, is

49

one in which a parent causes severe health problems for a child, often through strangling or suffocation, takes the child for emergency health care, and credits him- or herself with heroic steps that saved the child's life. The typical reason for the child's illness is temporary cessation of breathing. Some children who are victims of the syndrome die. Physicians and others began noticing that the same parents were bringing their children to emergency care on a regular basis with difficult-to-diagnose, dramatic, and life-threatening conditions. Hidden camera observations were used to show that parents were actually suffocating their children almost to the point of death. The issue—perhaps so small in its impact that it would be defined as the private trouble of children unfortunate enough to have parents who would harm them in that way—is increasingly being seen as a social problem, largely because the behavior is so deviant and the incidents so dramatic. The social problem was identified as such by human services workers.

Many other problems—such as the introduction of a new, dangerous, and illegal drug; the use of glues and other substances for sniffing, which can lead to brain damage and even death, by children; increases in long-term unemployment; and family homelessness—were identified by professionals, who noticed they were encountering repeated examples of them.

SOCIAL PROBLEMS VERSUS PRIVATE TROUBLES

In the human services identifying real social problems, rather than treating them as repeated examples of private troubles, is central. Social problems cannot realistically be solved case by case. Dealing with a widespread, pervasive social problem requires policies and programs. Appropriate policies and programs can resolve the difficulties faced by individuals and, perhaps more important, prevent the problems from affecting others in the future. Giving money to a person who requests it on the street will often be followed by another request from someone else. Job training and placement programs, financial assistance, and mental health treatment programs are potential solutions to problems that can have long-lasting and pervasive results.

THE PREVENTION POLICY EQUATION

It is axiomatic in the human services that policies, especially preventive policies, along with the programs or provisions that set those policies in motion, are the most efficient and least expensive means for dealing with human need. An example from the health and nutrition fields makes the point. Inadequate childhood nutrition can lead to delays or deficiencies in physical and mental development. Treating physical and mental deficiencies, which may be irreversible, can require hospitalization, institutionalization, and lifelong medical care, all of which may cost thousands of dollars per person per month. Yet a policy designed to prevent childhood nutrition deficiencies and programs such as food stamps or WIC (Women, Infants, and Children Program) provided during the early childhood years can, for a few hundred dollars, prevent the disabling conditions that later can only be addressed through expensive treatment.

Childhood immunizations against several severe illnesses are inexpensive. They are becoming even less expensive under the provisions of some new federal policies that will provide purchase of serums directly from manufacturers and under programs of universal immunization of all children. Compared to the cost of treating conditions such as polio and the complications of measles, the cost of preventing those conditions through immunization is miniscule.

Preventing severe child abuse or neglect, which could lead to expensive foster or institutional care for many years, is potentially much more cost-effective than identifying and dealing with cases of abuse or neglect after they occur. Prevention in that case can take many forms, including public education, financial assistance to low-income families, and mental health counseling. Early identification by schools or health services can pinpoint the families in which prevention efforts should be pursued.

Clearly, there is an element of efficiency associated with identifying and defining social problems. Doing so can lead to the development of policies and programs that may prevent the problems from spreading.

CONCLUSION

This chapter has presented the social problems component of understanding social policy. In order to understand social policy and the programs designed to implement policies one must also understand the phenomenon of social problems. It is from the identification of these problems that social policies are created.

Some of the ways in which private troubles or undiscovered phenomena become described as social problems are discussed in this chapter. The theories that classify social problems are also described, along with some of the means available for studying them. Public opinion and public

51

attitudes about social problems as forces in bringing them to public consciousness and concerted action are also described. In addition, the chapter outlines some of the areas of social problems that are currently crucial to human services professionals and programs. The responsibilities of human services workers to identify and deal with social problems are also covered.

Although the social problems component is only one part of the social policy process, it is a central component and one without which the others would have little reason for being realized. Problems—or, as some authors describe them, needs or discontents—are the source of the entire policy process.

DISCUSSION QUESTIONS

1. What do you consider your community's most severe social problem? In your opinion how did it come to be defined as a social, rather than a private, problem?
2. Social policies may play a role in preventing the spread of social problems. Describe a social policy, other than one of those discussed in this chapter, that may have prevented the spread or increase in magnitude of a social problem.
3. Many of those who write about social problems think there may be some ways to use scientific means to gauge problems and agree about what are, in fact, social problems. Discuss the truth or mistruth of that point of view. Why might those writers be correct or why might they be mistaken, based upon what you have learned about the identification of social problems in the United States?
4. This chapter has proposed that social problems arise from public opinion that the given problems are severe, that they represent need, and that they are sources of discontent. Do you agree with that position, or do you believe that there may be more technical, or positive, ways to identify social problems? If you agree, explain why you do; if you disagree, explain that point of view.

REFERENCES

Barker, R. L. (1991). *The social work dictionary,* 2d ed. Silver Spring, MD: NASW Press.

Branch, T. (1988). *Parting the waters: America in the King years, 1954–1963.* New York: Simon & Schuster.

Chicago Tribune. (1992, 29 Dec.) Parents who left kids arrested aboard plane. *Chicago Tribune, 364,* 1.

Cramer, L. (1992). Unpublished term paper on the social issues and social problems approach to social welfare policy and services. College of Social Work, University of South Carolina.

England, L. C., & Anderson, S. W. (1992). *The great American bathroom book.* Salt Lake City, UT: Compact Classics.

Jary, D., and Jary, J. (1991). *The HarperCollins dictionary of sociology.* New York: HarperCollins.

Manis, J. G. (1976). *Analyzing social problems.* New York: Praeger.

Maris, R. W. (1988). *Social problems.* Belmont, CA: Wadsworth.

Mercer, S. O., & Perdue, J. D. (1993, Jan.). Munchaussen syndrome by proxy: Social work's role. *Social Work, 38* (1), 74–81.

Merton, R. K. (1957). *Social theory and social structure.* Glencoe, IL: Free Press.

Mills, C. W. (1959). *The sociological imagination.* New York: Oxford.

Miringoff, M. L. (1992). *Index of social health: Monitoring the social well-being of the nation.* Tarrytown, NY: Fordham Institute for Innovation in Social Policy.

National Center on Child Abuse and Neglect (1993). *National Child Abuse and Neglect Data System, Working Paper 2, 1991 Summary Data Component.* Washington, DC: Author.

Pear, R. (1993, 9 Mar.) Clinton may seek lid on doctor fees and liability suits. *New York Times, 142,* no. 49,265, A 1.

Rittenhouse, C. A. (1991). The emergence of premenstrual syndrome as a social problem. *Social Problems, 38* (3), 412–25.

Ross, M. G., with Lappin, B. W. (1967). *Community organization, theory, principles, and practice,* 2d ed. New York: Harper and Row.

Schmidt, W. E. (1993, 23 Feb.) Two boys arraigned in Britain in killing of two-year-old. *New York Times, 142,* no. 49,251, A 4.

Schmidt, W. E. (1993, 26 Nov.) After murder, Britain asks why? why? *New York Times, 143,* no. 49,527, A 13.

Chapter 4

PUBLIC POLICY:
HOW GOVERNMENTS MAKE DECISIONS
ABOUT SOCIAL POLICY

Although not all American social policy is public, or governmental, most of it is. The evolution of social policy from the voluntary sector, especially from religious bodies, is traced in chapter 2. This chapter describes ways in which public policy is made by government in the United States. Public policies have an impact not only on programs that governments operate but also on the nongovernmental services that are an important part of social policy. Many believe that public policy is the essential activity of government. J. M. Burns, J. W. Peltason, and T. E. Cronin (1993) call public policy the substance of what governments do.

HOW GOVERNMENT POLICY AFFECTS THE
VOLUNTARY SECTOR

Social services that are voluntary such as the American National Red Cross, Boy Scouts and Girl Scouts, YMCA and YWCAs, family service agencies, church-operated children's homes, and thousands of others in the United States are directly related to government in several ways.

Taxation Policy

Perhaps the most important of the ways in which voluntary organizations are affected by public social policy is in taxation policy. In the United States most nongovernmental human services are exempt from taxes because they are usually delivered by nonprofit organizations. Their employees, of course, pay taxes on their incomes and sales taxes on their personal purchases. In some states, the organizations pay sales taxes. They do not pay income or businesses taxes, however, on the funds they raise.

They are also tax exempt recipients of donations. Individuals and corporations who help support them can make contributions and deduct the contributions from their state and federal taxes. Private foundations, which grant funds from the contributions of individuals and organizations such as corporations, are also exempt from taxes on the earnings of their funds. They use their earnings to support nonprofit activities, many of them human services programs. These tax exemptions are, in most cases, the single most important way in which public policy effects nongovernmental organizations.

Public Grants and Contracts

Many nongovernmental organizations today operate with government money through contracts and grants. For example, voluntary organizations, which are usually owned by nongovernment corporations or their memberships, or boards of directors, seek and often receive government funds. Their policies are made by their own members, or boards, but their real operations may be, primarily, activities connected with government objectives and supported with government funds.

Perhaps the best example of government-voluntary partnership is in the child care field, which is described in more detail in later chapters. It is important to understand that group child care facilities, or homes, operated by churches or community boards receive much of their financing from government. State departments of human services, mental health, or youth corrections, which are responsible for child care or treatment, place children in those homes and pay a monthly fee for the children's room, board, and services. In some cases specialized programs of treatment for emotionally disturbed children are operated by such voluntary organizations.

Many children's homes are former orphanages. Today there are few orphans in the United States and many fewer than there were when those homes were created. There is still a need, however, for substitute care for children who cannot stay in their own homes for any number of social, economic, and psychological reasons. Therefore, the former orphanages have become today's children's centers, or children's homes, and they operate largely with government money.

There are thousands of other examples of agencies that operate with federal grants to support mental health activities, housing programs, services to the homeless, programs for people with disabilities, including mental retardation, and educational programs for parents and others who are responsible for children with disabilities.

Not all social welfare organizations are either governmental or nonprofit. An increasing number of profit-making organizations provide human services. These include some mental health facilities, alcohol and drug treatment programs, hospitals, organizations that provide information to state agencies on potential adoptive parents, programs for people with developmental disabilities, and youth offender treatment services. Such organizations pay the same kinds of business fees and taxes as any other business might. They are not eligible for and do not seek nonprofit, tax-exempt status.

Licensing and Regulation

Governments also directly control voluntary social services organizations through chartering and licensing them. Even though the organizations may receive little or no financing from government, public policy generally requires that organizations that operate on behalf of people be regulated, in some ways, by government. Even though they may not be licensed or otherwise sanctioned by government, every organization that seeks tax exemption must receive certification from the government and must make periodic financial reports to government proving that it deserves to continue being exempted from taxes.

A PRIMER OF AMERICAN GOVERNMENT

It is impossible to discuss any human services in the United States without discussing the public policies of which they are a part. Knowing how government in the United States makes social policy requires an understanding of the ways in which American government is organized and operated, although it is beyond the scope of this book to provide a complete description of American government. Textbooks on American government and critiques of it are widely available and cover the subject in depth. Readers who have backgrounds in government or political science or have had thorough introductory or advanced courses in those fields may find much of this chapter elementary and redundant and, therefore, unnecessary.

One central theme that may not be familiar even to students of the general subjects of political science or government is the blurring of the public and the voluntary, or private, sectors, a subject that is addressed in several different contexts in this book. Although there may have been a time in which there were sharp separations between public and voluntary human services, in the 1990s most human services are mixed and contain both public and private elements.

The Federal System

The United States operates under what is called the federal system, or federalism, which is somewhat different than the government structures found in most other nations. The federal system evolved from earliest American history, when the nation did not exist but several states, then called colonies, did. After the Revolutionary War and the adoption of the Constitution the United States became a nation, and the federal, or United States, government was organized.

Even though there is a national government, however, it does not hold all of the powers of the nation. The Constitution specifies, in the Eleventh Amendment, that all of the powers not granted to the federal government in the Constitution are delegated to the states. Therefore, in most ways it is the state governments that exercise the greatest power over the lives of citizens. It is state government that has always been highly significant in the social welfare of the citizens of the United States.

For the most part social welfare programs are state programs, although the financial support of the federal government is often the basis for their financing and operation. Understanding the relationship between the state and federal governments is critical, and it is described in this chapter.

Although the federal government is supreme in cases in which there are conflicts, there are also specific powers reserved for each level; and the federal government, for example, does not become involved in exercising those powers that belong to the states. A good illustration is law enforcement. With the exception of federal crimes, law enforcement is a state power. The states both make and enforce the laws on crimes as fundamental as homicide, robbery, and embezzlement. Unless federal law has been violated, the federal government is not involved in enforcing local laws.

Yet even that distinction is overly simplified. The federal government has, for example, provided financial assistance to state governments for law enforcement. That is an appropriate, constitutional use of federal power. In some cases a criminal act may violate both state and federal laws. Thus, a murder, which is a state crime, may also involve violation

57

of the victim's civil rights, which is a federal crime. Understanding the details and complexities of state and federal relationships in all areas of government requires extensive study.

Separation of Powers

It is critical for understanding social policy in the United States to recognize that the United States government, at every level, operates under a philosophy called the "separation of powers." The three basic powers in American government are executive, legislative, and judicial. None of these is absolutely supreme: each requires the consent, cooperation, and support of the others; each is able, in one way or another, to affect the other two. Some observers call the separation of powers an arrangement of checks and balances, in which no one branch may dominate the others and, therefore, government and the nation. If citizens are unhappy with their state legislature or Congress, they may appeal to the governor or the president to battle for measures that will improve their circumstances. If they believe the legislative or executive branch has acted improperly, they may file suit in the courts. If they are displeased with the courts, they may ask the legislative branch to pass legislation that will negate or reverse court decisions. The separation of powers concept was designed to help avoid the development of a tyrannical government, such as the one in England which the earliest English settlers came to America to avoid.

The system of separation of powers is critical to policy-making, and to making changes in policy, in the United States. Yet most of the nation's citizens are unclear about the separation of powers concept. Many are baffled by, or have misunderstandings about, the ways in which government decisions and policies are made.

The concept of separation of powers in the United States Constitutions is based on three branches of government—the executive, the legislative, and the judicial. Each branch is generally independent of the others. The Constitution specifies the powers of each branch, incorporating a system of checks and balances that ensures that no branch exceeds its authority. This discussion illustrates the ways in which the three branches interact with and exercise checks and balances on one another.

The separation of powers concept applies to the federal government as well as to the states. In every state there are the same three branches— the executive, legislative, and judicial, as in the federal system. Although

58

there are specific powers that apply in every state, the relationships among the three branches vary from state to state. It is important for Americans interested in participating in government and social policy, to understand how things are done in their own states—because the patterns may be quite different than those in other states.

The state and federal governments constitute the main governing bodies of the United States. While we are attentive to and concerned about cities and towns, they are basically recognized as creations of the states. The powers of the cities are granted to them by the states in which they are located and can be taken away by those same states. The structure of American government is based upon the U.S. Constitution, which is a document that covers the states and the federal government, where the basic powers lie. Counties also exercise significant influence in the United States because they are also convenient subunits and arms of state government. The counties were developed by the states in order to implement the laws and policies of a state government throughout its territory.

The discussions of social policy in this book focus primarily on the federal and state governments because they are the sources of and the implementers of U.S. social policy, as opposed to local governments, although there are exceptions. Some states use the county and city governments as the principal operators of social programs.

The Executive Branch

The executive branch of government, as the word implies, executes the nation's laws, or, to state it another way, enforces the laws. In the federal government the executive consists of the president and the executive agencies or departments of the government. The president's "Cabinet" consists of the heads of those executive branch departments such as the Department of State, the Department of Defense, and, more relevant to human services and social policy, the Department of Labor, the Department of Health and Human Services, the Department of Education, the Department of Agriculture, and the Department of the Interior.

Each of these departments at the federal level carries out the laws made by the legislative branch, the U.S. Congress, or orders of the courts, as discussed later in this chapter. It is important to mention here that the executive branch exercises enormous power by deciding how to implement legislative actions. Part of its basis for deciding how to do this is the intention of the legislature, which it studies and cites as it proposes policies regulations.

Personnel. The people who operate the executive branch of government fall into two general classifications. In the United States government there are: elected officials and their appointees; and permanent "merit," or civil service, employees. The only elected federal officials in the United States government are the president and vice president. The president appoints many of the executive branch employees, especially the department heads, or members of the Cabinet, as well as a number of other top officials of each of the government departments.

Presidents also appoint judges, and that is the way in which the executive branch has influence over the judicial branch of the government. In addition, the president has appointment power for members of boards and commission and regulatory bodies, as discussed later in this chapter.

The other broad classification of employees are civil service employees. These are people who are appointed to their jobs on the basis of examinations or an evaluation of their qualifications. They stay on the job so long as the job exists or until they voluntarily leave, retire, or are terminated for failure to perform their duties satisfactorily.

Some government scholars refer to those who are appointed by the president as political appointees and the civil service, or merit, staffs as nonpolitical employees. The overall system that governs the selection of nonpolitical personnel is called the civil service system. All but a few of the employees in government are civil service employees.

Many of those appointed by the president serve at the will and pleasure of the president. That is, the president may ask the secretary of Health and Human Services, for example, to leave at any time, and the appointee does so. In fact, President Jimmy Carter terminated the appointment of secretary of Health and Human Services, Joseph Califano, who, of course, left the post immediately. The same has been true for many other executive branch employees.

Judges who are appointed by presidents, on the other hand, serve for life and cannot be removed by the president. The members of regulatory bodies or boards and commissions appointed by the president generally serve for fixed terms—usually longer than the four-year term of the president and vice president.

The U.S. Senate must consent to the presidential appointments of executive and judicial branch officials. A recent example was the appointment of former Senator John Tower to the position of secretary of Defense by President George Bush in 1989. The Senate refused to confirm the appointment and Tower did not serve. It is more rare for the Senate to refuse to confirm an executive appointment than a judicial. Several nominees for the U.S. Supreme Court have been denied confirmation in recent years by the Senate; the most dramatic example was in 1992 when the Senate came close to denying confirmation to current Supreme Court Justice Clarence Thomas, largely over a charge of sexual harrassment by University of Oklahoma Law professor Anita Hill.

The States

In the states the separation of powers operates similarly, although the rules and structures change from state to state. It is important for human services workers to understand how their state governments operate. Essentially, the pattern is for the governor to be elected and to have the authority to appoint most of the executive branch agency heads with state senate consent, much as the president appoints the Cabinet. In the states, however, there is usually more than one elected official. In many states there is a governor, lieutenant governor, plus several other executive branch heads, who are chosen by the voters rather than by the governor. Depending upon the state, these may include the state treasurer, state auditor, secretary of state, attorney general, superintendent of education, and secretary, or director, of agriculture. These individuals may not, of course, be removed by the governor. Their responsibility is to the electorate who chose them.

Election or Appointment—a Recurring Issue. A recurring issue in state government is the debate over the best method of selecting key state officials. Is appointing or electing them best for the programs and citizens of the state? Some political science theorists believe that a strong governor system is the best for efficient and effective administration. A strong governor can choose the people he or she wants, direct their work, and hold them accountable for the results of their efforts. If they are not satisfactory, they can be replaced. Electing officials, on the other hand, diffuses authority. They can ignore the governor's directions and may be inclined to take actions that will secure their own political bases and reelections rather than pursuing the best interests of the state. Some of those elected officials have relatively technical jobs, such as the secretaries of state, who issue corporate charters and perform other tasks that could, some argue, be directed by a relatively lower-paid appointed official. Those who favor a strong governor prefer that states elect only one or two officials, much as the United States government selects only

61

a president and vice president, and lets the others be appointed.

Those who prefer a larger number of elected officials believe that such arrangements provide citizens with more direct control over their officials. If they are unhappy, for example, with the educational program in a state that elects the superintendent of schools, they may replace that superintendent directly, by election. Of course, those who prefer a smaller slate of elected officials argue that the same voters can simply turn out the governor at the next election. Nevertheless, the more elected officials there are, the more individuals a citizen can contact directly to pursue specific government objectives. The argument is really over the degree of direct control citizens have over their executive branch officials. Most of the elected positions are spelled out in state constitutions, which are difficult to change, which is why most states have more elected executive branch officials than the experts on public administration would recommend.

Permanent Employees. The states, like the federal government, have merit systems and civil service employment for most of their employees, and the rules are similar to those of the federal government. In fact, many states originally instituted merit systems as a condition for receiving federal funds for human services programs such as AFDC and others established by the Social Security Act, which require the use of merit principles in employing staff. Most states have expanded merit system coverage to a majority of state employees.

The executive branch functions differently in some states, although the trend is toward a powerful governor who performs in many ways as the president does at the national level, making appointments, designing the government's programs through a staff, and taking the lead in financial matters. In a few states the governor is merely part of an executive committee, consisting of the governor and other elected executive branch officials, which makes decisions as a team rather than by the work of a single strong executive.

Budget. The basic power of the strong governor and, for that matter, the president is power over the budget. The governor, or president, proposes a budget, spends the budget, and administers the finances of the government. Nothing happens in government without money; therefore, the way in which power is exercised is by the control over money.

Generally, in the states the authorization of expenditures and the actual expenditure of money are functions shared by the governor with a state treasurer and, perhaps, an auditor. Their part, however, is merely to determine that the funds are available and that they are being spent legally. The decisions about how the funds are spent are made by the governor through the executive agencies, based upon the appropriations bills that are passed by the legislative branch.

Over the years the federal and state governments have developed large structures to deal with financial planning and forecasting, such as budget offices and, at the federal level, the Office of Management and Budget (OMB). Each executive agency also has staff and special units that devote their time and energy to financial management.

HOW THE EXECUTIVE BRANCH INFLUENCES
THE LEGISLATIVE

In the discussion of the federal system it was noted that the three branches have influence and power over one another. There are three separate, equal, and interrelated branches. The executive branch's influence over the legislative branch is important and not always thoroughly understood. There are, however, several ways in which the executive branch exercises influence over the U.S. Congress, in the case of the federal government, and the state legislature, in the case of state governments.

The most important way in which the executive branch influences the legislative branch is through the development and proposal of legislation. Most of the laws that the legislative branch considers come, in some way, from the executive branch agencies. In other words, when Congress deals with health and human services legislation, the legislation is likely to have originated within the Department of Health and Human Services. Even if the legislation has come directly from the thinking of a legislative committee or individual member of the legislative body, it is usually necessary for the executive branch agency to explain, through consultation with them or formal testimony before committees, how the legislative member or committee can achieve what they desire. Much of the advice given to legislative bodies about proposed legislation comes from the executive branch agencies, which often have to tell the legislative groups what can and cannot be done, how much the legislation will cost, and what impact it will have on citizens. The executive branch agencies prepare "fiscal notes" and other documents to assist the legislative body in making its decisions.

The executive branch also influences legislation by the ways in which it implements a statute or law. In many cases legislation is not as specific as it could be. The executive branch, in implementing legislation, may

63

decide where a building is going to be constructed, how a highway is to be located, or which agencies will receive contracts to operate services. The way in which a piece of legislation is implemented is often as important and influential on the subject of that legislation as is the actual bill that is passed.

There have been examples throughout recent American history of the executive branch refusing to implement laws passed by the legislative branch. In some cases an executive branch has simply refused to spend the money appropriated or has refused to implement the law, particularly when it applies to initiating or expanding programs. Both presidents Richard Nixon and Lyndon Johnson, for example, permitted the withholding of appropriated funds from social programs. They referred to their actions as recissions, "placing funds in reserve." During his presidency, Ronald Reagan appeared to define some legislation in ways that differed from the intent of Congress. For example, by executive order of the secretary of Health and Human Services, funds that might have been used for providing information on family planning were denied to organizations that provided or informed clients about abortion. In turn, when President Bill Clinton took office, one of his first acts was to reverse that executive action. The ability to do or fail to do what the legislative branch has passed is one of the most powerful influences of the executive branch over the legislative branch. The power of the executive branch in such matters has been tested in the courts and is not absolute. In many cases, however, it is legal.

THE ROLE AND INFLUENCE OF THE
LEGISLATIVE BRANCH

The legislative branch of government is a crucial and central part of government operation. Some would suggest that it is the most important and most powerful of the branches but, as has been suggested already, the three branches in fact influence one another and are, essentially, coequal. The legislative branches are different in each of the states and between the states and the U.S. Congress.

The U.S. Congress consists of 535 members, 100 in the U.S. Senate and 435 in the House of Representatives. Each of the fifty states has two senators, regardless of the size of its population. The House of Representatives members, however, are apportioned among the states based on population. Every ten years, after the census, which is required by the Constitution, some states lose members in the House of Representatives and others gain members. The number of members of Congress, 435, is set by the Constitution.

In contrast, each state has a different kind of legislative structure. All have two houses, or chambers, except for Nebraska, which has a one-house, or unicameral, legislature. There is usually a senate, which is called the upper chamber, and a house of representatives, or house of delegates, which is called the lower chamber. In many states the original structure was of a senate that represented each of the counties or a grouping of counties, much as the U.S. Senate represents the states. The lower houses represented the population.

The original theory behind these two houses was that there should be two kinds of influence operating in a state government and also in the U.S. government, a built-in form of checks and balances. Property, wisdom, and, perhaps, aristocracy would be the nature of the upper chamber's members. The hope was that the members of the senate would not be influenced by the popular passions of the times. Instead, the upper chamber would deliberate carefully, maintain a sense of history, and not allow anything too radical to happen too quickly. In most of the upper chambers, including the U.S. Senate, the members are elected for longer terms than the members of the lower chambers, reflecting that tradition.

Originally, in the U.S. government members of the Senate were not directly elected by the people of each of the states but, instead, were selected by the state legislatures, which moved them even farther from the popular feelings and passions of the day. That system was changed, and now all senators are elected by the people.

Despite the original designs of the state legislatures, the courts have held that it is unconstitutional for state legislators to represent anything but people: members of the legislatures do not represent trees or cattle or land in a region but only people, the courts have said. Consequently, each state must now base the election of members of both their senates and their houses on population alone. Therefore, many rural counties that once had their own representatives in the state senate have now been combined with many other counties for the sake of representation. Because they have small populations, they have less direct voice in the upper or lower chambers than larger metropolitan areas. These issues were decided in the U.S. Supreme Court cases of *Baker v. Carr,* 369 U.S. 186 (1962) and *Reynolds v. Sims,* 377 U.S. 533 (1964) (Plano and Greenberg 1989).

In today's legislative bodies only the U.S. Senate represents something other than population—by representing states. Today every legislator, with the exception of U.S. senators, has to represent approximately the same number of people as other legislators in his or her state. That policy was decided by the courts, which is an example of how the judicial branch exercises profound influence upon the legislative branch.

Operations of Legislatures

Legislative bodies have a number of characteristics that are not well understood by many citizens but which are important to comprehend when trying to analyze and influence legislative actions. One important consideration is that only a small portion of all the bills introduced in legislatures ever become law.

The Leadership. Every legislative body has a leadership structure, which is usually a small group of five to ten key members who are selected by their colleagues. That small group makes many of the decisions about the actions of the house or senate. The small groups are necessary because legislatures are bombarded with so much legislation that is highly technical and specialized that not all of the legislators can possibly understand and deal intelligently with everything. One bill may involve complicated issues of environmental pollution which are understood fully by only a few highly trained engineers. Another may deal with complex matters of health care. Still another may deal with the higher education system. Knowing about those systems requires extensive training and years of experience. Therefore, legistators know that they cannot be experts on all subjects. Consequently, they elect and defer to leadership groups.

The leadership usually consists of the top two officers of each house of the legislature. In the senate they are usually a president and a president pro tem. In the house they are typically a speaker and a majority leader. The other members of the leadership group often include chairs of some of the major committees, such as finance, judiciary, or ways and means, the chief financial committee in the house. The election of the leadership is obviously a pivotal issue in the operation of a legislative body. It is also where the political parties come into play. The political party that is dominant in the legislative body selects the leadership; the minority party has a lesser role. In fact, the minority often has no influence on the selection of the leadership. The majority party chooses whom it wants, in a private meeting called a caucus, and, because they are the majority, they always win when the entire house or senate votes. Therefore, the chairs and most of the members of the committees are from the majority party. A minority of the members of each committee are from the minority party, which has a parallel structure to the leadership for its own purposes. There is a minority leader, a minority whip, and other leaders who represent the interests of the minority party in the legislative body.

Another factor in leadership selection is seniority. The longer a person has served in some legislative bodies, including the U.S. Congress, the greater his or her prerogatives in assuming committee membership and leadership. In some state legislatures seniority is more important than in others. Ordinarily, however, elected leadership positions such as those described in this section are not based upon seniority, although those who have served longest often build a great deal of support and credibility with their fellow members.

Committees and Their Chairs. Most of the work of the legislative bodies is done by committees. Once a committee approves a bill, unless it is terribly controversial or important to large numbers of citizens, the bill is likely to pass the entire house or senate. The discussions, debates, and controversy take place in committees. The smaller amount of debate on the floor of the body usually is not truly important to the bill's passage. The subject matter is, as has been suggested, so complicated that members not on the specific committee may not understand the issues well enough to usefully participate in the debates.

Many inexperienced visitors to the U.S. Congress are disappointed and surprised that so few members are actually on the floor engaging in debate. It is not unusual to observe the Senate with one person speaking and only a handful of other senators listening. The same can be seen in the House. The members pour into the chambers for votes but are not likely to be present for debates. Some observers assume, then, that legislators are shirking their duties. In fact, the members are likely to be engaged in committee meetings at the time the debates are going on. That is where the real, detailed work goes on. The committee chairs govern the agendas, in most cases, which gives them a great deal of power. Their appointments emanate from the leadership.

There is at least one important role played by floor debate, however, even when the bill is not controversial, and that is the building of a record about the intentions of the legislative body. Because the legislation does not spell out all the details, the executive branch determines how

67

to implement much of the legislation. It has to justify its decisions, however, by citing the intentions of the legislative body. The floor debates provide a key source of information about what the legislative body intended the legislation to accomplish. Committee minutes are used in a similar way and have similar kinds of influence.

In some cases pieces of legislation have to clear more than one committee. For example, almost every piece of legislation has money attached to it, because it costs money to carry out almost any law that might be passed. Bills have to be taken before a subject matter committee, such as health, education, or human services, and also before a finance or ways and means committee, to make sure there will be money available to implement the law. The financially oriented committee may find that taxes will have to be raised to pay for carrying out the legislation or that the budget may have to be modified to include it.

Similarly, other bills may have impact on several different committees' responsibilities. A bill to license social workers, for example, may change the state laws regarding the practice of professions. Therefore, the bill might need consideration by the judiciary committee as well as the committee that deals with social services or health professions.

The Bill-Passing Process

There are several technical steps involved in turning a bill into a law. They vary among the states and between the states and the federal government. Each state makes information on its own procedures readily available, often through pamphlets describing the flow of a bill from introduction to being signed into law. Such pamphlets can be obtained from the state libraries and from the legislative bodies themselves. The mechanics, however, are themselves only a technical outline and guide to some of the procedures that are followed, such as "reading" a bill three times before it is passed; that typically involves the clerk of the senate or house reading the name of the bill, publishing it in the daily journal or record of the body, and then voting on it in final form. Rarely is the entire bill actually read aloud. Doing so would, in many cases, require hours. On some occasions members demand the actual reading of a bill, which is a form of filibuster, as a means of delaying action on it or otherwise preventing its passage. Unfortunately, the manuals or pamphlets that outline the bill passage process are not especially informative. They explain how things actually happen, but they obviously cannot explain the negotiation, bartering, and conflict that constitute the reality of legislation in U.S. politics. When legislators do favors for one another; or support or oppose issues largely on the basis of their own constituent interests, without regard to the larger good; or follow the lead of their party's governor or gubernatorial candidate; or kill a bill by referring it to more committees than might be necessary; or boost or deny the chances of a bill by the way in which they schedule the vote on it—in ways like these the subtle and complex realities of the legislative process come to light. Understanding the dimensions of how a bill does, or does not, become law requires sophisticated analyses and knowledge such as that found in political science books on the legislative process.

A bill introduced in one house only becomes law after it is passed by the second house and signed by the president or the governor. The president or governor may veto the legislation, but even that is not a final step in the life of a particular bill. If the U.S. Congress chooses to do so, it may pass legislation over the veto of a president with a two-thirds majority, likewise in the case of state legislatures and governors; most state legislatures, in fact, require a simple majority. If the bill is passed in such a fashion, whether or not it is signed by the governor or president, it becomes law.

It is worth noting that most governors have the "line item veto," while the president does not. That is, governors can veto parts of bills, while the president must either accept all of a bill or reject all of it. Some people believe that presidents should have the privilege of the line item veto and have introduced constitutional amendments to provide for one. Without it the president too often finds that Congress has included something the president does not want in a bill that the president badly wants to have passed. That kind of confrontation reduces the power of the president and enhances the power of Congress. The same sort of maneuver would rarely work in a state legislature because the governor is likely to have line item veto power, making it possible for him or her simply to strike the undesired program or policy while retaining the rest of the bill.

Conference Committees. More commonly, there are disagreements between the two houses of the legislature. In those cases "conference committees" are appointed. These committees are representative of both houses. They deliberate and bring forth recommendations to modify the legislation without the objections voiced by either of the two houses. The conference committees meet and make reports, and the house and

69

senate must vote for the proposal put forward by the conference committee if the bill is to pass. They cannot amend the legislation or otherwise change it. If they do not agree, the bill goes back to the conference committee for another effort.

Most legislation of any consequence goes to conference committees so that even the smallest differences between the two houses can be worked out. A bill is not considered to have been passed and does not go to the president or governor until exactly the same bill is passed by both houses of the legislature.

Legislative Staff

A development of more recent years has been the expansion of professional staff within legislative bodies. Both the federal and state legislatures employ large numbers of professionals to write legislation, conduct research, organize hearings, and otherwise administer the legislative process. Again, the complexity and amount of legislation are such that the individual members, on their own, cannot know enough or do enough to deal with it effectively.

State legislatures often centralize their professional staff in organizations called "legislative councils," or research services. These organizations have teams of professionals, many of them attorneys with expert knowledge in legislation. They are consulted by legislators who have ideas for new statutes. The organization staff converts the ideas into bills, which the legislators then introduce for action.

Professional staff members in Congress and in the state legislatures come from a variety of disciplines. Many, as mentioned, are attorneys with expert skills in legislation and the drafting of bills, which are specialized fields of law. Others have degrees in political science and public administration. In the human services areas many staff members are social workers, psychologists, counselors, or representatives of other human services disciplines. The roles of policy practitioners, which includes legislative staff members, are discussed in more detail in chapter 9. As the legislative process has become more complex, the numbers and responsibilities of legislative staff members have grown. Increasingly, those who want to have some impact on the legislative process in the federal or state legislatures must become acquainted with and work through staff members because they are often the most convenient and effective route to influencing the content of public policy.

70

It is worthwhile for those who want to understand the legislative process to also know something about the demands on members of Congress and state legislatures. Although the conventional definition of the job is that of studying problems and dealing with statutes about those problems, the reality of legislative work is that the first pressure on a member of Congress or a state legislature is in terms of constituent services. Constituent service means intervening with executive branch agencies on behalf of constituents, advising constituents on how to obtain services, often human services such as social security, and, on occasion, introducing legislation that will solve the problems of a constituent or group of constituents.

Members of legislative bodies are usually quite responsive to communications from constituents because their ultimate bosses are those constituents, voters. Legislators also respond carefully to political party officials, to executive branch officials, particularly the governor or president, as well as to trusted members of their own staffs. That is why it is sometimes more effective for people who have human services legislative concerns to work with and through legislative staff members than with legislators themselves. Staff members have major influence on legislators; obtaining their support for a program or a position can help ensure the action one seeks from a legislative body.

Lobbying and Lobbyists

One of the least well understood issues in the legislative process is lobbying and the roles of lobbyists. Lobbyists are simply people who represent various concerns or interests who attempt to influence the course (at times the passage, at other times defeat) of legislation or, at times, the implementation of legislation through the executive branch. Lobbyists often perform useful services for legislators such as bringing special issues to their attention, conducting research that helps inform legislators, and even drafting bills to deal with special issues for members of legislative bodies. The public stereotype of the lobbyist who spends money on legislators to try to sway a vote or draw attention to a cause is often accurate. Many times lobbyists find that the best way to get the attention of a legislator is to take him or her to lunch or dinner, which may be the only opportunity to capture the full attention of the member of Congress or a state legislature. Many states and the federal government, however, have limitations on the amount of money that can be spent for

71

entertaining legislators. Even when the limits are stringent, lobbyists can influence legislators because they have vast knowledge in special areas and, in fact, represent groups of constituents, who are important to legislators.

Many human services organizations, such as the National Association of Social Workers, the Child Welfare League of America, and the American Public Welfare Association, have lobbyists. They advocate improvements in human services, at least improvements in the organizations that sponsor their efforts, and greater attention to issues of concern to the organization.

There is a variety of techniques used to lobby, aside from having lunch and dinner; others are letter-writing, telegram, and telephone campaigns, all of which work best when the correspondence is highly individualized. When individual constituents write to members of legislatures about subjects of particular interest to them, they are more likely to be effective than if they had signed postcards all saying the same thing or sending obviously duplicated letters.

In any case, lobbying is a legitimate and effective practice in the process of influencing legislation. If it had not been for lobbying, there would not have been licensing laws for most of the human services professions, and program for human services would have been much less generously financed or even maintained without lobbying.

In most state legislatures and in the federal government those whose role is to try to influence legislation must be formally registered as lobbyists; they also must report on their activities and their expenditures. There is additional discussion of lobbying in chapter 9, which deals with human services workers who are involved in the practice of social policy.

THE JUDICIARY

The judicial branch is the third of the coequal branches of government in the United States. Most people are familiar with the courts and their deliberations in criminal and civil matters, in resolving civil cases such as lawsuits, and in adjudicating domestic matters such as divorce and child custody. The courts also play a role, however, in developing social policy, largely through their decisions about cases that are brought before them.

J. Figueira-McDonough (1993) suggests that the courts are of special importance in shaping current social welfare policy. Many of the reforms of recent years have come through litigation in the courts, especially the federal courts. Litigation has become vital in social policy development, although, according to Figueira-McDonough, the human services literature has not given that route of social change the attention it deserves. Judicial decisions, along with other policy changes, have the capacity to help whole groups of people, not just individuals. Also, as Figueira-McDonough points out, the rights of the most vulnerable individuals can be pursued in the courts more readily than they might through the lobbying processes. An individual who contacts a legislator may or may not be taken seriously, depending upon the group he or she represents and its influence. In the courts an individual is heard, and his or her concern must be addressed.

The principles of federalism apply to the courts just as they do to the other two branches of government. There are state and federal courts, each of which handles cases in its own areas of jurisdiction. In general, state courts hear cases about state matters and federal courts about federal matters. In certain situations a case deals with both federal and state laws and can sometimes be tried in both kinds of courts. Usually, however, cases are tried in only one jurisdiction. A federal court typically does not deal with matters of state law and vice versa.

There are different levels of courts. In the federal system there are three basic levels—district courts, circuit courts of appeal, and the U.S. Supreme Court. Similar levels exist in the states, although each state has its own unique arrangements. All but twenty states have no appeals court between the district, or "trial," courts and the supreme appellate courts, also called intermediate courts. Others have specialized appellate courts, and several have more than one supreme court—one for criminal and the other for civil cases, for example.

The lower courts are called trial courts because they are where the cases are actually tried. Trial courts decide issues of fact. Was the person guilty of the crime? Did one party injure another in a civil matter? Who is entitled to the property under dispute? Or how much financial compensation is the injured party entitled to receive? The appellate courts deal only with legal and procedural matters, such as whether or not the evidence used was properly introduced, the judge's instructions to the jury correct, and the indictment properly written. If an appellate court determines that a procedural or legal error was committed, it can order the lower court to try the case again. It cannot determine that a person found guilty by a jury is not guilty. It can, however, say that some element of the trial invalidated the guilty verdict and order that the whole matter be heard again. As a practical matter, many cases are dropped after they are reversed or the decisions invalidated by the appeals courts.

Appellate courts are typically the sources of social policy because they have the power to determine whether a statute passed by a legislature is inappropriate or unconstitutional. They may also invalidate an act of the executive branch by finding that it is improper under the law. The courts may determine that a statute or an act is in conflict with the constitution of the state or the U.S. Constitution. Not all cases of executive acts or statutes being overturned by courts have been done on constitutional grounds. Instead, they may find that another law makes this law invalid or that the implementation of a given statute was improper and outside the intent of the legislation. In general, courts assume that legislative bodies acted properly and that statutes are valid, and they are reluctant to overturn decisions of those who were elected by the people, unless the case for doing so is quite strong. The process of reviewing and deciding on the constitutionality of legislation is called judicial review.

Courts do not simply decide issues that interest them; they deal with cases that are brought to them. Appellate courts, however, can refuse to hear cases that are appealed to them. The U.S. Supreme Court, for example, hears only a small fraction of the cases that are presented to it each year; it must reject many others. When it agrees to hear a case it is usually on a writ of certiorari, the term used when a higher court calls upon a lower court to send up the record of a case for review (Plano and Greenberg 1989). Appellate courts cannot order an action, but they can stop a government from taking actions that are, in the court's decision, illegal. The case of *Roe v. Wade* (410 U.S 113 [1973]), which was decided by the U.S. Supreme Court in 1972, held that a state could not prevent a woman from having an abortion under some specific circumstances, among other things. The Court could not order states that did not permit abortions to do so, yet invalidated the laws that forbid abortion, which had the same consequences.

The executive branch is legally obligated to carry out the decisions of the judicial branch. Generally, the courts cannot execute their decisions with their own resources. They do not have implementers in the executive branch. They certainly do not command armies or police forces, which are the ultimate enforcers of laws. There have been situations in which the courts have taken steps to insure the implementation of their decisions. In several school desegregation cases courts appointed administrators to make sure their decisions were implemented because the executive branch agencies of the states in which the cases were heard were reluctant to desegregate the schools. Figueira-McDonough (1993) notes that in many cases judges have been asked to oversee the setting in place of the standards and changes they have ordered, although they have few resources of their own for implementing decisions. In general, it is the responsibility of the executive branch, which is the implementing branch of government and has the resources to enforce the law, to carry out the orders of courts.

In some cases state matters become matters for the federal courts to decide, if the parties think a federal issue is involved. That is true in death penalty cases, almost all of which begin in state trial courts but progress to federal appeals courts because constitutional issues are raised. In a famous 1992-93 case, a group of Los Angeles police officers were charged in the beating of Rodney King, a private citizen, in Los Angeles. King had been arrested on traffic charges and the police had difficulty subduing him. A video tape of King being beaten by the police was shown throughout the world. A California jury, however, found the police officers not guilty of improperly using force against King. The verdict caused widespread rioting in Los Angeles, and shortly after it was rendered federal officials charged the same officers with a violation of King's civil rights. Ultimately, two of the officers were found guilty of the federal charge.

In addition to the state and federal courts described here there are local courts that deal with more or less minor matters—small claims about financial issues, misdemeanor crimes, and other issues that, while important to the litigants, the accused, or the public, do not often lead to public policy changes.

Criminal versus Civil Cases

The key players in the judicial system depend upon the kinds of cases that are brought. There are two fundamental kinds of cases that come before the courts—civil cases and criminal cases. In some circumstances civil and criminal cases are handled by the same courts; in other cases there are separate courts for the two kinds of cases. Civil cases are those involving disputes between individuals over matters such as property, money, or relationships such as marriage and child custody. Criminal cases are between the government and individuals or groups of individuals who are charged with crimes. The courts resolve disputes, but they also specify actions, as the law requires, against those found guilty of crimes

75

against the people of a state, when they exercise their criminal court functions.

The role of the courts in criminal matters has less importance in the policy-making process than does their role in civil cases. The criminal function is important, of course, in such special areas of human services policy as corrections and juvenile offenses. The nature of crime, the penalties for it, and decisions about guilt and innocence are, however, typically determined by the legislation dealing with the crime, by juries, and by prosecutors. Although criminal cases occasionally have social policy implications, civil cases usually yield the most important social policy decisions because they deal so often with matters of interpersonal relationships, social programs, and human rights.

The key players in criminal cases are prosecuting attorneys, who are called solicitors, or district attorneys, in some states. These elected officials and their staffs determine which cases will be prosecuted. In some areas, for example, parents who are delinquent in their child support payments are rigorously prosecuted; in others they are not prosecuted at all. In some places laws against "sodomy" are prosecuted, which has major social policy implications for homosexual people; in others those laws are ignored. In some jurisdictions mothers who give birth to children with drug addictions are prosecuted for child abuse; in others no such cases are tried.

Prosecutors, on their own, do not bring cases to trial. They must present the case to a grand jury, which may choose whether or not to indict a person for a crime. The indictment means that there is sufficient evidence to try the person, who is, by constitutional right, presumed innocent unless proven guilty. In practical terms, however, the prosecutor exercises strong influence over the grand jury. If the prosecutor believes a case should be tried, the grand jury typically agrees. The process of sending a case to trial is usually called the process of issuing a "true bill" by a grand jury. If the prosecutor does not believe that the person should be tried, then the grand jury is unlikely to indict that person. There are exceptions, and some grand juries take actions opposite of those recommended by the prosecutors. But in the large majority of cases the wishes of the prosecutor and the grand jury are the same.

Perhaps the most important way in which courts influence policy is a result of the way in which law is really made in the United States. Some people believe that court decisions are based upon written laws, or statutes, passed by legislatures. That is true in some cases. Most of the content of the law, however, is based not upon statutes but, rather, upon earlier court decisions. In the American judicial system it is precedent—earlier decisions by courts—that counts. That approach to law is based upon the British judicial system. In fact, early British decisions are built into the law of the United States.

Common law is the name given to the American as well as the British system. In that kind of law each case is argued on the basis of earlier cases that were decided about the same or similar issues. Lawyers are educated by studying cases. They prepare for trials by identifying previous cases that held the position that they are pursuing on behalf of their client. Statutes, of course, take precedence when they are passed, but in many situations there are no statutes—only cases.

The opposite of common law is called Roman, or civil, law, which is used in many Latin American and most European nations. Louisiana law operates under the civil law approach. Under that system the laws are statutory and are modified by statute. Judges often have a larger role in determining whether or not the law has been violated under civil than under common law, partly because the statutes are more specific in the former case. In practice, however, many common law nations have statutes that define the law, and civil law nations may informally rely upon precedents in making legal decisions.

Selection of Judges

Federal judges are appointed by the president with the advice and consent of the U.S. Senate, which means that the Senate must approve the judges before they can take office. In the states judges may be appointed by the governor, elected by the people for specified terms, or in some cases chosen by the legislature.

In the federal system judges serve for life or until they choose to retire. They can only be removed from office by impeachment, which is one of the ways in which the Congress exercises power over the courts. In the states there are a number of different patterns, including lifetime appointments, long-term elections, reappointments after periodic evaluations, and a variety of other arrangements.

Social Policy and the Courts

Among the issues decided by the courts are many that deal directly with social policy. For example, the courts may remove children from their homes, finalize adoptions, and take other child welfare kinds of actions. They are also involved in the involuntary commitment of persons with mental disabilities to institutions. They deal with divorces, child support, and many other domestic matters that involve critical social policies. Of course, they are also directly involved in adjudicating juvenile misbehavior cases and in deciding the fates of persons accused of crimes.

The courts enter, at some point, into almost all of the issues of American social policy. In many cases when a court makes a decision it is also making a policy. For example, a child custody case that works its way through the judicial system to the U.S. Supreme Court can impact the ways in which other courts will decide child custody cases. If the Supreme Court were to decide, for example, that courts must presume that a child is best cared for by its mother, except in unusual circumstances, that would have an impact on all other U.S. courts deciding similar cases. The Supreme Court would have made a policy. The rights of juveniles who are in conflict with the law, the rights of nonresidents of states who seek public assistance in those states, the rights of assistance clients to hearings when they think they are being mistreated, and many other social policies have been determined by the courts.

Again, one of the most important social policy functions of the courts is judicial review. Recall the Dorothea Dix–inspired federal support for mental hospitals, discussed in chapter 2. It was judicial review by the U.S. Supreme Court which overturned that piece of legislation.

Some Practical Sources and Ideas

One of the most graphic and best illustrations of the ways in which courts actually operate can be found in the writings of John Grisham, an attorney and popular American novelist. In his most current book, *The Client* (1993), there is an instructive discussion of the ways in which government attorneys attempt to compel a child to testify about the murder of a United States senator. The eleven-year-old child is afraid to testify because he has been threatened with harm to himself or his family if he does so. The courts are capable, under some circumstances, of compelling citizens to testify.

In Grisham's novel the legal maneuvering between the government attorneys, who want the information so they can prosecute, and the defense attorney, who the boy has hired to help him, provides insight into the ways in which contending parties conflict in legal procedures.

Perhaps the most instructive element is the commentary of the judge. This juvenile judge has to work with the child's defense attorney and with the government attorneys to determine whether or not the child must tell what he knows. If he does so, his life will be in danger. If he does not, he could be held in contempt of court and imprisoned in a juvenile facility. The judge rails at the prosecutors and advises the child's defense counsel. Most important, he scrupulously upholds the law, which says that the child has no right to refuse to provide the information that he has about the crime—even if he is in danger.

Judges are immensely powerful within their own purview. Individually, they have greater power than most other public officials in American government. There is very little that can be done to force a change in the mind or the behavior of a judge on a matter within his or her jurisdiction. Judges have great power over the passing of sentences on people who are convicted of crimes; in their instructions to juries—they can tell the jury what the law is and is not and the jury is bound to follow the judge's instructions about legal matters; and they do not tolerate misconduct or lack of respect toward themselves.

Judges are generally scrupulous about applying the law accurately and correctly. They rarely make decisions that they do not feel are justified by law. And, of course, the law is both the common law decisions that have been passed down over the generations as well as the statutes that are part of the code of laws that the judge applies. Judges resist taking actions that might be counter to the law because of their general desire to be competent, as do all other professionals, but they also dislike being reversed by appellate courts. A reversal of a decision may be considered a mark against the judge's wisdom and professional competence.

Judges are able to have close personal relationships with lawyers from all sides and with clients but also able to separate their personal sentiments from their professional actions. When I served in state government I had many personal experiences with lawyers and judges. In fact, one of the functions of state officials in appointed roles often is to be sued by people who think laws are being improperly applied. Therefore, many state officials have their names attached to important common law cases, even though they were not directly involved in the cases and may not have even appeared in court when the cases were heard. There is a case dealing with child custody in removal of children from their biological parents called *Gibson v. Ginsberg,* which had some notoriety, for example. In that case, Gibson and several other parents charged that the Department of Human Services improperly removed children from their homes without guaranteeing families the services they needed to properly care for their children, and without giving them the right to improve their child care before their children were taken from them. The case was settled after lengthy legal discussions. Changes were made in the child removal policies of the Department of Human Services because of the case. I also testified in other cases, including some of the early Medicaid abortion cases.

One of the more frightening elements of relationships with courts came when our Medicaid fraud investigative unit believed that a pharmacy in a small community was abusing the Medicaid program by substituting low-cost generic medicines for high-priced name-brand medicines and charging the state for the name brands. Our agency, under my name, suspended the man from participation in the Medicaid pharmacy program. He employed an attorney, and I personally conducted a hearing on his charges which was very much like a trial, one of my obligations as a state commissioner. After the hearing I was persuaded that the man had committed the acts, and, therefore, I implemented his suspension. Within a few hours his lawyer appealed to a judge in their local community, and the judge overruled me and restored the man to the Medicaid program. My lawyers, in turn, went immediately to the State Supreme Court of Appeals, the only appellate court in West Virginia at that time, and it overruled the local judge in favor of the Department of Human Services and allowed the suspension of the man from the program.

Within a few days the judge who had been overruled demanded that I appear in his court, which was some distance away from the state capital, on a routine food stamp abuse case—totally unrelated to the pharmacy case. The Department of Human Services staff around the state regularly brought charges against food stamp recipients and took them to court so that the stamps they took could be recouped. Never before had it been ordered that I, as the state commissioner, with no special knowledge of the particular case, appear in court. My lawyers checked with the judge, however, and it was clear that he wanted me there in person, on time, and ready to testify.

I appeared in the court and listened to the case. Every lawyer in the county, it seemed, was also there to witness the judge chastise the department for its handling of the case. After disposing of the case, the judge called me into his office, and we had a friendly conversation.

My concern, knowing about the power of judges, was that the judge could have called me into his county's jail for whatever reason. I traveled to the court with a lawyer and two other staff members. I also took the precaution of notifying a friend in the state police that I might find myself in jail and that I hoped he would find some way to help me get out without spending the night there. I had done nothing wrong, and I was confident that it would not be difficult for me to be released. Yet I had heard of the unsavory kinds of things that can happen to people in jails overnight, and this was not something that I anticipated with pleasure. The problems never occurred, and all I really had to do was show up, on time, in that court. Nevertheless, the situation was more than slightly intimidating to me.

Conversely, I was friendly with a number of state Supreme Court of Appeals justices when I served as a state commissioner. I attended the wedding of one, socialized with others, and generally found close friendships with the membership. Yet I frequently lost cases in that same court. In one case the Court ordered the Department of Human Services to provide care for homeless people under a statute that, I contended, had not been written to deal with the homeless. It was a statute dealing with adult protective services, and the homeless did not, it seemed to me then, fit the definitions of adults needing protection. Parenthetically, since that time—in reflecting on the case, the law, and the Court's actions—I think they were quite correct. Homeless people are in need of protection and met many of the emotional and mental deficiency definitions that were considered in the statute. At the time, however, because of the immediate demands of my job, I was probably more concerned about maintaining a balanced budget than I was scrupulous about providing services to people who surely needed them. In any case I lost. Similarly, I lost another case involving services for youthful offenders—expensive services in therapeutic environments. I never noticed the judges providing me with any special kindness based on our friendships; they always sought to read the law the way the law was written, and, although I disliked losing cases, I found their behavior reassuring in the long run.

For a variety of reasons the judicial branch is the least well understood part of the federal system and, as Figueira-McDonough (1993) suggests, the least likely to be mentioned in the human services literature. In fact, this branch of government exercises great power and authority, as a coequal with the executive and legislative branches.

81

INDEPENDENT AGENCIES

In addition to the three branches of government, there are relatively new kinds of organizations in government called independent agencies. These are bodies that are appointed by presidents or governors and approved by senates which typically regulate some highly specialized area of government. They are intentionally separated from the political branches so that they can operate independently and do what is technically most sound without fear of losing their employment or otherwise facing unpleasant consequences because of their decisions; in other words, their jobs are for specified terms. Organizations such as the Securities and Exchange Commission, the Federal Communications Commission, and the Interstate Commerce Commission are examples. They deal with such subject matter as stocks and bonds, the rates that transportation companies may charge, and the licensing of radio and television stations.

These groups are sometimes called quasi-executive, quasi-judicial, and quasi-legislative bodies because they perform the functions of all three branches of government. That is, they may make rules and regulations, as if they were an executive branch agency or a legislative group; they administer programs and functions such as licensing, as executive branch agencies do; and they resolve disputes, as the judicial system might do. In some cases they assess penalties for those who violate their own regulations, which makes them comparable to judicial bodies.

These organizations are not very active in human services areas at the federal level, but in some states they are directly associated with programs such as social welfare, health services, licensing of human services facilities, and the like.

CONCLUSION

This primer of how government makes policy provides fundamental information on the social policy process which is crucial to a full understanding of that process. Subsequent chapters, as they discuss social policies and programs, will require an understanding of the executive, legislative, and judicial branches of the federal and state governments, which are the main actors in the making of public policy.

The next chapter talks about economic policy, which is a special case in the United States policy process, and it describes some of the ways in which social policy is impacted by the economic policies of the federal government.

DISCUSSION QUESTIONS

1. Discuss some of the ways in which executive policy-making and legislative policy-making differ.
2. Visit an attorney's office or a law library and read a human services case decided by the U.S. Supreme Court. There are cases in the areas of child welfare, adoption, mental health, and other fields, which you will be able to find with the help of the attorney or a librarian. Try to determine what the issues in the case were and note what the Supreme Court decided. Was there any invalidation of existing state or federal law on constitutional grounds? Did the Court uphold or reverse a lower court decision?
3. What are some of the virtues, in your opinion, as well as some of the deficits of the federal system followed in the United States? Why do you think the United States has continued that historic arrangement, even though transportation, the size of the population, and communications have changed so much since the system was first developed over two hundred years ago?
4. Discuss the ways in which the three branches of government are coequal. How does each exercise authority over each of the others?

REFERENCES

Burns, J. M., Peltason, J. W., & Cronin, T. E. (1993). *Government by the people,* 12th ed. Englewood Cliffs, NJ: Prentice-Hall.

Figueira-McDonough, J. (1993, Mar.). Policy-practice: The neglected side of social work intervention. *Social Work, 38* (2), 179–88.

Grisham, J. (1993). *The client.* New York: Doubleday.

Plano, J. C., & Greenberg, M. (1989). *The American political dictionary.* New York: Holt, Rinehart & Winston.

Roe v. Wade, 410 U.S. 113 (1973).

Much of the content in this chapter has come from the author's study of and personal experiences in politics. For a detailed review of information on the structure and function of American government, readers are encouraged to consult current introductory texts in the field of government or political science. The most widely consulted and comprehensive of these texts is:
Burns, J. M., Peltason, J. W., & Cronin, T. E. (1993). *Government by the people,* 15th ed. Englewood Cliffs, NJ: Prentice-Hall. Earlier editions of this

work contain basic information on the public policy process which is sufficiently current to understand some of the concepts discussed in this chapter. (Note that the twelfth edition of the book is cited in the references for this chapter.)

Chapter 5

PUBLIC ECONOMIC POLICY

The ways in which a national government operates its economy—in general, the total of all the nation's goods, services, and wealth—is a complicated subject that ought to be studied in depth by anyone engaged in social policy analysis and development. The components of social policy can be understood only by grasping the fundamental ideas of political science and economics.

Government economic policy has an impact on all social policy. Public economic policy in the American system is made by the executive and legislative branches, primarily. It is also made by some of the independent agencies, especially the Federal Reserve Board, which runs the American banking system and which, in large measure, governs the U.S. economy.

BASIC ECONOMIC CONCEPTS

Classic Free-Enterprise Economic Theory

There are several economic theories underlying American government. Among the most important and pervasive are the classic economic theories of Adam Smith (1910). They include the belief in capitalism and free enterprise as fundamental to a viable economic system. Among Smith's classic theories is the belief that the government that governs best is the government that governs least. Smith's laissez faire (the French term for "to leave it alone") economic theory, in particular, suggests that government should let the economy operate through the activities of individuals who are trying to maximize their own gains and avoid losses. The desire to maximize one's wealth is, according to this classic theory, the essence of economic development. It is the philosophy that has been followed for much of the history of the United States, from early American times through the Great Depression era of presidents Herbert Hoover and Franklin D. Roosevelt. It was also the predominant theory of Ronald Reagan and, to an extent, informed the presidency of George Bush. Although other theories have been added to fundamental American economic practices, the basic ideas remain those of Adam Smith's classic economics.

85

Many classic American economic practices and beliefs follow the nation's commitment to free enterprise. The requirement under American policy that businesses avoid collaborating and work, instead, to compete directly and aggressively with one another comes from the thinking and writings of Smith, as well as other economic thinkers who share his beliefs. These convictions about the wisdom of government staying out of the economy were the basis, during much of American history, for the nation's refusal to deal with problems such as poverty and national health care. It was only the crisis of the Great Depression that turned the nation in a new direction, toward undertaking to solve pressing social problems as a nation.

The capitalist tradition in the United States is so strong that it is almost taken for granted. One author, E. S. Greenberg (1989), has written a complete descriptive text on American government that asserts that the whole system—executive, legislative, and judicial—is set up to support and maintain the capitalist tradition in the nation. His text emphasizes the maldistribution of wealth in the nation, the use of government to keep workers in line and capitalists on top, and the clear, although often unstated, premise that American democracy and capitalism are inseparable.

A nation that totally believed in Smith's classic approach would make little room for social welfare programs that promote social justice through the redistribution of wealth. Instead, classically-oriented policymakers believe, the economy ought to be left alone and allowed to flourish; when it does everyone will be better off, and social and economic justice will prevail. The American commitment to avoiding involvement by the national government in the economy is also a product of the federal system. Under the Constitution, before it was amended, most government activities directly affecting individuals came from the states. The national government only dealt with major national concerns, such as the money system, international relations, and defense (Ginsberg 1987). Direct contact between the national, or federal, government and individual citizens did not occur. Over the years, however, through amendments to the Constitution, there have been more and more direct connections built between the federal government and its citizens.

Again, the fundamental concept underlying our economic system is free enterprise capitalism, and with it comes dislocation, which may, for example, cause people to lose their jobs, require them to move, or otherwise endure changes that they would prefer not to make. In the classic economic philosophy such disruptions are essential to a healthy economy:

86

those within the labor force who are situated where they are not needed ought to relocate to places where they are needed. Unemployed people, if left alone, the theory states, will make rational decisions that provide for their economic well-being. It is that pursuit of economic advantage by all the actors in the economy which builds economic viability. Any interference drags the economy downward.

Adam Smith was writing in the eighteenth century, at a time when small merchants, shopkeepers, and tradespeople dominated economic activity. The notions of unbridled free enterprise and competition made good sense in such times, before there was instantaneous international trade and communications and before giant conglomerates, the antithesis of classical theory, could dominate large segments of the market.

Competition could, Smith envisaged, benefit everyone. Shoemakers, for example, would sell their shoes at the best price they could get. They would also compete with other shoemakers for quality production. Customers would flock to those with the best products and prices, and, thus, consumers and producers alike would benefit. The producers would use their earnings to expand their businesses or embark on other economic ventures, which would employ still more consumers. The free market, if left alone to pursue its own activities and values, would make everyone prosperous.

Although P. R. Popple and L. Leighninger (1993), among others, call the adherence to the classic ideas of free market economics a "conservative" approach, it is probably the case that this model is central to the U.S. economic system. Most national economies, including that of the United States, are mixtures of several different economic theories; nevertheless, belief in the value of the free market guides and colors many elements of American economic policy. American policy generally supports such principles as the virtue of competition, the negative consequences of fixing prices, and the belief that businesses must earn profits or fail. Many Americans believe in these ideas, elements of a strong national tradition, although they may do so without thinking of themselves as advocates of the philosophy of Adam Smith.

Marxism and Social Control of the Economy

A second approach is the planned, or socialist, economy, in which government controls and attempts to manage all economic activity. The theories behind these concepts are many but most of them emanate from the concepts of Karl Marx and Friedrich Engels (Hirsch, Jr., Kett & Trefil 1988). Marx's ideas laid the basis for the political system of communism as well as the economic system of socialism. Other philosophers, such as Claude Henri de Saint Simon (Bullock and Brass 1977) contributed to theories supporting an economic system based on socialist, or cooperative, ideals.

Under socialist economies governments own the basic tools of production such as manufacturing, transportation, and utilities of various kinds. The former communist nations of Europe and parts of Asia have followed this philosophy, which is often attractive because it emphasizes the fair distribution of resources and wealth, fairness in the economy, the desire that no one suffer, that there be adequate housing, and so forth. Many of these economic concepts have been rejected by the former communist governments, many of which are trying to develop free market, or capitalist, economies, along the lines of that in the United States.

Of course, Marx's theories were more complex than what has been stated here. He and Friedrich Engels, his close associate for many years, believed that market economic systems exploited workers for the advantage of capitalists, who in fact "stole" the labor of their workers; profits, in this view, actually belonged to the workers. When a product is produced the owner might provide the tools and the materials, but the real value is the labor that goes into making the materials into something worthwhile. Workers are never paid the full value of their work, according to this theory, and the difference between what they earn and the price of the product goes to the owner in the form of profits; therefore, labor was exploited by capitalists, who enriched themselves through the work of others. Marx envisioned an ideal society in which all of the people owned all of the tools of production; in which people received what they were entitled to, based upon their needs; and in which everyone worked as well as he or she could, because society belonged to everyone. A classless society without needs and a people with plenty was the Marxist ideal (Hirsch, Jr., Kett & Trefil 1988).

Popple and Leighninger (1993, 15) call those who support these Marxist approaches "radicals" who "would prefer an economic system where workers have control over the conditions of their work; where goods are produced for genuine need and not to satisfy whims created by advertising; where money is not the measure of worth; and where basic rights, such as medical care and housing, are not reduced to commodity status and sold in the marketplace to the highest bidder." They add that some such radicals want a government that organizes and delivers medical care, housing, and social welfare benefits for all citizens. Of course, it is not just these so-called radicals who seek such changes. So do many liberals and conservatives and others who support what is termed by some the pursuit of social justice.

Current Critiques of Nonmarket Economies. Socialist, or planned, economies, in theory, appear to have the advantage of distributing resources satisfactorily, providing essential services, and making sure there are no absolute poor. On the other hand, critics of planned, or nonmarket-based, economies demonstrate that in truth in such economies everyone is relatively disadvantaged, people tend to lose incentive and entrepreneurial spirit, and, generally, everyone has subsistence earnings and resources in socialist economies but not much more than that.

In my own experience in communist countries there does appear to be a sort of shared misery rather than a shared prosperity. When I visited Cuba in 1990 I was astonished at how poor virtually everyone was. That was, as likely as not, however, a consequence of the U.S. boycott of Cuba as much as of the communist system under Fidel Castro. When I visited Romania in 1992 and 1993 I saw the remnants of communist government; here, again, there were certain basic advantages of the system which were quite humane. People were well educated, medical services were readily available, and there was plenty of food, although the variety and quality were poor. Prices were low; people had places to live, although they were often unattractive dwellings in large apartment houses, which some of the people said they did not enjoy. But, of course, there are variations among Marxist nations. In Cuba, for example, which has remained communist at a time when many such countries have rejected communism, citizens are permitted to own their own homes, which was not always so for those living in the former Soviet Union.

Other critics insist that capital is necessary for the operation of a national economy, and they believe that without the profit incentive there will not be sufficient investment in capital. Capitalists make a vital contribution, they say, by investing their wealth in new or expanding enterprises.

Of course, a society that has no economic problems, which is the Marxist ideal, probably would have no other problems to be addressed by human services workers. Generally, Marxists believe that most social ills are economic and that, if the economy is just, there will be a just society. In many of the former communist countries, therefore, psychology, social work, and some other human services professions were eliminated. By the 1990s many of those countries—my own experiences have been in Romania—had no social work and psychology schools nor professors and practitioners. I was pleased to be part of the efforts to help Romania reestablish its human services professions.

Some point to the Western European socialist nations, which seem to combine some of the more humane elements of socialism with some of the virtues of free enterprise economics so that life is relatively good for most people—in, for example, the Netherlands, Scandinavia, and the former West Germany—as worthy models. Although few are terribly rich, taxes are high, and the population is not fully satisfied with every aspect of its economic life, basic needs are met.

At the same time, the nations with a fundamentally free enterprise system also seem to be doing well. Many are in Asia. For example, *Newsweek* reported on what it called the "Saigon Virus" (Moreau 1993), which is the name being used for the strong, free enterprise economy of the former capital of what was South Vietnam. Saigon, which has been called Ho Chi Minh City since the Vietnam War, is a city of four million inhabitants, which is only 7 percent of the Vietnamese population; they account, however, for one-third of the country's industrial production, much of it based on small, family-run businesses that would have fit the definitions of a proper economy developed by Adam Smith. Much of Southeast Asia follows similar patterns. Hong Kong, Japan, Singapore, and Taiwan are among the most prosperous economies of the world, yet in some of these nations the people work long hours and lack the wage and hour protection and other labor law advantages that those in more mixed economies have. There is little doubt that strong capitalist, free enterprise operations have helped Asian nations become economically powerful.

A good bit has to do with those nations' resources. Wealthy nations with abundant natural resources, well-educated people, and capital appear to function well under free enterprise economics. Overpopulated, impoverished nations of the world, on the other hand, have sometimes pursued socialist, central planning as a means of preventing great economic need.

MANAGING THE ECONOMY—THE INFLUENCE OF JOHN MAYNARD KEYNES

The theories of government's ability to manage the economy—cooling it off when it is too hot and growing too fast, and becoming too inflationary, or heating it up and making it more effective and more responsive to economic needs—come in part from the works of John Maynard Keynes (Pennant-Rea & Emmott 1983).

In the U.S. system Keynsian economic theory has governed American thinking for much of the time since the presidency of President Franklin D. Roosevelt, which coincided with Keynes's writing and the popularization of his theories. In fact, even the free enterprise–oriented, capitalist administrations of Ronald Reagan and George Bush tended to follow some of the fundamental teachings of Keynes. Despite the fact that authors such as Popple and Leighninger (1993) call supporters of Keynesian economics "liberals," the reality is that most public officials appear to embrace Keynesian approaches, treating them as valid economic principles rather than aspects of some political point of view.

Keynes, who was from England, visited the United States during the Great Depression of the 1930s (Burns, Peltason & Cronin 1984). He insisted that, if people did not consume or invest enough, the national income would fall. He proposed that government find ways to increase expenditures on consumer goods and also investments in heavy industries such as steel and shipping facilities. If private business could not do it, government must, he said.

In many ways the 1930s New Deal programs were based upon Keynesian economic theory. Rapidly injecting money into the economy was one of the purposes of such employment and training programs as the Works Progress Administration and the Civilian Conservation Corps. After World War II the U.S. Congress passed the Employment Act of 1946, which was designed to provide mechanisms for managing the economy but also to stimulate the economy and to pursue high levels of employment (Dolgoff, Feldstein & Skolnik 1993). The act created the Council of Economic Advisors, one of the federal executive branch's primary mechanisms for monitoring and fine-tuning the economy. President Harry S Truman, recognizing the need for the government to take steps to maintain the health of the economy and high levels of employment, proposed the legislation (Burns, Peltason & Cronin 1984). The policy of trying to guarantee employment to all employable people was reaffirmed in 1978 through the passage of the federal Humphrey-Hawkins Full Employment Act (Dolgoff, Feldstein & Skolnik, 1993). The goal of full employment, by requiring the government to create jobs and employ those who would not otherwise be employed, has not been implemented or seriously pursued, according to Dolgoff, Feldstein, and Skolnik (1993).

The *multiplier* and *leverage* effects are among the concepts provided by Keynes. They are discussed in more detail in a following section on

91

the money supply. The emphasis on consumption to stimulate economic growth, referred to above, is an example of the multiplier effect, and the emphasis on investment is an example of the leverage effect. Keynes also was one of the first to show how deficit financing can help government grow—that, by borrowing in the short term, governments can expand their economies. He also showed the other side of the lesson—that, when things are moving along well in an economy and the economy is close to inflation, governments best serve their people by contracting the money supply, by making it more difficult to borrow, and by reducing economic activity. Keynes was one of the first to show how governments, by public policy, are able to tune an economy in ways that make it possible to keep the economy in balance, so that most people are employed, goods and services are equitably distributed, there is sufficient growth, and there is only modest inflation.

As suggested earlier in this section, it appears that conservative and liberal politicians alike concur about the value of the Keynesian approach. His findings constitute something of a law in economics—a law that is operational. Historically, as discussed in chapter 2, the most severe economic crisis ever to hit the United States was the Great Depression of the 1930s. It was the policy of the New Deal, which began in 1933, to apply Keynesian theory to modern government. The economy did, in fact, expand, and the Depression did end, and since the 1930s there has never again been as severe an economic crisis as that one. Whether or not such economic disaster will occur in the future, despite efforts to prevent it, is still unknown.

These discussions of Keynesian economic theory and government spending are crucial because many times government's expenditures are for social welfare programs. Programs for creating jobs, providing housing and financial assistance and improving education are among the solutions to social problems; at the same time they serve those in need, these solutions add money to the economy and thus stimulate it along the lines suggested by Keynes.

The tendency throughout the world is toward mixed economies that follow the Keynesian model, provide the humanity and protection of the socialist and communist approaches, and allow the relatively free activity of economic markets under the free enterprise system. In truth, most governments, particularly Western governments and especially the United States government, use a mixed approach. That is, in the United States, for example, there is a high degree of emphasis on capitalism, competition, and other manifestations of the Adam Smith free enterprise ap-

92

proach to government. At the same time, governmental attempts to improve the economy by speeding it up or slowing it down, following the theories of John Maynard Keynes, have been encouraged. There are also many examples of government involving itself directly in human services and the redistribution of wealth, which are in some ways Marxist ideas. Government in the United States is, thus, largely mixed—although the fundamental tenets underlying it support free enterprise and capitalism.

TAXATION

One of the ways in which government affects social policy is through tax policy. By giving special advantages, for example, to social agencies and those who support them, government supports social welfare programs.

By definition, all taxation is a means for distributing the cost of government in ways that are considered just and fair by the government and its people. Taxes are not primarily a means for raising revenue, although that is typically the way we think of them. Instead, they are a way of raising revenue in a manner that citizens may believe to be rational and equitable (Snider 1965).

Governments may simply take—and have taken—the property of citizens and use it for governmental operations. It may take people and force them to labor on behalf of the government. Taxes are simply a way of making the rules explicit and of trying to find a way that distributes the burden fairly and in line with the beliefs of the society. In many ways taxes reflect the values of a nation's population. When we provide tax deductions for charities and charitable contributions, for health care expenditures, and for older people, we are expressing our belief in their worth over other kinds of activities and people.

Governments always make sure they have the money to do what they want to do. The questions are simply over how they will obtain that money, from whom they will obtain it, and in what amounts.

There are three general classifications of taxes—*proportional, progressive* and *regressive*. R. Pennant-Rea and B. Emmott (1983), among others, claim that a proportional tax is blind to income, that it takes the same proportion of a wealthy person's funds as a poor person's. A flat 10 percent tax on all incomes, without regard to the circumstances of the taxpayer, would be a proportional tax, which is seldom used.

Progressive taxes require people to pay on the basis of their wealth. The more money they have, the larger share of their money is paid in taxes, and, similarly, the lower their incomes, or wealth, the lower the taxes they pay. The U.S. federal personal income tax is a progressive tax. It charges higher rates at the upper levels of income and lower rates at the lower levels; in fact, people with the lowest incomes pay little or no personal income tax.

There is a bias in the income tax toward those who earn their money from working as opposed to those who earn their money from investments. Those who earn money from investments may pay a larger tax on their earnings than those who earn their money from working. There is also a bias in favor of families. Those who support children and other family members pay fewer dollars in taxes than those who support only themselves. As noted, too, there is a bias in favor of those who give money to charitable causes. They pay lower taxes because they do not pay taxes on the amounts that they contribute to charitable causes. Thus, the income tax, like all taxes, reflects a variety of values and government goals.

A regressive tax is one that places its burden more heavily on lower-income people than on upper-income people. The favorite example used by those who write about tax policy is the sales tax, which is charged at some rate—5 percent is a common amount—on purchases. Some say that the sales tax is fair because it charges everyone the same amount, that everyone faces an equal burden. In reality, however, the sales tax is regressive, because the lower one's income, the larger the percentage of one's earnings that is spent on items for which sales taxes are paid, such as food and clothing. People with great wealth spend smaller proportions of their entire wealth on items that they purchase in retail stores. They use much of their money for savings, investments, insurance, and the like, on which sales taxes are usually not charged. Therefore, there is a great difference in the percentage of one's income that is paid in sales taxes, based upon one's overall income. In some states sales taxes are not applied to necessities such as food, clothing, and shelter, which mitigates against the regressive nature of the sales tax; the lower-income families, who spend the largest parts of their incomes on such necessities, are not taxed on them, thus making the sales tax less regressive.

In 1993 President Bill Clinton said that his administration was considering using a Value Added Tax (VAT) as a means of financing his new health care reforms, although it was not part of the plan being discussed when this book went to press. The VAT, according to Pennant-Rea and Emmott (1983), is widely used in European nations, Mexico, and other nations but, thus far, not in the United States, Canada, and

94

Japan. The VAT is somewhat akin to the Marxist notion of the value of labor. When a raw material is turned into a finshed product, it is taxed every step of the route, from beginning to end, but ultimately only the consumer pays the tax. For example, a rancher sells a head of cattle to a packing house. That rancher pays the VAT of 10 or 20 percent but passes it along as part of the price to the packing house. The packing house sells the meat that it takes from the head of cattle to a food store and also pays the VAT and passes the tax cost along to the food store. The food store sells the product to the consumer, who pays the VAT and is the only participant who does not pass along the tax.

Ultimately, the VAT can quickly and easily raise extensive revenues for the government. The consumer pays what amounts to a large national sales tax. Is the tax regressive? Perhaps it is, because it is applied to products at all stages of their manufacture. Lower-income people spend disproportionately more for products than upper-income people. This tax, however, is supposed to be easy to administer and raises revenues efficiently, and it could, in theory, replace all or part of the income tax.

Some suggest that the social security tax is regressive. Everyone pays the same rate on his or her earnings up to a maximum salary of nearly $60,000. The lower-income person pays his or her percentage, matched by a comparable amount from the employer—up to that maximum. The amount of one's earnings does not affect the rate paid, only the amount, thus the wealthier person pays only to the maximum and nothing above that. Social Security benefits, however, are related to one's earnings and the amount of one's contributions over time. Therefore, the lower-income worker can expect benefits upon retirement or if he or she ever becomes disabled which are related to the amount paid into the system.

Some assert that social security is not a tax at all. They view it as an insurance premium that protects one against retiring in poverty, early death, or disability. Participants receive the amount they should, based upon their contributions. Benefits are based on money paid in, not on the special needs of the beneficiaries.

There are many other kinds of taxes. Some are called "sin" taxes. These taxes are placed on alcohol and tobacco, for example. The assumption is that government wants to discourage the use of these products and, therefore, makes them more expensive by applying extra taxes. There are also "luxury" taxes on such things as jewelry, expensive vehicles, boats, and other costly items. Taxes of this kind are based on the notion that people who can afford such luxuries ought to pay more in taxes than those who cannot afford such luxuries.

95

There are fuel and energy taxes as well. Governments that want to control the use of fuel and energy will raise the taxes on these commodities as a way of discouraging people from wasting energy. In some European nations gasoline costs three times as much as it does in the United States.

There are also a number of tax incentives, special breaks in tax structures, to encourage some kinds of purchases or behaviors and to discourage others. For example, some states exempt food and clothing from sale taxes. Others exclude medical care and prescriptions from the sales tax. These, again, are means for making the sales tax less regressive.

There are a number of ways in which government expresses its policies and preferences through the tax structure.

THE MONEY SUPPLY

The amount of money in circulation and the value of that money is also a product of governmental policy. When government wants more money in circulation it makes it easier for banks to borrow money from the federal government and make loans to citizens. The loaning of money by banks actually creates money and expands the money supply. The more money banks loan, the more money there is in the economy. When government wants to reduce the money supply and cut down the amount of money in circulation, it makes it more expensive and difficult for banks to make loans (Snider 1965).

Government needs to control the money supply as a means of controlling inflation, which occurs when there is more money in the economy than there are available goods and services, or to spur economic growth, when there is not enough money being invested in the economy. Increasing the interest rate slows down the economy and helps prevent or at least control inflation. Lowering the rate tends to lead to economic investment and growth.

In the United States the executive branch of government influences the money supply, often based upon the advice of the Council of Economic Advisors, a group of three members appointed by the president with the consent of the Senate. In addition, the president annually must report to Congress on the nation's economy. The establishment of that report and the creation of the Council of Economic Advisors resulted from the passage of the Employment Act of 1946 (Burns, Peltason & Cronin 1984). Other entities, such as the Federal Reserve Board and the

Department of the Treasury, also play significant roles in studying and molding the economy.

The process of creating money works by consumers and businesses borrowing money from banks and from investment in capital growth. Banks are able to loan money, based upon their assets and their reserve requirements. For example, if the bank has a current reserve requirement of 10 percent, and it makes a loan of $10,000 it must have $1,000 in assets to back the loan. The other $9,000, however, is new money, and when the borrower pays back the loan, plus the interest, the bank now has greater assets. It actually created the $9,000 by the use of its account with the Federal Reserve Bank, a federal government independent agency which is, in essence, a bank for banks. The banks can borrow more money from the Federal Reserve, which increases its assets, and make more loans. The Federal Reserve makes it more costly for banks to borrow when it wants to restrict the money supply and less costly when it wants to expand the money supply.

Parenthetically, paper money and coins have very little to do with the amount of money in circulation. There is a great deal more money in circulation than there are bills or coins to cover it. Cash is simply a convenience that is used for some transactions. Most of the money in circulation is simply numbers in checking accounts which are transferred from one account to another (Snider 1965). If one thinks about it, little of the money people spend is in cash. Instead, it is spent through writing checks. With the widespread use of credit cards there is even less need for cash. People charge their expenditures to their credit cards, they are billed for those expenditures, and they write checks to pay the credit card bills. In the whole process no cash ever changes hands. Again, money is created by banks, when they make loans; the loans are generally made in the form of credits to the customer's checking account.

One of the ways in which the money supply increases is through expenditures. Government is a major spender of funds, along with businesses. Businesses spend to increase their profits. Governments spend most often in order to carry out their programs; however, they sometimes spend to improve the economy. When governments and businesses spend money, on anything, they increase the supply of money in the economy. When governments spend money at the lower levels of the economy, by providing assistance to low-income people, for example, the money is spent almost immediately. As it circulates through the economy—to the stores in which the people spend the money, the banks where the stores deposit their receipts, the manufacturers or farmers who make the products that are purchased or grown—the amount of money is multiplied. Therefore, government jobs programs, cash assistance programs, and food stamp programs, in addition to improving the lives of people, are means to introduce more money into the economy. Putting money into the hands of any people puts money into the hands of all people. The effect of putting money into the economy, through assistance programs, stimulates what is referred to as the multiplier effect, a concept developed by Keynes.

The leverage effect (also a Keynesian concept), on the other hand, occurs when money is introduced into the economy "at the top"—by providing financial assistance, contracts, and other benefits to large corporations and to wealthy individuals. The money, once used, again moves through the economy, although not always as rapidly as when it is introduced at the lower levels of the economy. One of the approaches tried for increasing the resources at the top of the economy has been "supply side economics" (Pennant-Rea & Emmott 1983), a central tenet of Reagan's early 1980s policy. When a major manufacturer or a very wealthy person is provided with a government contract or a tax cut, or any other means of providing relief to the top of the economy, the theory goes, the money circulates and provides employment, and money in other forms, to everyone else.

Some people refer to the leverage effect as "trickle down" economics: provide money to the top earners in the economy, and they will invest it in new production, purchases, and home construction, among other things; eventually those funds will trickle down to reach everyone else. Conversely, if you put the money into the base of the economy, such as in the Aid to Families with Dependent Children program, the money will eventually "trickle up" to the wealthiest. Spending money simply adds to economic activity and wealth.

Of course, when governments spend more than they have or more than they can justify, based upon the wealth of their nation, they cause inflation. That is, if they spend money that is not worth very much—given that the wealth of the nation determines what the money is worth—they cheapen the money and stall the economy with devalued money. Inflation is simply devaluation of money; it is too much money chasing too few goods. When on a given day $100 purchases only half of what it would have been able to purchase a day or month earlier, the cost has been inflated and has lost half its value.

Inflation typically results when money no longer reflects the value of the nation's wealth. Simply printing money, without an adequate economic base to back the amount that is printed, leads to inflation.

Social policy is affected by monetary policy in many ways, and social policies influence the money system. In the simplest terms, when there is a large supply of money available there are more resources for social services of all kinds, and governments are more likely to appropriate those funds for such services than they are when money is in short supply. Similarly, social programs usually benefit the lowest-income individuals and families in the nation most directly. Those individuals and families, of necessity, spend nearly all the money available to them. In some cases, through borrowing, they spend more money than they have available. The multiplier effect comes rapidly into play when the money is spent, and the trickling up through the economy is often dramatic. The ultimate result is often a stronger or at least more active economy as well as increases in tax revenues, often larger in amount than the social services expenditures were.

When the money supply contracts and interest rates increase there is less investment by businesses, which often results in reduced employment. This, in turn, can cause greater social needs. In many ways social policies are a central factor in the operations of an economy and represent significant economic as well as social functions.

Deficit Financing

There is extensive discussion in the United States about the virtues and vices of federal deficit financing. Deficit financing is another form of governmental finance in which government borrows money and uses that money for its own operations. It is a tax because, ultimately, the repayment of the money and the interest on the debt, which is paid to those who loaned the government money, is paid by taxpayers. According to the *Pocket Economist* (Pennant-Rea & Emmott 1983), deficit financing is the act of allowing a budget deficit as a way of putting money into the economy and expanding the demand for goods and services. Governments may sometimes simply expand the amount of money in circulation but, in the United States, the money is borrowed from lenders and paid back to them.

It should be noted that deficit financing is only an option for the federal government. Only sovereign, or autonomous, nations, which control their own money supplies, are able to add to the nation's economy through some of the mechanisms already discussed. Similarly, only

99

sovereign nations—such as Germany and Mexico—can issue bonds to spur investment and participate in the kinds of borrowing and lending discussed in this section. Most state governments, by law, must operate on strictly balanced budgets. They must show that their revenue estimates will pay for their planned expenditures. If their revenue estimates fall short and less money is available than was anticipated when the budget was developed, they must reduce expenditures for the rest of the fiscal year so that it will end with a balanced budget.

Of course, some states are permitted to borrow—from retirement funds and other trust funds and from banks—but they must pay back the loans plus interest, just as they would pay for any other expenditure. Only the federal government may determine that it wants to borrow money and authorize itself to borrow and spend more through the issuance of bonds, Treasury notes, and other financial instruments. State governments generally must spend only as much as they receive in taxes. If they need more money, they must borrow it from banks, just as families must.

Despite the criticism and expressions of concern, however, deficit financing is often a convenient and efficient way to improve a nation's economic situation. Like individual citizens, nations are able to do things through borrowing which they could not do with cash. An individual might want to purchase a house and does so by borrowing money. Saving the money for the house, on the other hand, might require twenty years of waiting and saving. Borrowing the money and paying off a mortgage may make it possible for the person to live in the house twenty years sooner. That is not terribly different than a national government borrowing money to undertake new projects without cutting back on other services and without waiting to save the money through tax revenues.

There is one essential difference between borrowing by a national government and individual borrowing: the individual must eventually pay back the money. Individuals and families ultimately die, while nations do not. One always hears, in discussions of deficit financing, that, by borrowing money, we are mortgaging the quality of life of our children and grandchildren. That sounds reasonable, but, in reality, a nation's debt can go on forever. The children, grandchildren, great-great grandchildren need not pay the debt back either. They can simply continue paying interest and borrowing more to pay off old debts, into infinity. The nation is not going anywhere and does not have the same constraints a family has.

This does not mean there are no consequences for nations that do not pay their debts. They may find it impossible to borrow, to buy the products of other nations, or even to sell their own goods on world markets. Nations that have become economically unsound have typically experienced widespread poverty, revolutions, and other severe problems.

The interest payments on the debt are, however, a major item in the national budget. Paying for the interest competes with all other demands for money, including social welfare programs. The national debt occupies a larger and larger share of the national budget and thus reduces the amounts of money available for appropriation for social needs.

It is important to note that deficit financing is far from a universally accepted idea. Many political figures campaign against it. There has been a national movement to introduce and adopt a new amendment to the U.S. Constitution which would require the government to operate with a balanced budget, the so-called balanced budget amendments (Burns, Peltason & Cronin 1993). At times the movement has been strong and popular, although, at the time this is being written, it is not often reported in the media as a change that is being actively pursued. Nevertheless, President Clinton campaigned on a promise to reduce the federal deficit over a period of several years and has been proposing fiscal measures that would achieve that goal. Congress has also attempted to reduce the deficit through legislation, the most important being the Graham-Rudman-Hollings bill, which focuses on balancing the budget.

Some observers point out that deficit financing has further policy implications. When the government operates through borrowing, who receives the interest? Generally, the debt is to other Americans, often the most wealthy Americans, who own the Federal Reserve notes and other fiscal instruments through their own investments. Therefore, the interest goes to the wealthy. K. Phillips (1990) points out that during the presidency of Ronald Reagan the U.S. debt and deficit increased because taxes were reduced without a comparable reduction in spending. The borrowing, which was necessary, increased U.S. expenditures on interest paid on the debt, which went from $96 billion in 1981 to $216 billion in 1988. Because taxes were reduced at the same time, fewer dollars earned with that interest were repaid to the federal Treasury as taxes. Phillips points out that the increase in the deficit combined with the decrease in taxes had a great deal to do with the U.S. redistribution of wealth which took place in the 1980s. During that time the wealthiest

Americans had major increases in their incomes; the middle-income groups either stayed the same or experienced slight increases in wealth; while the lowest-income individuals, who have few investments and whose benefit programs were either reduced or not expanding, declined (Ginsberg 1992). Therefore, it is clear that deficit financing has an impact on individual taxpayers and the distribution of the burden of paying for government services.

THE BUDGET PROCESS

Economics and finance are such important components of social policy that they are central to much of the work done by the executive and legislative branches every year in the form of budgeting and budget preparation. The budget process continues throughout the year in the federal and state governments. (For a current, sound, and detailed discussion of the budget process, see Burns, Peltason & Cronin 1993). The budget process begins well before the end of the budget, or fiscal, year, which, at this time, is 1 October–30 September in the federal government and which varies among the state governments. The most common state fiscal year is 1 July–30 June, although some use the calendar year as the fiscal year.

In the federal executive branch the president proposes a budget to the Congress each year, which is based upon the estimates and requests of all the government agencies. The executive branch has an agency called the Office of Management and Budget (OMB), which studies all of the budget requests and makes a recommendation to the president for the new fiscal-year budget. The president proposes the budget, which is a massive document, to Congress, where it is again studied by a number of groups but, especially, the Senate Finance Committee and the House of Representatives Ways and Means Committee. Congress has an agency called the Congressional Budget Office, which serves as something of an auditor and planner on financial matters for the Congress.

The Office of Management and Budget and the Congressional Budget Office both have large staffs of those who are experts on every phase of government. They carefully study the agency budget requests and try to determine the impact of those requests as well as the impact of any recommended changes in them. How many fewer people might be served, for example, if the budget for food stamps were reduced? What level of health care will be available with the recommended appropriation for Medicaid? The policy experts in these two offices are familiar enough with the programs to make knowledgeable recommendations for budget or appropriations levels. Those who work within the programs find that influencing the staff of these two organizations may be more significant in producing results than anything else they might do in trying to improve their programs.

Ultimately, the president's executive budget, which specifies both income and expenditures, is acted upon by Congress, after careful study by the two committees. There is intense negotiation, at times conflict, between the executive and legislative branches about the budget. In fact, it is the budget that has caused most of the recent conflicts between the federal executive and legislative branches. The tax increases passed by Congress and signed by President Bush during his term of office were a source of conflict and of strong political maneuvering. In fact, the issue of taxes was probably the most widely discussed subject in the 1992 presidential campaign, which followed. By 1993 President Clinton engaged in—and prevailed in—a major conflict with Congress over the economic program he was proposing for the coming fiscal year.

The president retains some control over the budget through the use of veto power. Yet in the federal government, the president must agree to or veto the whole appropriations, or budget, bill because the president does not have line item veto power, as is mentioned in chapter 4. Under the Constitution, a president may only veto a whole piece of legislation, not just a portion of it. Therefore, a president who wants improvements in social welfare programs may have to compromise by accepting a larger defense budget than might be desired in order to have those improvements.

The federal budget also shows, at this time, deficit financing such as the amount that will be borrowed, the amount of interest expected to be paid, and the overall balance sheet of anticipated revenues, expenses, borrowing, and deficits.

Budgets are essentially plans. Less money may come to the Treasury from taxes than is anticipated, or more money may be raised. Agencies may not choose to spend all of the money appropriated for them, or they may receive some additional money during the fiscal year to carry out a specific objective or to avoid reducing services to clients.

The state budget process is in some ways similar but also strikingly different than the federal process. For example, states, in general, must always present and operate under a balanced budget. It is a violation of the law, in most states, for the state to operate·in a deficit position. And in most states, as mentioned, the governor has line item veto power and can eliminate or reduce a specific budget item without vetoing the whole appropriations bill.

Like in the national government, on the state level there are professional staffs in both the executive and legislative branches whose members know about all the various state agencies, study their budget requests, and help develop the final budget legislation. In most states it is the governor who presents the executive budget, which is, as it is in the federal process, the most important working document in the fiscal planning process. In a few states a board of the key elected officials develop and present the budget on behalf of a kind of executive committee. Those are generally states with weak governors. Even in those states, however, the governor presents an executive budget, although it does not have the same importance as the executive budget has in states with strong governors. Even in the weak governor states the governor has the line item veto power and exercises it often in creating the budget bill.

The bill that is finally passed is usually a combination of the executive budget and changes made to it by the legislative branch. Battles over the budget are so important that in many states, and at times in the federal government, the budget does not pass the legislative body and become law until the fiscal year ends. In those situations the state often passes a kind of bill called a "continuing resolution," which allows government to spend money at the same level as the prior year for the functions specified in the now-expired budget. Failing to do so, which has happened from time to time, may mean that essential services are abandoned and that government employees are not paid for their services or required to work. Such situations usually last only a few days because they paralyze the government so that everyone works to resolve the problems and pass a budget.

An issue that often becomes critical in budget debates is the efficiency of government, or its avoidance of duplication of services. The Congressional Budget Office and many private groups, including lobbying groups, study the budgets of the state and federal governments and look for ways to eliminate waste and conserve funds. A current popular book, *Government Racket* (Gross 1992), summarizes the problems of duplication and waste in a variety of federal government programs.

In American state and national government there is nothing quite so fascinating as the ways in which presidents, governors, Congress, and state legislatures deal with the budget. It is the budget that contains the real details of social policy, and it is the budget that reflects what government wants to do and will do in a multitude of specific programs and procedures.

CONCLUSION

The levels of and the ways in which government finances itself have great impact on the levels of human services programs that government is willing to sustain. Spending money on social welfare programs may have a very positive impact on the economy through the multiplier effect. Spending too much may cause inflation, which is often harmful to everyone because, no matter how little or how much money they have, it is worth less than it would have been had there been less or no inflation.

It is important to understand that economic policy and social policy are closely connected and to understand that government can increase and decrease the money available to citizens through its own policy decisions. Budget and finance policies are the highest form of social policy, in some ways. In fact, there is no such thing as a social policy that does not have some financial implications. Therefore, understanding social policy also requires an understanding of economic policy. What is and is not done in the social policy field is always related to some forms of economic issues.

DISCUSSION QUESTIONS

1. Are social welfare programs more likely to have an impact through the "multiplier" or the "leverage" effect? Explain your answer.
2. This chapter suggests that free market, classic Adam Smith economic theory is fundamental in the U.S. economy. Try to list three examples, not already used in the chapter, of the ways in which free market economic principles are followed in the U.S. economy.
3. Describe some of the ways in which the U.S. economy appears to be a "mixed" economy. Identify elements from all three economic approaches discussed in this chapter.

4. John Maynard Keynes is considered a giant in economic theory because of the contributions he made to showing governments how they might control their economies. In your own words describe what you believe are some of the practical consequences of Keynes's economic discoveries.

REFERENCES

Bullock, A., & Stallybrass, O. (1977). *The Harper dictionary of modern thought.* New York: Harper & Row.

Burns, J. M., Peltason, J. W., & Cronin, T. E. (1984, 1993). *Government by the people,* 12th & 15th eds. Englewood Cliffs, NJ: Prentice-Hall.

Dolgoff, R., Feldstein, D., & Skolnik, L. (1993). *Understanding social welfare,* 3d ed. New York: Longman.

Ginsberg, L. (1992). *Social work almanac.* Washington, DC: NASW Press.

Greenberg, E. S. (1989). *The American political system: A radical approach,* 5th ed. Glenview, IL: Scott, Foresman, Little.

Gross, M. L. (1992). *Government racket: Washington waste from A to Z.* New York: Bantam.

Hirsch, E. D., Jr., Kett, J. F., & Trefil, J. (1988). *The dictionary of cultural literacy: What every American needs to know.* Boston: Houghton-Mifflin.

Moreau, R. (1993, 12 Apr.). The "Saigon virus": It's catching—business is booming in South Vietnam. *Newsweek,* 12 April 1993, *71* (15), 34–38.

Pennant-Rea, R., & Emmott, Bill. (1983). *The pocket economist.* Cambridge: Cambridge University Press.

Phillips, K. (1990). *The politics of rich and poor.* New York: Random House.

Popple, P. R., & Leighninger, L. (1993). *Social work, social welfare, and American society,* 2d ed. Boston: Allyn & Bacon.

Smith, A. (1910). *The wealth of nations.* New York: Knopf (Everyman's Library). Original edition published in 1776.

Snider, D. A. (1965). *Economic myth and reality.* Englewood Cliffs, NJ: Prentice-Hall.

106

Chapter 6

THE DESCRIPTIVE COMPONENT:
ECONOMIC ASSISTANCE AND ENTITLEMENTS

A fundamental requirement for understanding social policy is understanding social programs. Throughout this book programs—or, as they are sometimes called, provisions—are discussed as the outcomes of social policy. Problems are addressed through the development of policies, and programs are developed to implement the policies and resolve the problems.

In this book programs are discussed and described as examples of public policy and analysis and as benchmarks in the historical development of social welfare and social work. This chapter and the chapter that follows are designed to describe the basic categories of social welfare programs and certain facts about the programs in order to provide an understanding of the American social welfare system and the ways in which it operates.

Although social programs are an important part of overall American government and charitable activity, they are not as well known as one might expect among American citizens. It is critical, however, that human services workers, especially social workers, have a detailed and working understanding of social programs. In many ways social programs are the subject matter of social work and other human services professions, just as medicine is the subject matter of physicians and law the subject matter of attorneys. Social programs are what social and other human services workers use, in addition to their own professional skills for serving clients, to help people. A knowledge of social programs is indispensable for every kind of practice in every kind of situation, yet it must be understood that even the most experienced human services professionals cannot know the details of all the programs that are available to their clients at all times and in all places. Learning about programs and keeping up with their development is, for the human services worker, the equivalent of the physician maintaining current knowledge about medical advances.

107

FAMILIARITY WITH SOCIAL PROGRAMS

There are several reasons why social programs are not as well known to the general public as other programs such as education and health care. First, information about social programs is not typically taught to students in elementary or secondary schools. In most cases students in higher education—unless they happen to be students of social work or social problems or policy courses in fields such as political science, psychology, and sociology—learn little about social programs. In college curricula there is usually no core requirement for the study of such issues, although students may be exposed to them through elective courses or through the selection of specific social sciences as part of their basic undergraduate requirements.

For many social work students at the baccalaureate and graduate levels social work courses are the first in which they learn about such fundamental social services as Social Security, mental health, child welfare, and corrections.

Second, most Americans, especially younger Americans, do not have very much contact with social services systems. We all pay Social Security taxes and Medicare taxes. We may hear about or read about social services programs in the media, and we may even have relatives or friends who are recipients of social welfare programs and services. Yet, personal involvement with the social services is not a typical experience for healthy, relatively prosperous American young people and their families. Many people come to social agencies for the first time when they encounter a disabling personal or family crisis such as mental illness, unemployment, or severe illness and have no knowledge or skills for gaining access to the services that are available to them.

As other parts of this book demonstrate, the recipients of social welfare services are typically special groups, such as older people; young mothers who, because of lack of support from the fathers of their children, need financial assistance; children who cannot live with their own families and therefore become part of the foster care or adoption systems; aspiring adoptive parents; foster parents; people with a variety of physical and mental handicaps; and those who encounter difficulty with the law.

Even when they are all added together the groups who receive social services constitute a relatively small proportion of the American society. More important, they are often isolated geographically and generationally from college students and many employed adults. At some point during their lives, most Americans have some contact with social programs—when they retire, when their parents are ill, when they become unemployed—but, so long as everything in their lives is satisfactory, most have little or no contact with social services programs or agencies.

Third, even political figures are reluctant to discuss social welfare programs in great detail during elections. Those who speak most about social welfare programs typically oppose them, using them as a surrogate enemy that stands for "government waste," poor economic policy, and a number of other negative indicators against which political campaigns may be launched. Consequently, a detailed knowledge of American social welfare programs is a requirement for most people who are newly exposed to the human services professions.

WHAT ARE THE PROGRAMS?

It is a practical impossibility to describe, in detail, all of the social welfare programs that operate in the United States. The programs are extensive and complex. Many who work in them full time for decades do not know every detail of all of the programs in their own organizations.

A conscientious study of social welfare programs would include some comparative analysis of services in the United States with services in other nations. Adding the international dimension makes it even less likely that a human services curriculum would be able to describe comprehensively all of the relevant programs and services. Even if it were technically possible to do so, it would also be challenging because the programs are constantly changing through judicial, legislative, and executive actions, as chapters 4 and 5 suggest. But even if all the roadblocks to describing every program in detail were removed, doing so would probably prove to be so boring for most students that instructors and authors would not attempt such comprehensive descriptions.

Reference works such as the *Encyclopedia of Social Work, 18th ed.* (Minahan et al. [eds.] 1987), *The Social Work Dictionary, 2d ed.* (Barker 1991), and *Social Work Almanac* (Ginsberg 1992) provide the kinds of descriptive information on individual programs which can help students understand enough to write about them or bring them to the attention or benefit of their clients. Information and referral services operate in most communities so that those who are in need of services can find out what the services are and how they operate.

It is necessary for beginning students as well as those at any level of professional practice to remember that there are several broad categories of services. The eligibility rules and the nature of the specific services available to specific individuals or families vary considerably.

Income Maintenance

Income maintenance services are those that help people with their basic financial requirements such as buying food, paying rent, paying for medical services, purchasing clothing, and meeting other fundamental needs. In the United States income maintenance is subdivided in a variety of ways. The basis for most income maintenance programs in the United States is the Social Security Act of 1935, the development of which is described in chapter 2.

A Non-Means-Tested Program. Income maintenance programs are divided into those that are "means tested" and those that are not. R. L. Barker (1991) says that a means test is one that evaluates a person's financial resources and uses the results to determine that person's eligibility for services. The largest and most important income maintenance program in Social Security is the Old Age Survivors and Disability Insurance, or OASDI, which is available to elderly, blind, and disabled people as well as to survivors of persons who were covered by Social Security but who are deceased. The amount of OASDI depends upon a variety of factors, including the length of time the person worked in employment for which Social Security taxes were paid, age, and income when he or she worked. In the case of families that are collecting benefits under the coverage of a deceased wage earner, the amount paid depends upon the factors already mentioned plus the number of children in the family who are eighteen or under.

OASDI is an example of a non-means-tested program. The means of the recipient are not a factor in determining benefits, just as they are not a factor in receiving benefits from a private insurance policy. That is, the wealth or poverty of the recipient is not a factor in determining eligibility or the amount of the benefit. A very wealthy person may receive a significant amount of money in monthly benefits, based solely upon his or her earnings, age, and the number of years in which payments were made to Social Security. A very poor person may receive no more than the legal minimum, no matter how great his or her needs may be. The average monthly benefit for a covered worker who becomes aged, in 1991 was $629 (Committee on Ways and Means, U.S. House of Representatives 1993). When blind and disabled persons were included, the monthly amount was slightly less ($623).

110

Of course, there are regulations governing OASDI which prevent recipients from collecting maximum benefits while continuing to work for relatively high earnings during their early retirement years. And recipients who have other income must pay taxes on a portion of the OASDI benefits. Ultimately, therefore, wealth has some impact on the benefits one may retain after taxes. Yet to calculate the specific benefits no means test is used.

Entitlement Programs

One of the complicated terms in social welfare is *entitlement*. According to Barker (1991, 75), an entitlement is "services, goods, or money due to an individual by virtue of a specific status." He goes on to define an entitlement program as a government-sponsored benefit that is due to people who are in a specific class. It is important to note that entitlements are provided as a right, not as charity. That is true not only of the benefits to which people contribute, such as OASDI, but also of assistance that is paid for with general government funds raised through taxes. A service is an entitlement because the laws establishing it say that people in a specific class are legally entitled to that service. Governments have no discretion over eligibility; if someone fits the defined status or class, he or she need only apply for the service to receive it.

Income maintenance is provided under a variety of means-tested entitlement programs. These benefits are provided to people who can demonstrate they lack the means to take care of themselves completely and that they are in need of help. The two largest means-tested income maintenance programs are Aid to Families with Dependent Children and Supplemental Security Income (which are described, in terms of their historical development, in chap. 2).

Aid to Families with Dependent Children. AFDC is available only to families in which there is a child eighteen years of age or younger and in which the family is unable to meet its basic living requirements without help. AFDC, which is often simply called "welfare" in the United States, is administered by state governments, but half or more of the costs are paid for by the federal government, based on the wealth of the individual state. The benefits vary according to the size of the family and by state, with a median per-family grant of $372 in 1992. In 1993 the lowest AFDC grant for a family of three in the United States was $120 per month in Mississippi, and the highest was $924 per month in

111

Alaska (Committee on Ways and Means, U.S. House of Representatives 1991). Some states have a maximum amount, no matter how large the family may be, while others provide additional amounts of assistance for each additional family member.

Most families that receive AFDC are one-parent families. Typically, the household is headed by a mother whose husband or the father of the children is not providing them with support because he is not present in the household. In 1990, 92 percent of AFDC homes had no father present (Committee on Ways and Means, U.S. House of Representatives 1993).

There is an important federal-state program designed to locate parents who should be but who are not paying child support. It is called the Child Support Enforcement Program, and it is required to operate in every state. The failure of families to receive adequate child support is the most important reason for their eligibility (Committee on Ways and Means, U.S. House of Representatives 1993). Therefore, families are required to cooperate with the Child Support Enforcement Program if they receive AFDC so that the state can attempt to find the absent parent and obtain support from that parent. The Child Support program is also available to non-AFDC families. For a small fee—as little as one dollar in some states—the program will attempt to locate the absent parent through Social Security numbers and other data provided by the parent receiving assistance, if the parent's whereabouts are unknown; arrange for a court to determine the absent parent's child support liability; and enforce the court order with deductions from the parent's wages, tax refunds, and benefit payments. The objective is for the child to receive financial support as well as to force absent parents to meet their obligations, sometimes through punishment such as fines and imprisonment.

The policy associated with child support programs is that legal parents or guardians of children are expected to pay for their care. In addition to the public programs for securing support payments that result from court orders, there are also a variety of private resources, such as certain business-like organizations, or attorneys who specialize in obtaining child support—that help families that are having difficulty receiving the support they are entitled to.

Supplemental Security Income. Supplemental Security Income (SSI) is a national program for aged, blind, and disabled people. It is administered through the federal government's Social Security offices and the costs are paid by the federal government. It paid $422 per month to an individual and $633 to a couple living in their own households in 1992. Those who live in group care facilities, nursing homes, and mental

112

health institutions receive smaller monthly benefits. Some states supplement this federal program with additional funds so that SSI recipients receive different amounts in different states, although the federal payment is the same for all recipients, no matter where they live. In 1991, for example, Connecticut residents received supplements of $325 per month but Oregon residents only $2 per month. Many states provide no supplement at all (Committee on Ways and Means, U.S. House of Representatives 1993).

Of course, all three of these income maintenance programs can work together. One family may have a Social Security recipient, for example, who may also be eligible for Supplemental Security Income because the Social Security payments are less than SSI would provide. In such a case the recipient would receive a combined payment of no more than the SSI payment level. The children in the family may also make them eligible for AFDC. The complexities of calculating the amounts of payments and the degrees of eligibility are great and often require specialized computer programs for definitive answers.

The programs that have been described are cash income maintenance programs. That is, clients receive cash assistance that they can use for necessities. In some few cases in which assistance clients demonstrate that they are incapable of properly caring for themselves or their children—because they spend their assistance funds without paying for their necessities—states may establish "vendor payments" in which the government directly pays landlords, utility companies, and other debtors so that the family's basic requirements are fulfilled by the assistance (Ginsberg 1983).

Workers' Compensation Programs. Another of the important income maintenance programs in the United States is provided under the title of workers' (or, in some states, workmen's) compensation. Those programs compensate working people and their families for illnesses, injuries, or deaths that are connected with employment. Each state has a program, but each state program, and the levels of compensation they offer, is different. In general, the programs are funded by taxes or insurance premiums paid by employers. In some states the government collects the fees and pays the benefits. In some states companies purchase coverage from private insurance companies, which administer the benefits. In yet other states there is a combination of state-operated and insurance company–operated programs.

Workers' compensation is paid to those who sustain injuries in connection with their work or who become ill because of that work. The

113

coverage, however, is not only for industrial accidents or illnesses. Employees who are injured in auto accidents while they are on duty, for example, may be entitled to benefits such as payment for their medical care and financial support while they are recovering. If they are killed in the accident, their families may receive financial support. Industrial illnesses caused by environmental problems in the workplace and other factors may make the worker eligible for health care and income maintenance assistance.

Workers' compensation is not means tested. That is, eligibility is based upon the fact that the worker was injured or killed in connection with work. That, and not the financial needs of the worker, is the criterion.

Pensions and Insurance.   Individuals such as self-employed people and those employed by others may also be covered for income maintenance and retirement pensions through public or privately financed insurance programs. In some cases individuals purchase their own coverage, and in others their employers pay all or part of the costs. Employees of government typically receive some kind of retirement benefits, and the same is true of most employees of large corporations and many other organizations. When the individuals retire they receive pensions that may be combined with Social Security retirement. These pensions may be the basis for retirement and may, in many cases, be much larger than the Social Security benefits. Government assists with these programs through tax incentives. Private employers may deduct the costs from their taxes. Public employers operate the programs, in part, through appropriations. Employees usually contribute part of the costs, but they also receive tax incentives, in that they may often exclude their payments from their taxable incomes and only pay taxes on their contributions when they retire and receive them. Retired people are typically in lower tax brackets than those who are working.

There are also insurance plans that provide income to people who become disabled. These plans, which may also be paid by the employee and the employer or by one or the other, provide payments to workers when they are ill or injured and unable to continue working.

As is discussed earlier in this chapter, all of these programs may work together and may have some impact on one another. For example, the amount of workers' compensation payments may be deducted from the Social Security disability payments. All or some of the private or public resources of individuals are considered in their income tax payments.

114

Health Care Financing

A major form of income maintenance is assistance with the financing of one's health care, especially when there are catastrophic, expensive medical needs. The two basic public health care programs in the United States are Medicaid and Medicare, which are authorized as parts of the Social Security Act. Medicaid is provided to pay the costs of care for low-income people or people who would be of low income if they had to pay their own medical care costs. It generally is available to those who receive AFDC and SSI as well as other people who would be eligible for AFDC or SSI if they paid their own medical bills. The levels of coverage and eligibility vary, however, from state to state. In most states Medicaid covers hospital care, physicians' services, some prescriptions, and nursing home care. The costs are paid by the federal and state governments, with the federal government providing half or more of the costs, following basically the same formula as it uses for AFDC.

Medicare is an insurance program to which employed people and their employers contribute. It is provided to all people sixty-five years old or older, no matter how much, if anything, they have paid. It also covers some other categories of people, including, under some circumstances, those covered by Social Security disability. It provides coverage for hospital care and many other kinds of expenses. Recipients may also pay additional premiums under "Part B," which provides coverage for physician costs and other services. Although Medicare is a federal government program, it is often administered by private insurance companies, under contracts between the government and the companies, an example of the blurring of the private and public sectors which will be discussed later in this chapter.

The two programs work together, in many cases. For example, many states purchase Part B coverage for their elderly Medicaid recipients so that Medicare pays for costs that might otherwise have to be covered by the state. People who are in need of health care may receive Medicare benefits for part of their costs and Medicaid benefits for the rest.

There are many rules, regulations, and procedures that are required in the Medicaid and Medicare programs. For example, providers of services may bill Medicare recipients for the difference between the amounts Medicare pays and what the provider usually charges. It is a violation of federal law, however, for a provider to bill a Medicaid recipient for those additional amounts. Special efforts are made by the

115

federal and state governments to hold down the costs of these expensive programs, a major public policy concern. There are also special efforts to prevent fraud or abuse of these programs, which have been problems in many parts of the United States.

In addition to these programs there is also a federally financed program for crippled children, which is administered in each state. In most cases there is a means test to determine how much assistance will be provided, but the levels of need are often higher than they are for Medicaid. That is, families of modest but not necessarily poverty-level incomes may obtain help for children with disabling conditions or illnesses. In some states mentally ill as well as physically disabled children are covered.

Some health care financing is also available through local and state governments. Free hospital care for the indigent or payments for that care are sometimes provided.

At the time of publication of this volume, there was a national debate over reform of the nation's method of financing health care.

Employment and Training Programs

Assistance to the unemployed is another example of income maintenance services. These are services provided by state employment services agencies with funds that are usually totally provided by the federal government with revenues collected from payroll taxes paid by employers. These programs provide unemployment compensation for those who are without work for a period of time, without regard to the assets of the unemployed persons—although they must report and deduct income received from other employment. Unemployment of the wage earner or wage earners is a financial disaster for most families. It is also a problem that affects large numbers of families every year. In 1992 the projected unemployment rate in the United States was 7.2 percent of the civilian labor force. The average weekly benefit in that same year was about $169, although the amounts vary among the states. The range in 1992 was from $118 average per week in Louisiana to $240 in Hawaii (Committee on Ways and Means, U.S. House of Representatives 1991, 1993).

Those who collect unemployment compensation must have lost their jobs for reasons other than their own misconduct or unwillingness to continue working. Employees who misbehave on the job or resign voluntarily are not eligible. Generally, unemployment compensation continues until the recipient finds work or for twenty-six weeks, whichever comes first. In times of severe economic problems the federal government may extend the period of eligibility beyond twenty-six weeks.

There is also a human services element associated with unemployment compensation services. The unemployment agency makes referrals to jobs and training programs, which are ways of helping people overcome their unemployment problems. They are also a condition of receiving financial assistance. Those who are assisted must be available for work in their general area of skill, must demonstrate that they are seeking work, and must report to the unemployment office periodically to receive their compensation.

There are also many kinds of training programs that are financed by government and industry or, most typically, by a combination of government and industry efforts. Programs such as the Job Training Partnership Act provide federal training funds to states, which, in turn, use those funds to train or retrain workers. Some of that training is in the form of apprenticeship programs, other parts are in more formal courses, and other portions are in work experience activities, in which trainees learn basic job skills by working for public and private employers. Some work experience programs are associated with AFDC, which requires most recipients who are physically able to do so and who do not have infant children to work or participate in work training. There are efforts to involve the private sector heavily in such programs. Part of that involvement is in the training itself, and part is in the form of tax incentives. In some programs, such as the Work Incentive Program (WIN), which is a cooperative effort by public assistance and unemployment agencies, special federal tax benefits are provided to employers who hire WIN participants.

General and Emergency Assistance

Federal programs are usually entitlements for people who meet specific needs requirements. Many of those who are desperately in need of help are not blind, disabled, or elderly, however, so they do not qualify for SSI; do not have children, so they do not qualify for AFDC; are not recently unemployed, so they do not qualify for unemployment compensation—they are just poor. Many such individuals are women who have recently become single because their male wage-earning partners have left them or have died. If they are younger than Social Security age, have no work history, and have no disabilities, they do not qualify for the basic programs.

117

Therefore, there are many local and state general assistance programs that help people who need assistance, without regard to their characteristics other than poverty. Those programs vary dramatically from place to place. That is because there are no national standards for such assistance. State or local governments may provide whatever kinds of help they choose. Some states have regular, monthly assistance programs. Other states provide help only once and then for only one month's needs.

Emergency assistance is similar to general assistance in its variability, except that the federal government does provide some help for families that are receiving or who would be eligible for AFDC. Specific emergency assistance programs may include temporary housing, food, medical care, and other in-kind assistance as well as limited cash assistance.

Emergency and general assistance may be provided by county or other local governments or by the same agencies that provide AFDC. Frequently, one of the tasks of the worker in the AFDC program is to help needy clients connect with some of these limited assistance programs to help them overcome their immediate needs.

In-Kind Programs

There are also a variety of entitlement or income maintenance programs that are paid "in kind." As the chapter on social welfare history describes, benefits have traditionally been provided either in the form of cash or in-kind payments, with in-kind benefits providing greater control of the nature of the assistance received and the ways in which it is used. The largest of the in-kind benefits in the United States is the food stamp program, which provides coupons on a monthly basis to individuals and families who cannot meet their basic food needs with their incomes. Again, the amount of food stamps depends upon the size of the family, its income, family assets, and other factors. Although the food stamp program is administered by a different federal agency than AFDC and Social Security—by the U.S. Department of Agriculture—at the state and local levels, food stamps are generally provided through the same agencies that provide AFDC.

Another important nutrition program is called WIC, which is the Special Supplemental Food Program for Women, Infants, and Children. The program is national and is typically administered through health departments at the local level. It provides nutrition education, health services, and food checks to buy milk, eggs, cheese, juice, cereal, and infant formula for pregnant and breastfeeding women and young children.

There are also many other income maintenance assistance programs provided on an in-kind basis. There is low-cost public housing; subsidized housing in privately owned apartments; and assistance with utility payments, especially in the winter, when utilities are important for providing heat, through the Low Income Energy Assistance Program, which is discussed in chapter 7. Nutrition needs are also addressed through emergency food rations and food banks directed by charitable or government antipoverty organizations and often supplied by food manufacturers. There are also programs that assist with clothing, emergency shelter for the homeless and dispossessed, and a great variety of other kinds of direct help, based upon the local community's interests and abilities to assist people in need.

Many of the in-kind programs and services are provided by voluntary charities rather than by governments. Churches, neighborhood centers, and civic clubs often organize in-kind services projects such as clothing and food distribution programs for those in their communities who need help.

These income maintenance services are discussed first because they are so fundamental to the needs of those who receive social welfare assistance. There are many kinds of human need, but, if basic financial needs are not met, the others cannot be effectively addressed.

LOCATION AND OPERATION OF SERVICES

Another way to describe services is in terms of the level of government or the location in which they are provided. Generally, government or public services are provided at the federal, state, and local—which includes counties, regions, cities, and towns—levels. As indicated, some services are largely local, while others are national or statewide in scope. There is great variability within the United States in the kinds and levels of services provided.

In the United States many services are provided through joint financing by the federal and state governments. The services, however, are usually delivered at the local level—in counties, cities, or regions. Very few services are provided directly from the federal government. Social Security, some services to Native Americans, and veteran's benefits are the primary examples.

It is a truism of American government and the federal system, discussed in chapter 4, that services are largely financed by the federal government, partly financed by state governments, and delivered at local levels, although often by divisions of state government. Services may on occasion be financed by county or city governments with locally collected taxes. That is especially true of certain services that are relatively new in the social services system, such as domestic violence shelters, rape crisis programs, and self-help groups as well as others that have not had the long history of mental health, corrections, mental retardation, and vocational rehabilitation services, which have long been established with financing from federal and state sources.

Another distinction made in describing the structure of services is whether the auspices of the services are religious or secular. Many of the social services provided to people in the United States are developed, administered, and financed by Roman Catholic, Protestant, Jewish, and other religious bodies. These services may include child care, counseling, financial assistance, health services, or any number of other aids to people who are in need. A variety of nonsectarian, or secular, organizations also provide human services. These include civic clubs such as Kiwanis, Lions, Rotary, and Civitan.

In addition, other nonreligious private, voluntary, charitable groups organize and deliver human services. Groups of people with special interests, such as parents of children with mental retardation, and advocacy groups, such as the Alliance for the Mentally Ill, which is composed largely of family members of persons with mental illness, are also examples of nongovernmental, nonsectarian services.

There are also a large number of well-known organizations devoted to the resolution of specific personal or health problems, such as the March of Dimes, Cystic Fibrosis, the Tuberculosis Association, Easter Seals, the National Association for Mental Health, and numerous others.

A detailed description of all the services and auspices under which services are provided is, of course, impossible because of the dynamic nature of social services. Services develop, go out of existence, combine with other services, change patterns, become affiliated with government agencies, and otherwise modify themselves or are modified periodically by others.

FINANCING

To pursue another theme that pervades this book, understanding the financing of human services is crucial to understanding the services themselves. Although this chapter, so far, has suggested that there is a clear distinction between governmental and nongovernmental, or between public and private organizations, that distinction is more traditional or historical than it is real. As chapter 2 discusses, for much of human history there was no governmental involvement in human services. In the United States it was not until the 1930s that the federal government became involved in the organization and delivery of services to residents.

One of the least well known but most important developments in the human services is the blurring of the lines between governmental and nongovernmental programs. Although the distinctions once were absolute, there are now many programs in which federal and other government funds are used to support nongovernmental services. These examples usually involve contracts or grants in which a government agency employs a voluntary program to carry out some governmental functions or to achieve some of the objectives of a governmental program. Although that is more likely to be the case in personal social services—services other than those that are designed to assist people in maintaining their incomes, as described in chapter 7—that pattern can also be true in financial assistance programs. In some states, for example, the distribution of AFDC checks and food stamps is handled by banks, finance companies, private check-cashing companies, or other financially oriented institutions. Governments pay the organizations a fee for carrying out those responsibilities, and government believes it saves money and increases efficiency by doing so. Some refer to this trend as the "privatization" of services (Barker 1991).

Some of the newer experiments in the food stamp program involve the use of electronically encoded cards that look and function like debit cards of the kind issued by corporations such as Mastercard or Visa. Instead of receiving a book of food stamps, the client receives a credit to his or her account each month. That account information is maintained in a central place. When the client purchases groceries with his or her food debit card the amount of credit is reduced by the amount spent on the groceries. The cards are usually produced and maintained by a private corporation, as are the records and the special machines used in the food stores, under contract with the governmental agency responsible for food stamps.

ANTIPOVERTY PROGRAMS

A variety of efforts first developed under the Economic Opportunity Act of 1965 continue to help clients with basic needs. Although these

121

are not typically income maintenance organizations or programs, they often assist with helping low-income people obtain help that is not covered by major programs such as SSI or AFDC. They may provide weatherization services to help low-income people keep their dwellings warm during the winter months; maintain food and clothing emergency supplies for people who need them; and operate advocacy and information programs for people who need economic assistance of one kind or another.

PLANNING AND FUND-RAISING AGENCIES

There are also a number of agencies that are organized to serve other agencies. The United Way organizations, which are found in most communities, are perhaps the best example. They raise funds in a coordinated way to provide help to voluntary agencies in their communities. These organizations have the support of the local governments and business communities for a variety of reasons. First, they are usually able to raise money for less administrative cost than would be true if the dozens of agencies they represent were to conduct their own campaigns. One single, efficient campaign is conducted each year on behalf of large numbers of individual, voluntary member agencies. The agencies request budgets each year, and the United Way determines the amount it will attempt to raise for that organization. In turn, the agency agrees that it will not embark on public campaigns for funds but will, instead, contribute to the overall United Way effort.

United Way agencies also contribute to the rational financing of voluntary agencies by setting budgets that appear to be reasonable for the community. They try to insure that the most important community needs are served and that the role of emotion in determining who receives what is minimized. For example, certain disabling conditions that largely affect children may have strong appeals in the community, even though the number of children affected is small. The "health" organizations established to deal with specific conditions may raise more money than their problem warrants in the community. When such organizations are parts of United Way fund-raising efforts such problems are reduced, and the United Way board members put the health problem in perspective so more appropriate funding levels are provided. Combined campaigns reduce the amount of work time that might be devoted to raising funds for worthwhile causes by concentrating the whole effort on one campaign rather than dozens of smaller efforts.

122

Typically, the United Way raises voluntary funds for most of the longest established local and national charities such as the YMCA and YWCA; Boy Scouts, Girl Scouts, and Campfire; family service agencies; as well as many others. Most of the services it supports are not income maintenance oriented, although a few, such as the Salvation Army, help individuals and families meet some of their fundamental needs through the provision of food, clothing, and lodging. As mentioned earlier, the United Ways function as policy-making organizations in their communities.

Although they remain popular and important in communities, United Way organizations faced some serious problems in 1992 when it was reported that the chief executive officer of United Way America, which is the national coordinating body for all local United Ways, was paid an unreasonably high salary and was also spending the organization's money lavishly on his personal expenses. Several local United Way organizations withheld money from the national body and also scrutinized their own administrative expenditures to see if similar abuses might be occurring. An excellent and detailed book on the United Way was recently written by E. L. Brilliant (1990).

Coordinating and planning councils also operate in many communities in ways designed to help those communities rationally and efficiently provide services without duplicating them and without duplicating assistance to the same clients or groups of clients. Such organizations have a long social policy history oriented to the objective of avoiding the duplication of services. Readers will recall that avoiding duplication and the possible waste of limited resources have been preoccupations in social services for as long as those services have existed.

In the classic example of the centralized planning council records are maintained on all of those who seek and receive services. Then, before an organization helps someone, it checks to determine whether or not the person has already received or is continuing to receive help. In some communities computer-stored records are used to investigate such possibilities.

Because, however, government provides most of the financial assistance that is available and government agencies are required to maintain and consult specific records on all those they help, the need for a community central registry has declined. Planning and coordinating councils are now more likely to devote their efforts to studying and trying to find the means for dealing with human need. Such groups may discover that there are special housing needs for abused spouses and may work to find a solution for them. Or they may find that the real need is for

123

information on services and establishing an information and referral service for those who call. Or they may discover that, although there are ample services, those who need them most are confused by the application procedures or not received enthusiatically when they apply for help. Thus, the planning council may focus its efforts on providing "advocacy" services—on making sure someone is available to help applicants obtain what they need.

Some central planning efforts are focused on coordinating services rather than providing new services. In some cases central locations are developed so that an individual who needs help may apply for a variety of services in the same building or, ideally, with one application, which is then duplicated and distributed to all the programs and services with potential resources available to the client. Some central planning bodies provide "case managers" to clients—people who coordinate the services that the client is receiving or ought to be receiving.

CONCLUSION

It is clear that publicly funded and administered human services are a complicated and extensive part of American community life. Understanding everything there is to know about these services is, of course, impossible, yet those involved in social work and related fields must be aware of the broad structures and categories that describe and govern the human services. Perhaps more important, one must be able to understand and analyze social policy in one's locality to better understand how to gain access to those services for clients.

This chapter has covered many of the public and voluntary, cash and in-kind, income maintenance programs found in the United States. These are, in many ways, the keys to social policy in the United States. Although human needs are numerous and varied, financial need is often a key ingredient of other kinds of needs, whether for mental health assistance, child protection, or health care. Financial assistance and income maintenance programs are thus fundamental to all social programs.

DISCUSSION QUESTIONS

1. List and define three income maintenance programs that fall in the category of "entitlements" and three that do not.
2. What are some of the differences between means-tested and non-means-tested programs? Why, do you believe, have both of these

kinds of programs been developed and maintained as part of the U.S. human services system?

3. What are the advantages of cash and in-kind programs? What are some of the reasons, in your opinion, that social policy leans toward most programs being organized around cash rather than in-kind assistance?

4. This chapter describes a large number of income maintenance programs for many different groups of people. Do you think there are any gaps in the provision of assistance to Americans? If so, who are the people affected? Why would they be left out of the benefits available to people in need?

5. Carry out some practical exercises. Visit your local Social Security office and obtain a special postcard that enables you to inquire about your Social Security account. The office will send you an up-to-date report about your earnings and contributions while in the program and your potential for retirement benefits. While there, obtain pamphlets and brochures about Social Security.

REFERENCES

Barker, R. L. (1991). *The social work dictionary,* 2d ed. Silver Spring, MD: NASW Press.

Brilliant, E. L. (1990). *The United Way: Dilemmas of organized charity.* New York: Columbia University Press.

Committee on Ways and Means, U.S. House of Representatives (1991). *Overview of entitlement programs: 1991 green book.* Washington, DC: U.S. Government Printing Office.

Committee on Ways and Means, U.S. House of Representatives (1993). *Overview of entitlement programs: 1993 green book.* Washington, D.C.: U.S. Government Printing Office.

Ginsberg, L. (1992). *Social work almanac.* Washington, DC: NASW Press.

Ginsberg, L. (1983). *The practice of social work in public welfare.* New York: Free Press.

Those who want current, detailed information on these programs may find what they need within current government documents, especially those published by the Social Security Administration. The series of House Ways and Means Committee "green books," two of which are cited above, provides one of the best compendiums of data on all entitlement programs. In addition, the annual "Statistical Abstracts" published by the Bureau of the Census are a good source of information.

125

For additional information on the programs described in this chapter, see the above sources; and A. Minahan et al. (Eds.) (1987). *Encyclopedia of Social work:* 18th ed.; and L. Ginsberg et al. (Eds.) (1990). *1990 Supplement.* Silver Spring, MD: NASW Press (the 19th ed. of the *Encyclopedia* is scheduled for publication in 1995).

Chapter 7

THE DESCRIPTIVE COMPONENT CONTINUED: SPECIAL CARE FOR SPECIAL GROUPS

Chapter 6 described the economic assistance services that are the foundation of social programs in the United States. This chapter describes the other side of social services—the personal social services, which R. L. Barker (1991, 172) says are designed "to enhance the relationships between people and between people and their environments and to provide opportunities for social fulfillment.... (They) include counseling and guidance, developing mutual help and self-help groups, family planning, and services for the aging and for children." Barker quotes Sheila Kamerman's (1983) exclusionary definition, which says that personal social services are those that do not provide money, health care, education, or housing.

Personal services are crucial, and developing and administering them is the focus of most professional human services jobs. They require high levels of professional skill because services are individualized to meet the requirements of a multitude of clients. The economic assistance programs described in the last chapter, for example, can make a dramatic difference in the lives of clients, but one has to know just what programs are available, how they can best be applied to a particular case, and what the limits are. Once policies and programs are established, however, people with less professional human services education, and even computers, are able to make basic decisions about and run them. In today's human services programs it is the personal social services for which most students are educated and in which most human services professionals are employed.

The care of people with special needs is a distinctive area of social policy in the United States. Although the poor have traditionally been viewed as the primary category of those with needs and the major subject of social policy, the vulnerable and disadvantaged include many subcategories of individuals such as widows, orphans and other dependent children, the elderly, people with mental and physical disabilities, those suffering from illnesses, people found guilty of breaking the law, and others. The establishment of the human services profession is part of that history of developing services for people with special needs.

INSTITUTIONAL CARE

Institutional care has long been a factor in the social services for people who cannot care for themselves, as chapter 2 describes. According to C. A. Alexander (1987), in the eighteenth century a number of institutions were established for people with specific needs. A privately financed home for mothers and children was established in New Orleans by the Ursuline sisters, for example, primarily to care for survivors of Indian massacres and a smallpox epidemic. A public mental hospital was established in Virginia in 1773. A public orphanage was founded in Charleston, South Carolina, in 1790. Schools, often residential, for the deaf and blind were founded in many parts of the United States, as were schools for persons who were mentally disabled and for juvenile delinquents. Prisons had, of course, existed from the beginning of the nation, but in that earlier time they were not considered part of the social welfare system. Institutional care remains one of the primary means of serving people in the late twentieth century.

CARE FOR CHILDREN

Children have traditionally been the focus of many of the resources provided for personal social services. Although it may be difficult for current readers to imagine, children were not always treated specially by society, as if they were any different from adults. Although they are obviously smaller, weaker, and less skillful, generally, than adults, children were not always considered a special population group with special needs and requiring special care; that concept is relatively new, a development from late in the last century.

Children constitute a large population group everywhere in the world. In the United States it is estimated that more than 20 percent of the population will be under fourteen years old in the year 2000. In the world as a whole, however, people in that age group will constitute 31 percent (U.S. Bureau of the Census 1990). More than one third of the members of the National Association of Social Workers (NASW) are involved in serving children and their families (National Association of Social Workers 1992).

CHILD LABOR REGULATIONS

Even prohibitions against children working within the same kinds of circumstances as adults are relatively new developments. Not only was there no social policy prohibiting child labor in earlier U.S. history; in some ways it was encouraged. P. J. Day (1989, 147) noted that child labor was "viewed as beneficial to both child and society, teaching the sanctity of work and the evils of idleness." Although there were concerns earlier, policies to end child labor were not in effect until the twentieth century. In certain industries, such as mining, children were prized because they could reach places that larger workers could not reach, and since they were not responsible for supporting families, they could be paid lower salaries than adults. If they were injured or killed in industrial accidents, the impact, it was felt, would not be as great as if a principal family wage earner, such as a father or mother, had been injured or killed.

Many of the states have had laws against child labor for much of their history. Yet there was no federal prohibition against it until the early twentieth century; in 1916 the U.S. Congress passed a law called the Child Labor Act, to forbit interstate commerce in goods that were manufactured by children. The bill was declared unconstitutional by the Supreme Court, however, in 1918 (Alexander 1987). The states enacted strict laws prohibiting child labor, work in dangerous occupations, and required school attendance.

Child labor is reemerging as an American social problem (Dumaine 1993). An article appearing in *Fortune* magazine in 1993 by B. Dumaine pointed to current examples throughout the United States which suggest that employers are hiring children for long hours and to do dangerous work, in fast food restaurants, garment factories, and grocery stores and in door-to-door sales at night of such things as candy. Children are also working with their parents as migrant workers in agriculture. Clearly, the provisions that now exist to prevent the use of child labor are in need of revision or better enforcement.

The Children's Bureau and Policy Concerns for Children

Congress established the Children's Bureau in 1912 (Alexander 1987) to work toward the protection of the rights of children and to promote children's well-being. Despite the Supreme Court invalidation of the Child Labor Act, the Children's Bureau was given directives to prohibit federal contractors from using child labor (Jansson 1993), another example of executive branch policy-making which worked even though the legislative and executive branches were unable to implement the same policy.

The Children's Bureau, one of the oldest of the federal agencies that deals with human services, has throughout its long history monitored

129

the problems of children in the United States and advocated better treatment of young people. Its creation followed the precedent-setting 1909 White House Conference on Children, the first to be held (Alexander 1987); these were continued for the rest of the century in some form—although the national, high-profile conferences were dropped during the presidency of Ronald Reagan. That first conference was initiated under the sponsorship of another Republican president, one of the most innovative of all American history and an activist, Theodore Roosevelt. These conferences pushed for programs that eventually led to the Social Security Act and many others.

Current children's services are many. In fact, most of the money spent for human services in the United States is devoted to improving the well-being of children. The largest and most expensive of these efforts is, of course, public education. Substantial amounts are also spent on the economic assistance included in the AFDC and OASDI programs, among others.

Child Welfare Services

The major programs providing help to children, apart from financial assistance and education, are called child welfare, which falls into several different categories. In every category, however, it is fundamental to child welfare policy that the focus is on the well-being of the child. The best interests of the child, always and without question, are supposed to be the fundamental concern of those who administer child welfare policies, including agency personnel and the courts. The goal is that the best interests of the child be served, even when his or her interests may conflict with the wishes of parents, relatives, and other interested parties. And very often the child's best interests are the same as those of the child's caretakers. One of the social policy themes that permeates child welfare is that children ought to be able to remain with their families—biological, adoptive, or of any other kind—whenever possible. But a related policy theme is that children should be removed from abusive family situations, when a satisfactory resolution and reunification cannot be expected, so the child may be placed with another family on a permanent basis. Obviously, delaying proper care for children too long is equivalent to denying children their childhoods. Waiting too long can mean waiting until near adulthood, when having a satisfactory childhood is no longer a possibility.

130

Child Protective Services

The most important of the categories of child welfare is *child protective services,* which is a collection of services provided to children who are in danger of neglect or abuse by their parents or others who are caring for them. In every state there are child protective services provided to children whose need comes to the attention of the child protective agency. Children who require protective services fall into a number of categories, such as those who are victims of physical abuse, sexual abuse, emotional abuse, and neglect. In 1987 there were nearly 2.7 million children reported to authorities as abused or neglected (National Center on Child Abuse and Neglect 1993). The data on the nature of child maltreatment is sketchy, but most studies show that over half the children who require protective services have been neglected rather than abused. In many cases, however, children suffer from a combination of maltreatments, which is one of the reasons it is often difficult to isolate neglect from abuse. In general, younger children are the ones most often neglected and older children the ones most often abused (National Center for Child Abuse and Neglect 1993). The differences are not as important as they might initially seem because both abuse and neglect endanger the lives and well-being of children.

Fundamental to the concept of child protective services is that children are vulnerable and, therefore, in need of special protection by society. That idea emanates from the twentieth century redefinition of children as a special category of people, just as the laws against child labor emerged from a new cultural ideal that children should not work, especially in dangerous occupations.

Informing the Authorities about Child Abuse and Neglect

In recent years there have been large increases in reports of child maltreatment. According to the American Association for Protecting Children (1989), the rate of reports per 1,000 children of child abuse and neglect increased from 20.1 cases in the United States in 1982 to 34.02 cases in 1987. In more recent years the rates have continued to rise. Many believe the increases are a result of the legal requirements for reporting maltreatment now being strengthened by law, rather than an increase in the actual rate of child maltreatment. Public knowledge of the problem has also expanded, and the media regularly report on child maltreatment cases. Greater public awareness has led to more reporting of suspected abuse and neglect. The legal requirements, in almost every state, now compel those who have contact with children—such as nurses, physicians, teachers, child care workers, social workers, psychologists, and almost all other professionals—to report promptly to the state child protective services agency any suspicions about possible neglect and abuse. Failing to do so, in most states, is a crime, and a professional who fails to report a suspected case could be fined or imprisoned.

When a report is made the child protective services agency—which is often a division of the same social services organization that provides AFDC and food stamps—is required to investigate the report, often within a day. The investigation attempts to uncover whether the complaint is legitimate or unfounded. In some situations reports are made mistakenly because the observer thinks a child is being abused or neglected when, in reality, a family has merely punished and not abused a child. Or perhaps the child suffers from an illness or has sustained an injury that appears to be the result of maltreatment but, in fact, is not. Sometimes the child protective services system has been used by an angry relative, former spouse, or a neighbor as a means to retaliate for some reason against parents. No matter what the suspicions of the child protective agency or worker, however, in most states a complaint must be investigated.

When a report is confirmed and neglect or abuse is verified, the protective services agency and its worker may exercise one or more of several options for dealing with the problem. Parenthetically, the popular media often suggest that child protective matters are investigated and addressed by law enforcement agencies; in truth, almost all such investigations are handled by the child protective services agency staff. Police departments are more likely to report the problem to child protective agencies rather than investigate them. Much of the involvement of law enforcement officers is in visits to homes under circumstances that may appear to be dangerous. In those cases, when the worker has reason to believe that there might be an assault by a parent or caretaker, the police may be asked to come along to protect the worker. It is true that most forms of abuse and some forms of neglect are crimes. Occasionally, a child's caretaker may be arrested and tried for such a crime, yet those cases are only a small fraction of the many handled every year. Even child sexual abuse and abuse that leads to serious physical injury are not always handled within the criminal justice system.

132

The options that may be used, which are spelled out in some detail in the agency's policy manuals, include the following:

1. Counseling with the household, in which the worker talks with household members about the nature of the problem and helps them plan to avoid future incidents of maltreatment.
2. Emergency removal of the child or children. If the children in the household appear to be in imminent danger, they may be removed to an emergency shelter, which may be a group home, institution, or another household that receives children for temporary, emergency protection.
3. Foster care. One of the solutions often used is foster care, which is temporary care in another home. The foster parents may be relatives of the child or strangers who are recruited and paid by the protective services agency.
4. Long-term or permanent substitute care. It is the philosophy and strategy of child welfare services programs to place children in as few different substitute care arrangements as possible. Child welfare workers believe that the well-being of children is compromised when they move from one foster home to another. Therefore, their preference is for longer-term care with a single family so that, if a child is removed from his or her household, there is placement in only one other home until, and if, the child may be returned. If the child cannot be returned, there is often an effort made to make the foster home placement permanent or to arrange for the child's adoption. These approaches follow the mandates of federal and state policies that carry out the provisions of the 1980 Federal Adoption Assistance and Child Welfare Act, which emphasizes *permanency planning* for children, so that they are not lost in the system (DiNitto 1991).
5. Referral to specialized services. When it appears to be potentially useful, members of the household are referred to counseling and mental health services in order to help them overcome their problems associated with caring for the child or children. In some cases, especially neglect cases, caregivers may be referred to financial assistance agencies so that they can better meet the material and health needs of the child through programs such as AFDC, food stamps, Medicaid, and public housing.
6. In cases in which it is doubtful that the family can improve, the agency may take steps to call upon the courts to terminate legally

the rights of the caregivers to be guardians of the child so that the child can be placed in a more permanent foster care arrangement or be adopted.

In some states reporting requirements apply to almost everyone, and private citizens, like professional social workers, are required to tell the protective services agency about suspected abuse and neglect. In all states any person can make such a report and cannot be charged with making a false report, even if his or her suspicions are unfounded. The social policy is that government seeks the widest possible range of reports, which can be culled and rejected when appropriate. Child welfare matters of almost every kind are treated as confidential everywhere in the United States. Court proceedings are secret, reports by child welfare workers may not be divulged, and the names of the children and their families are kept out of the press.

Another critical social policy is that children should not languish in temporary care—that they should either be returned to their households or placed permanently with foster or adoptive families. Families are permitted, by social policy found in the state statutes, to have a period during which they may try to improve the care of their children, often through the services offered to them. When they are unable or unwilling to improve, the children may be removed. As suggested, these policies are long-standing, but they are underscored in the 1980 Adoption Assistance and Child Welfare Act (DiNitto 1991).

The whole area of protective services, including removal of children from their homes, has become controversial in recent years. There is a national organization, Victims of Child Abuse Laws, or VOCAL, which says it has members in every state and some other nations who are battling public agencies because, VOCAL claims, they are targeting parents who discipline their children but are not abusers, yet have been charged as such (Zupan 1993). Media reports are common about discontented parents who believe the protective services systems has harmed them. These protests have become more frequent as the number of reports, and other activities by the system to combat child abuse and neglect, have grown.

Substitute Child Care

The discussions above deal with foster care, which is one of the three main forms of substitute care of children; the others are adoption and group care. Much of the foster care provided in the United States is by relatives rather than strangers. The official foster care population in the nation is well under 1 percent of the child population (Fender & Shaw 1990). Although foster care is an important program and one that many social policy specialists believe requires additional attention and reform, it does not affect large numbers of children.

Adoption. Adoption, the permanent, legal placement of a child in a substitute family, is also a complicated area of social policy. The circumstances under which adoptions can be made is not the same in all states: some require that adoptions be handled through licensed public or private child welfare agencies; others allow families to arrange adoptions independently between themselves, but only with a prior study by a licensed agency, which conducts an investigation and makes a report to the court that is hearing the case. In other states adoptions may be handled privately, often through attorneys or medical practitioners who know about the availability of an infant (usually because a young, unmarried woman plans to release the child for adoption after it is born) or an older child.

In 1986 there were over 104,000 adoptions in the United States. Half of all these adoptions were by relatives (U.S. Bureau of the Census 1991). In many states adoption by relatives is not handled through agencies at all, even though adoption by strangers might be. In many cases those relatives are stepfathers or stepmothers who merely formalize their parent-child relationships. In other cases children are adopted by their grandparents, or by aunts and uncles. Many times, these family members already are the child's primary caretakers and have been for a long time.

Social policies to protect children in adoption situations are abundant. Those that require pre-adoption interventions by agencies are examples. In those cases human services professionals study the potential adoptive home and interview the parents to insure that the child's best interests will be served. In addition, many states have policies that forbid an adoption becoming final less than a few days after the birth. Other states require that adoptions become final only after a trial period of several months, with visits by human services professionals during those months to insure that the families remain suitable. In 1986, of the 51,000 adoptions that did not involve relatives, 20,000 were arranged through public agencies, 15,000 through private agencies, and 16,000 were independently arranged (U.S. Bureau of the Census 1991).

Group Care for Children. One of the substitute care arrangements used for children who cannot live with their caretaker families is group care, which is provided in a number of forms by many different groups.

The traditional group care service for children was the orphanage, which generally cared for children whose parents had died. In modern American society there are few true orphans, largely because of the extension of the adult life span. For decades there has been no need for orphanages in the traditional sense of the concept.

There have been, however, consistent needs for group care to serve children who cannot live with their families. Therefore, over the years many of the orphanages that did not go out of existence when there were no more orphans to serve changed their function to that of providing care for children who were not able to live at home. These facilities, which house varying numbers of boys and girls, are typically used for children who cannot live with relatives or in foster homes. Many such children are placed in group care because, for instance, they are one of a group of siblings who do not want to be separated from one another; because they are older and, therefore, more difficult to place in foster homes; or because they have behavioral or emotional problems that make it difficult for them to be placed in private homes.

Group care homes have various kinds of organizational structures. Some have their own schools, for example, while others send their children to public schools. Some are religiously affiliated, following the tradition of the orphanages from which they came, while others are operated by nonsectarian community boards. Others may belong to governments and are operated by counties, cities, or states. Most carry out fund-raising to pay for any costs that are not otherwise covered. Many of the children in group care facilities, however, are supported by state child welfare agencies, which provide a fixed monthly stipend to the agency for caring for the children. In some states the agencies are paid the audited cost of caring for the children. In others the state provides a flat amount, often the same as is paid to the foster parents who maintain children on their own. The balance of the cost of caring for the children, which is often more than the direct costs of foster parents, is raised from donations, endowments, or the support of the sponsoring organization such as a church or civic group.

Modern group care is expensive for several reasons. Group care facilities require paid employees twenty-four hours per day along with the operation and maintenance of buildings, which is also expensive. Those who study caring for people who cannot care for themselves have begun to believe that in almost every case large institutional or group care is not the first choice. Not only is it expensive, it is typically less desirable in human terms—more family-like care is preferable.

There are many interesting policy issues associated with group care, many of them dealing with money, which, as noted, is a central feature of social policy. For example, many children in group care also attend the local public schools, even though their official residences may be in other communities. Where does the state per-child education allocation go—to the district that is the official residence or the district in which the group facility is located? For another example, what are the legitimate costs that public agencies ought to pay for children, beyond food and shelter? Should the public pay for their school pictures, Scout dues, prom dresses, class rings, and football game tickets, just as parents typically do for their children? In many cases these issues are resolved informally, with voluntary contributions. Some agencies cover certain of these costs, as a matter of policy.

Small group homes also are operated for children who need group care. These may house a small number, such as two or three children. Care is provided by houseparents, whose profession is the operation of the small group home. In some cases therapeutic or specialized foster care homes are developed to house children with severe emotional or physical problems. In those cases the adult caregivers earn their living by serving as substitute parents; that is their sole employment. Small group homes are used, in particular, with children who have physical or mental disabilities or histories of juvenile delinquency. They often arrange for care and treatment by social workers and psychologists as well as routine medical services.

Although there is discussion later in this chapter of the special services for people with physical, mental, and behavioral disabilities, the general pattern in child welfare is to treat children as children. A juvenile delinquent is not a special species of humanity but is, the child welfare policies of the nation assert, a child with special behavioral problems. That is, a child is first a child; special characteristics or problems are considered secondary issues.

Child Day Care. For several complex social, political, and economic reasons child day care for preschool-age young people has taken on new importance in American social policy. Increasing numbers of children require care outside their homes during the day. The trend toward requiring AFDC recipient families to work or train for work (the original philosophy of the program was to provide assistance to families so that

137

mothers, especially, would be free from working and could remain in the home and care for their children) has also accelerated the need for day care.

Social policy recognizes two general kinds of day care: care in centers and family day care. The first is familiar to most Americans; the second is also widely used. Parents, often mothers who have their own preschool-age children, care for others' children during the day. Many families have used such arrangements for years. The United States has long been an industrial nation with a large labor force, which has always included large numbers of women, many of whom have needed day care or after-school care for their young children. (Current debates about equal employment opportunity for women have more to do with the quality and level of women's work than with whether or not women should work. Historically, women have been employed in manufacturing and service industries, among other work.) Family day care has and commonly continues to be called "babysitting." In some cases the family day care providers are relatives of the children they are taking care of. Some states and localities have training programs for family day care providers, while others do not.

When children are in day care so that their parents may participate in compulsory employment or employment training programs, the cost of the care is normally borne by the agency that requires the employment or training. Therefore, a sizable proportion of day care in the United States is paid for by human service agencies.

Nutritional Assistance to Child Care Facilities

In addition to financial payments and training for centers and family day care providers, under some arrangements and in some states food or cash to purchase food is provided to day care programs, including family day care centers. Food or money for food is provided through the U.S. Department of Agriculture to group child care facilities. The policy is to make nutritional assistance available to the children and to facilitate group care and day care services without adding financial burdens to the institutions or families. Of course, the primary purpose of Department of Agriculture programs is to maintain the food production capacities of the nation and to insure that the farming industry is sustained. Purchasing and redistributing surplus food is a by-product of those policies. Payments are provided under the same agency, the Food and Nutrition Service, which operates the food stamp program.

Licensing Policies

One of the major elements of social policy is the control of facilities for children. It is the policy of all the states to license facilities that care for children as well as the aged and other groups. Each state's licensing laws and procedures are different, but the essential features of all cover specific elements of the facilities' operations. These include:

1. Fire and other safety controls. Facilities must comply with fire prevention strategies, have extinguishers available, store hazardous materials properly, be constructed in ways that will allow for people to exit burning areas safely, organize regular fire drills, and avoid dangerous structural features and materials that may cause injury or death. Such arrangements are, of course, especially important when institutions house vulnerable groups such as children, people with disabilities, and older people.
2. Public health inspections to insure properly maintained food preparation areas, environmental safety, general good health practices, and general cleanliness.
3. Programs that can help the residents with their problems or basic needs. These parts of the licensing process usually involve human services professionals who try to insure that there are sufficient numbers of qualified staff and that the facility operates a program that can educate, develop, and treat or maintain the morale of the residents. A facility that has no program beyond eating, sleeping, and watching television—which many do not—may find its license threatened.

Operating a facility without a license is a violation of the law, so facilities treat the licensing requirements seriously. In some states, however, facilities that are operated by religious bodies are not subject to the licensing requirement. The belief is that the children's home or facility for the aged is a "church" and, as such, is not subject to state regulation. Of course, that is not a constitutional issue. A facility that provides care for people, no matter what its sponsorship, is not automatically constitutionally exempt from state regulation—just as the profit-making business enterprises of a nonprofit organization are subject to taxes, even though the nonprofit organization, itself, may not be. An anomaly of social policy in some states is that religiously affiliated human services facilities are legally exempted from licensing laws. Many of those facilities are of high quality and would have no difficulty in meeting licensing requirements; others may operate in ways that are detrimental to their residents.

For a more detailed study of child welfare services, see Kadushin and Martin 1988, one of the most complete and reliable texts on the subject.

YOUTHFUL OFFENDERS

Children who have had difficulty with the law pose a special set of social policy issues. Child welfare specialists tend to include *juvenile offenders* with children who face other problems and to view them as people who are in need of treatment or supervision rather than punishment. In U.S. tradition a child who violates the law is not treated as a criminal; in fact, the assumption is that a child is not capable of knowing that he or she is violating the law—that the concept of crime is one that children do not fully comprehend. There are, of course, exceptions. Children who commit what would be serious crimes if they were adults, such as rape, armed robbery, and murder, are in some states treated as adults and may be punished as adults, including capital punishment. But most legally established juvenile offenses would be considered crimes if they were committed by adults. Because of the age of the perpetrator, however, the act is not considered criminal. Cases are heard in special courts. Policies prohibit releasing the names or photographs of the children who are involved. Sentences for offenses are not viewed as punishment but, rather, as a means of controlling the child's behavior, rehabilitating the child, and treating the child so that he or she learns not to commit future crimes.

Status offenders are young people who commit acts that may be forbidden for children but are not offenses when they are committed by adults. Status offenses include such acts as consuming alcohol, engaging in sex, and staying on the streets past a specified curfew.

For many years juveniles whose acts would be considered criminal if the perpetrators had been adults and status offenders were treated in the same way by the juvenile courts. Many were—and in some states continue to be—held in juvenile correctional facilities. In recent years, since the 1970s, there has been a trend, spawned in large part by a federal policy that rewards states that distinguish between the two groups, to separate the treatment of juvenile delinquents and status offenders. It is now unusual for children who have committed status offenses to be held in correctional facilities.

Although there is a decreasing emphasis on institutional care for juveniles who have been in trouble with the law, just as there is for other children and the disabled in institutions, national data reflect an increase in the numbers of children who are being held in facilities. Small group homes and foster care are used for youthful offenders, just as they are for children who cannot live with their biological or legally constituted families. Some of these facilities are private rather than public and, as can be seen in other forms of care discussed in this chapter, there has been a shift from the public to the private. Yet the total number of children in custody has increased. In 1975, for example, there were 74,270 juveniles held in custody. By 1987 there were 91,646 children being held. There were, however, somewhat greater increases in the private facilities than in the public. The number of public facilities grew less than 10 percent, while the number of private facilities grew by 28 percent between 1979 and 1985 and by 10 percent between 1985 and 1987 (U.S. House of Representatives 1989).

INSTITUTIONALIZATION TRENDS

The shift from public to private facilities for those who need institutional care can be seen in most areas of services. Care for the infirm and aged, dependent children, youthful offenders, persons who are mentally disabled, and persons with mental illness has moved from public to private resources. Some observers of social policy, as noted, refer to the shift as the privatization of services.

Public policy has swung in the private direction for a variety of reasons. Private care is often viewed as potentially more humane and, in some ways, less costly than public care. The care can be provided by contracts with care providers, which can be cancelled or allowed to expire. When government builds facilities and staffs them with permanent employees it takes on fiscal obligations that continue indefinitely and often expensively.

SERVICES FOR PEOPLE WITH MENTAL ILLNESS

One of the more complex areas of social services for people who need help is the care of the mentally ill. As chapter 2 points out, institutions for the mentally ill were an innovation and reform in the nineteenth century. Before the development of the asylum movement the mentally

141

ill might be incarcerated along with prisoners who had violated the law, chained, and even executed. The segregation of the mentally ill and the provision of humane treatment to them in asylums was a major reform pursued by Dorothea Dix and other advocates. The history of care for the mentally ill in America has been described in a fascinating, classic work by A. Deutsch (1949).

In later years, however, the mental hospital–asylum reform movement became its own problem, because such institutions were found to fall short of high-quality, humane care for the large population of Americans with mental illness.

The Discrediting of Mental Hospitals

In the twentieth century another famous reformer, Clifford Beers, became an important figure in mental health. His book, *A Mind That Found Itself,* written in 1908, following his own recovery from mental illness, spoke about inhumane treatment by the staff within punitive asylums—the very organizations that were originally designed to improve the treatment of the mentally ill and make it more humane (Beers 1957; Quam 1987). Beers helped organize state, national, and international organizations concerned with mental illness, which evolved into such groups as the National Association for Mental Health.

The social policy for much of the twentieth century had been to place mentally ill people in mental institutions, where they could be safely treated for their conditions. Yet as Beers and others reported, the institutions presented new kinds of mistreatment of that vulnerable population. In the 1960s other students of mental illness and mental health studied and wrote about the poor, often punitive treatment to which the mentally ill were subjected. Perhaps the two most important works were *Asylums* (Goffman 1961), which described, on the basis of a participant observation, the social structure of a major mental hospital. The portrait's truth was persuasive. It demonstrated that treatment for patients in such institutions was unlikely to be a high priority. The second work, *The Myth of Mental Illness* (1961), is by a psychiatrist, Thomas Szasz; in it he effectively questions the notion that there is actually something that can be called mental illness, in the same sense that a physical condition is an illness. This book, and several that followed, challenged the mental health system in the United States, especially the system of committing people to institutions without their consent.

A development in the 1960s and the years that followed was a series of court cases that challenged the involuntary commitment aspect of the mentally ill laws which had for so long been the basis of social policy covering the mentally ill. One of the most important, *Wyatt v. Stickney* (1972), was a federal Alabama case that held that a person could not be confined in a mental hospital against his or her will unless treatment was provided to that person. It became clear that the mental health policies, as they had operated, could no longer continue because many mental hospitals had neither the programs nor the personnel to provide the treatment required. The states also discovered that supplying treatment to their mental patients was much more expensive than the essentially custodial care that had been provided for much of the history of the asylum movement. Therefore, many states began discharging patients who, prior to the court cases and the community mental health legislation, might have spent the balance of their lives in mental hospitals. The new requirement was that the mental health system and the mental hospitals become treatment centers designed to help and not simply restrain or isolate the mentally disabled.

Meanwhile, treatment had become more of a possibility with the development, beginning in the 1950s, of sophisticated drugs that could be used with severely mentally ill people in place of mechanical restraints, locked cells, and other artifacts of past methods. It became increasingly possible, because of these new drugs, for more people with mental illnesses to live in the community and carry on near normal lives.

Not all mentally ill people, even though they may not need hospital care, can live unsupervised in their communities. Therefore, there have been small group facilities established for the mentally ill, often operated by private individuals who house several patients who might otherwise be in hospitals; these facilities are not terribly different in structure than the small group homes described for children who cannot live in their own homes. In many cases the adult residents pay for their care with payments from Supplemental Security Income or Social Security Disability, for which they are eligible because of their disabilities. This is another form of the movement toward private rather than public care for vulnerable people.

Although some observers continue to believe that mental illness is simply a metaphor for socially unacceptable behavior (Szasz 1961), there appears to be strong societal acceptance of the idea that mental illness is, in fact, an illness and that it is treatable; psychoactive drugs have increasingly provided means for treating the kinds of behavior defined as mental illness.

Other observers have been bitter critics of the social policy to remove mental patients from hospitals, a process that is called *deinstitutionalization*. E. F. Torrey (1988) is one who insists that the removal of such individuals is directly related to the problem of homelessness. It is one of the ironies of current U.S. policy that many persons who would have once been held in mental hospitals, because they have symptoms of mental illness, are now residing in homeless shelters, which are typically not as attractive or humane as today's mental hospitals. Mental hospitals, especially after they were required to provide treatment to their patients, became so expensive that it was in the interest of the state governments to reduce their populations. Therefore, some observers believe that the whole shift from hospital to community services is an effort to save money more than an effort to preserve the rights and enhance the well-being of the mentally ill.

D. Mechanic's 1989 book is devoted solely to the whole issue of mental health and social policy. His book and other literature on the same subject are of increasing importance because it is clear that mental health is currently less a problem of medicine and treatment than it is a problem of social policy—for instance, policy about such fundamentals as deinstitutionalization.

Another currently important book is Elliot Liebow's (1993) *Tell Them Who I Am*. Liebow, an anthropologist, worked closely with homeless women in shelters and centers near Washington, D.C. Such shelters have in some ways replaced mental hospitals in housing people with mental problems. Although he does not specifically identify the women he met as mentally ill, Liebow notes that those who do need mental health services are not likely to receive or be able to effectively use them. He writes, "Even if one can overcome the initial problem of locating such persons and persuading them that they need what the program offers, there remains the even more difficult problem of getting those persons to remain in one place long enough to receive continued treatments over time" (41–42).

Community Mental Health Centers

Perhaps the major current policy response to the issues of mental health and mental illness has been a series of statutes establishing and financing a network of community mental health centers. That development was initially a product of President John F. Kennedy's New Frontier program. The statutes on community mental health were passed in 1963, 1975, and 1980. Those Community Mental Health acts established local services for the mentally ill and were part of the virtual revolution in the care and treatment of the mentally ill which began in the 1960s. D. Chambers (1992), in his social policy analysis text, provides a detailed discussion of the community mental health legislation and policies.

By the 1990s community mental health centers dotted the United States to the point that virtually every citizen was covered by a program. The programs are generally less accessible to those in rural areas than those who live in cities, but the services are still available, to some extent.

Community mental health programs provide for mental health counseling, the provision of drugs, "club houses" for people to spend their days, hospitalization in community hospitals for people who require it for short periods of time, employment referral and training, and community education about mental health problems. Today's community mental health centers typically provide screening for those who appear to need mental hospitalization. The effort is to prevent commitment to an institution and to serve the patient in the community instead. Similarly, the centers are charged with the responsibility of following up with patients when they are discharged from hospitals so that they are able to be served in the community and to avoid rehospitalization.

Who Are the Mentally Ill?

Although this section has discussed the mentally ill as if they were a single group of people, that is not the case. The mentally ill include those who are diagnosed with existing mental illnesses, those with behavior problems, those who abuse or are addicted to substances such as drugs and alcohol, as well as older people who suffer from dementia and children with mentally disabling conditions. Some mentally ill people are defined as dually diagnosed; that is, they may be addicted to drugs or alcohol and also diagnosed as mentally ill, or they may experience mental illness as well as a developmental disability such as epilepsy.

One of the key policy sources in defining mental illness and its treatment is the *Diagnostic and Statistical Manual of Mental Disorders* (3d ed.) of the American Psychiatric Association (1987). The manual specifies and codes mental illnesses. It is the basis for billing insurance companies and government agencies for mental health services as well

145

as for separating those who are mentally ill from those who are not. Although it was not designed to serve as a policy manual, it has, in effect, become one.

People with Developmental Disabilities

Another population group whose care has evolved over the years is the developmentally disabled, a category that generally includes people with mental retardation, autistic people, those with cerebral palsy, and those with epilepsy. Historically, each of those groups has been handled in ways that are comparable to those used with the mentally ill. In the past they have been restrained, isolated, punished, and killed. There have also been major changes in the care of the developmentally disabled, toward deinstitutionalization and a shift from public to private care, such as in the case of the mentally ill and juvenile offenders. Over the past several years there has been a remarkable reduction in the number of persons with mental retardation housed in state facilities. In 1977 there were 186,743, but by 1988 that figure had dropped to 99,327 in 1,177 facilities. There have, however, been almost comparable changes in private facilities. In 1987 there were 89,120 in private facilities, but by 1988 that figure had jumped to 171,275 in 35,365 facilities (U.S. Bureau of the Census 1991). Clearly, the movement has been from state institutions, which were typically large, to smaller community institutions.

A series of statutes and court decisions have also begun more aggressively to protect the rights of disabled people, including those with physical handicaps, to live as close to normal lives as possible. The policies of the nation now require schools to enroll and serve disabled students in public schools and higher education programs (sometimes in special classrooms for all or part of the day), require transportation companies to provide service to those who need special help, and require that public buildings be accessible to all.

Persons with developmental disabilities may also be provided with a variety of community services such as day centers, recreation programs, special education activities, and various other programs to enhance their lives and well-being.

People with disabilities, including the mentally and developmentally disabled, are eligible, as the preceding chapter makes clear, for Supplemental Security Income, if they are of low income. Those who have

146

worked prior to becoming disabled—who tend to be mentally or physically disabled, since developmental disabilities begin, in many cases, at birth—may receive OASDI.

Recipients of SSI are usually eligible for food stamps and for social services provided by state human services agencies as well. These may include chore services and homemaker services, to help clients and their families handle their everyday living situations more effectively, as well as transportation assistance. They are also normally eligible for Medicaid, to help pay the costs of their health care.

Offenders against the Law

A relatively new area for human services professionals, including social workers, is work with criminal offenders. Again, for much of human history law violators were simply punished for their behavior. The assumption was that people were conscious of their own misbehavior and chose to commit any illegal acts. Therefore, punishment was the appropriate response. As time has passed, however, social policies have changed. Perhaps the most important of the changes has been the assumption that physical punishment is not the appropriate response to all misconduct. In fact, the Bill of Rights to the U.S. Constitution forbids cruel and unusual punishment. Incarceration and isolation from the larger community are acceptable, partly as the kind of punishment that can be imposed on those who violate the law and partly to protect the public from law violators. Capital punishment—the death penalty—is also permitted in many states.

Policy alternatives to imprisonment, such as probation, and early releases, such as parole, have required human services workers to supervise and otherwise monitor offenders while they are serving their probationary periods. Even prior to sentencing, many courts rely upon professional workers to study convicted offenders and assess the best sentences for them, in terms of community justice and the possibility of preventing the prisoner from committing future offenses. Incarceration in prisons, although not as expensive as mental hospitalization, is still a costly alternative. When it is possible social policy suggests the need for community care of offenders so they may be employed and so they are able to pay their own living costs. That trend is another example of the shifting of responsibility from the government to other resources. Although the trend is not as pronounced in adult corrections as it is in some of

147

the other fields discussed in this chapter, some states are experimenting with contracting with private vendors to run all or a part of their corrections systems.

Current social policies have led to the employment of human services professionals not only in probation and parole programs but also within institutions themselves. A number of social problems are now encountered within correctional institutions which were not commonly found in the past. These new phenomena include the following:

1. Many more people are currently in prison or on probation or parole than there were in the past. There was an increase from 1991 to 1992 of some 60,000 total state and federal prisoners in the nation. In 1991 there were 824,133 prisoners and in 1992 883,593. The rate of incarceration in the United States has more than doubled since 1980, so there are now 329 people out of every 100,000 in the United States incarcerated (either in prison or under corrections supervision). The numbers alone have led to prison overcrowding and the problems associated with it (Gilliard 1993).

2. Many more women are entering prisons than in the past, although the large majority of all prisoners are men. The number of women in state and federal prisons in 1980 was 13,420. By 1989, there were 40,556 (Greenfield & Minor-Harper 1991). Many of those women are mothers, and they require human services workers or others to help them arrange for and maintain care for their children. Other women enter prison pregnant. Many penitentiaries have nurseries to care for newborn children, although when they become older most of the children are placed with family members in the community.

3. Large numbers of prisoners have problems with illegal drugs, although fewer are in prison because of drug offenses. A 1991 study of prisoners in state institutions found that some two thirds had, at some time, been drug users on a regular basis (Beck, et al. 1992). Thirty-two percent had used cocaine on a regular basis, compared to 22 percent in 1986. However, there was a small decline from 56 to 50 percent in the percentage who used drugs in the month before the offense in 1991, compared to 1986. There was a comparable drop, from 36 to 31 percent, in those who were using drugs at the time of the offense. The problems of drug users, as well as the problems of drug use within prisons, often require the intervention of human services workers.

148

4. Long prison sentences, which have often been associated with public policies designed to reduce drug use and abuse, have created an elderly prison population. It is not unusual for state and federal prisons to house inmates in their senior years, which creates a need for the kinds of health and human services other elderly people require (Harbert & Ginsberg 1990).

5. It is clear to many observers that law violators often suffer from mental disabilities, especially mental retardation and mental illness. Many also have learning disabilities. Such inmates often benefit from the services of human services workers who can help prisoners overcome or cope more effectively with their problems.

CRIME VICTIMS

According to L. D. Bastian (1992), people over age 12 living in the United States in 1991 were victims of 34.7 million crimes. That figure actually represented a decrease of 16.2 percent from 1981. Of those crimes, 15.8 million were household crimes, 12.5 million were personal thefts, and 6.4 million were violent crimes.

Another developing social policy is that victims of crime ought to be compensated and helped. Most states now have crime victim programs, which include restitution plans for offenders to compensate their victims (Schultz 1987). Victims also receive counseling and similar services to help them overcome the consequences of the crimes against them, including the trauma they experienced.

PROGRAMS FOR THE ELDERLY

Another special group that has traditionally been the target of social policy is the elderly. Older adults are probably the most diverse population in the United States. That is, the aging process affects different people in different ways. Health and economic status, mobility, and appearance all vary dramatically from person to person, within and among age groups. Some seventy-year-olds are healthier than some forty-year-olds; some sixty-year-olds need to retire, while some eighty-year-olds continue full-time employment. Given those variations in circumstances, it is not surprising that there are difficulties in developing social policies that make sense for the total population of older people.

Many of the programs for the elderly are contained in the Social Security Act, which is discussed in other sections of this book. The social services needed by and available to older people come from various sources, but largely from the Older Americans Act, which was passed in 1965 (DiNitto 1991). That legislation provides funds to the states for the establishment and operation of various programs for older people. Those programs include low-cost meals; home-delivered food; the operation of local "senior centers," which sponsor educational, recreational, and health programs; transportation services; telephone reassurance (in which older people who live alone receive daily telephone calls to check that they are all right); and many other activities and forms of assistance chosen and designed, in part, by the older people themselves. By policy the funds are allocated and administered through state commissions on aging and local-area agencies on aging. Conscious efforts are made to insure that the programs meet the needs and interests of the elderly.

Low-income elderly people are eligible for SSI, as are the mentally and physically disabled. They may also receive the social services that disabled people may obtain through state human services agencies. An important distinction between social services and income maintenance is that the latter is an entitlement, while the former is not. Agencies may provide their social services on a discretionary basis because they have only limited funds and are not required to spend them equally on all clients, which is the case for economic assistance entitlement programs.

OTHER SERVICES

Many other policies establish agencies and programs for the benefit of Americans. It is beyond the scope of this book to catalog all of them, and, as has been suggested, they change so frequently that it is not productive to try to develop an exhaustive listing.

Some of the more important programs that are part of the social policy of the United States and are designed to improve the well-being of individuals in the nonfinancial assistance realm include:

1. Community Action Programs, which are outgrowths of the War on Poverty or Economic Opportunity Act of 1965, discussed in chapter 2.
2. Vocational Rehabilitation, which finances programs in each state, largely with federal funds, to train or retrain people for employment. Many of the beneficiaries have physical or mental disabilities.

3. Family service agencies, which provide family counseling, some adoption services, consumer credit counseling, and counseling services for employees under contract with employers, among other services that vary with the individual, local agency.

4. Informal education and recreation agencies such as Boys and Girls Clubs, Jewish Community Centers, YMCA and YWCA's, Boy Scouts, Girl Scouts, Campfire, Big Brothers and Big Sisters, and a variety of comparable organizations that are local.

5. There are also many self-help organizations, including the Alliance for the Mentally Ill, Alcoholics Anonymous, programs for parents of children with disabilities, and similar organizations for people facing other problems.

6. Employee Assistance Programs, which operate in government agencies and corporations to help employees with personal problems such as alcohol and drug abuse, marital difficulties, and other forms of counseling and assistance.

7. Veterans' services, which are provided to veterans of various war eras. They include health and mental health care; pensions, especially for those injured during wars; education grants; and various other benefits, some of which are means tested.

In addition to the government and nonprofit agencies that have been discussed in this chapter, there is also an array of proprietary, businesslike organizations that provide human services. These include private practice counseling services and hospitals for those who are facing personal problems.

CONCLUSION

This chapter has provided information on the current operations of many of the most important human services, especially those that are targeted for special groups of people with special needs. The services delineated are not, by and large, entitlements, as are those described in the preceding chapter. They are, however, widely available to those who need them. They represent what some call the personal social services, in that they help people with their personal, functional problems rather than their economic needs. They constitute a critical part of U.S. social policy and represent the nation's specific efforts to address tangible human problems with appropriate policies and programs.

DISCUSSION QUESTIONS

1. Contrast the services provided to persons with mental illness with those provided to the aged.
2. What are some of the ways in which the services described in this chapter are different than the entitlements discussed in the last chapter.
3. Discuss some of the factors that have caused offenders against the law and the correctional system to become a concern of social policy.
4. Analyze some of the reasons for the shift from institutional, or group, care of children, mentally ill people, and offenders to community, or family, care.

REFERENCES

Alexander, C. A. (1987). History of social work and social welfare: Significant dates. In Minahan, A., et al. (Eds.). *Encyclopedia of social work,* 18th ed., 1:777–88. Silver Spring, MD: NASW Press.

American Psychiatric Association. (1987). *Diagnostic and statistical manual of mental disorders,* 3d rev. ed. Washington, DC: Author.

Barker, R. L. (1991). *The Social work dictionary,* 2d ed., Silver Spring, MD: NASW Press.

Bastian, L. D. (Oct. 1992). *Bureau of justice statistics: Criminal victimization, 1991.* Washington, DC: U.S. Department of Justice.

Beck, A., et al. (May 1992). *Bureau of justice statistics: Survey of state prison inmates, 1991.* Washington, DC: U.S. Department of Justice.

Beers, C. W. (1953). *A mind that found itself.* Garden City, NY: Doubleday.

Chambers, D. (1992). *Social policy and social programs: A method for the practical public policy analyst,* 2d ed. New York: Macmillan.

Day, P. J. (1989). *A new history of social welfare.* Englewood Cliffs, NJ: Prentice-Hall.

DiNitto, D. M. (1991). *Social welfare: Politics and public policy.* Englewood Cliffs, NJ: Prentice-Hall.

Deutsch, A. (1949). *The mentally ill in America: A history of their care and treatment from colonial times,* 2d ed. New York: Columbia University Press.

Dumaine, B. (1993, 5 Apr.). Legal child labor comes back. *Fortune, 127* (7), 86–95.

Fender, L., & Shaw, D. (1990). *The state of the states' children.* Washington, DC: National Governors' Association.

152

Gilliard, D. K. (1993) *Bureau of justice statistics bulletin: Prisoners in 1992.* Washington DC: U.S. Department of Justice.

Ginsberg, L. (1992). *Social work almanac.* Washington, DC: NASW Press.

Goffman, E. (1961). *Asylums.* New York: Anchor.

Greenfeld, L. A., & Minor-Harper, S. (March 1991). *Bureau of justice statistics special report: Women in prison.* Washington, DC: U.S. Department of Justice.

Harbert, A., & Ginsberg, L. (1990). *Human services for older adults: Concepts and skills,* 2d ed. Columbia: University of South Carolina Press.

Jansson, B. S. (1993). *The reluctant welfare state: A history of American social welfare policies,* 2d ed. Pacific Grove, CA: Brooks-Cole.

Kadushin, A., & Martin, J. A. (1988). *Child welfare services,* 4th ed. New York: Macmillan.

Liebow, E. (1993). *Tell them who I am.* New York: Free Press.

Mechanic, D. (1989). *Mental health and social policy,* 3d ed. Englewood Cliffs, NJ: Prentice-Hall.

National Association of Social Workers. (1992, June). Unpublished data from membership data base.

Quam, J. K. (1987). Beers, Clifford Whittingham (1876–1943). In Minahan, A., et al. (Eds.). *Encyclopedia of social work,* 18th ed., 2:912. Silver Spring, MD: NASW Press.

Schultz, L. G. (1987). Victimization programs and victims of crime. In Minahan, A., et al. (Eds.). *Encyclopedia of social work,* 18th ed., 2:817–22. Silver Spring, MD: NASW Press.

Szasz, T. S. (1961). *The myth of mental illness.* New York: Harper & Row.

Torrey, E. F. (1988). *Nowhere to go.* New York: Harper & Row.

U.S. Bureau of the Census. (1990). *Statistical abstract of the United States: 1990,* 110th ed. Washington, DC: U.S. Government Printing Office.

U.S. Bureau of the Census. (1991). *Statistical abstract of the United States: 1991,* 111th ed. Washington, DC: U.S. Government Printing Office.

U.S. House of Representatives, Select Committee on Children, Youth, and Families. (1989). *No place to call home: Discarded children in America.* Washington, DC: U.S. Government Printing Office.

Wyatt v. Stickney. (1972). 493 F. Supp. 521, 522.

Zupan, F. H. (1993, 31 Mar.). Critics organize against "heavy-handed" DSS. *Columbia State* (SC), 3B.

Chapter 8

ANALYZING SOCIAL POLICY
AND MODELS FOR POLICY ANALYSIS

Fundamental to understanding and working with social policy is the ability to apply policy analyses. In human services education, especially social work education, the emphasis in social policy curriculum is on learning to analyze policies effectively and accurately. One cannot deal with policies as a practitioner or even intelligently apply social policy without a clear, systematic understanding of what the policies are and how they operate.

Part of the competence of a professional is systematic knowledge of one's roles and the reasons for one's work. In the human services the simple following of rules and regulations, which implement social policy, minimizes the professional role of the professional. One should know why the policy is being applied; the social values the policy reflects; the alternative ways in which the policy might be applied; alternative policies; the sources of funding and the financing alternatives; and the effectiveness of the policy. A well-prepared professional will want to be sure that he or she fully comprehends the policy and ways that it might be improved. Human services professionals should think and act beyond their daily tasks to the larger concepts of social change and human services delivery planning.

The Curriculum Policy Statements that govern accredited baccalaureate and master's social welfare policy and services curricula, for example, state that "students must be taught to analyze current social policy within the context of historical and contemporary factors that shape policy" (CSWE 1992, 9). Such an emphasis on policy analysis can be traced to Boehm's 1959 study of and recommendations for the social work curriculum. Volume 12 of the landmark thirteen-volume study of what social work education should teach and what social workers should know was written by Irving Weissman (1959), who was then a professor at the Tulane University School of Social Work in New Orleans. Its title, *Social Welfare Policy and Services in Social Work Education,* standardized the name of that curriculum area. The concepts were actually developed by an eighteen-person panel of social work educators, organization leaders, and federal officials (Weissman 1959). They based their ideas on their

154

own thinking and experience as well as on an examination of course outlines from many of the schools that were teaching social work at the time.

As an analytic framework, the study presented a three-part model for understanding and evaluating social policy, a model that remains useful for current policy analyses and which appears to be implied in all of the current models that are suggested for social work. The model presented by Weissman (1959) and his colleagues said that there were three elements necessary for understanding social welfare policy and services:

Problem
Policy
Provision

Their theory was that policies developed from the understanding and definition of social problems. *Problems,* Weissman (1959, 32) wrote, were those situations that could not "be worked out with available resources institutionalized in society." Chapter 3 discusses in greater detail the social problems orientation, which deals with the definitions of how a phenomenon becomes a social problem.

Policy, Weissman and his colleagues believed, "refers to the process of social decision-making by which a course of social action is determined, formulated and promoted . . . as well as the product of that process" (32–33). In other words, once a problem is identified and agreed upon as a problem society determines policies that are designed to deal with the resolution of the problem.

The way in which the policy is implemented is defined as *provision,* which deals with making resources available to meet social problems or implement policies (Weissman 1959). Clearly, one of the first systematic models for understanding social work and social welfare was this three-part model. It is interesting and perhaps historically significant that three-part analytical models were well regarded in social work. In fact, the most fundamental conceptualization of the social casework, or direct practice, approach that was originally developed by Mary Richmond and later defined more specifically by G. Hamilton (1940) had three phases—study, diagnosis, and treatment. That conceptualization was widely used at the time of the *Social Work Curriculum Study* (Boehm 1959) and was likely to have influenced the model chosen by those who developed the concepts for social welfare policy and services. In more recent years, as this chapter will demonstrate, much more detailed and longer lists of elements have been developed for policy analysis. Similar expanded

155

conceptualizations of direct practice are also now used (Meyer 1987).

The fundamental reasons for the emphasis on policy analysis in social work education are discussed in chapter 1. In order to effectively serve people, social work believes that it, in the corporate sense of the whole profession, and its individual practitioners must influence social policies —that policies are a major tool for helping those in need. Most of the current textbooks on social policy place their greatest emphasis on policy analysis.

ELEMENTS OF UNDERSTANDING

R. L. Barker (1991, 175) says policy analysis consists of "systematic evaluations of a policy and the process by which it was formulated. Those who conduct such analyses consider whether the process and result were rational, clear, explicit, equitable, legal, politically feasible, compatible with social values, cost-effective, and superior to all the alternatives, in the short term and in the long term."

Effectively analyzing policies presupposes a variety of kinds of knowledge. One cannot analyze social policy by simply understanding and applying a policy analysis framework. Instead, one must have some knowledge of the public policy-making process, politics, public opinion, public finance, the structure and function of the social welfare system, and economics. That is why policy analysis is only one of the components of understanding social policy, as it is discussed in this book. One needs the background information provided by the other components of understanding social policy as well as the learnings associated with other areas of the curriculum, especially research and human behavior and the social environment.

A person from another planet, for example, might develop an analysis of a social policy and a strategy for changing it which might objectively appear reasonable but that might be horrendously inappropriate and unattainable. For example, when I was a state human services commissioner in the 1970s, my staff told me about a budget crisis in the line item for providing services to adults. They suggested that we make some simple modifications of the "chore services" program, which paid people to care for adults with disabilities in their own homes with cooking, cleaning, and personal care. The staff suggested that we simply tell those chore service providers who were relatives of chore service recipients that we would no longer pay them for their help. It seemed reasonable that

156

relatives ought to take care of one another without the state paying them. Because it seemed to be a worthwhile policy that ought to be well understood by all parties, including legislators, we decided to announce it to the chore services providers and recipients.

When we implemented the policy we learned more about the issue than we had known. First, we discovered that half the chore services providers were relatives. In other words, half of the people who were receiving the services were being helped by their relatives. Second, we learned that the providers had chosen, or had been persuaded, to supply care for their disabled grandparents or aunts or uncles or cousins in lieu of working in the regular economy. If they were not paid, they would have to quit providing services to their relatives. The families wanted their disabled family members to remain at home, which they could only do with financial help. The state had an interest in maintaining the arrangements as well, because care in the clients' own homes was much less costly than nursing home or institutional care. Other relatives, legislators, the press, and other groups pointed to the impropriety and wastefulness of the policy change. A reasonable-sounding policy proved totally unreasonable, and we quickly abandoned it.

Candidates for political office have had similar difficulties with Social Security, which appears to many to be a dispensable source of funds which can be cut in order to reduce budget deficits without hurting anyone too badly. Republican candidate Senator Barry Goldwater proposed converting Social Security to a private program when he ran against President Lyndon Johnson in 1964. It was a major factor in his decisive loss. President Reagan made similar suggestions early in his presidency but quickly abandoned the position, although he made some changes in benefits for college-age survivors of recipients. They were essentially eliminated from receiving Social Security payments. He was also able to implement a tightening of eligibility requirements for persons with physical and mental disabilities. Those targets were young people and people with disabilities, who are not as effective advocates as the elderly. President Bill Clinton's administration spoke of taking action to waive the annual cost of living adjustment for Social Security beneficiaries and of increasing the income taxes on the benefits they received. Those moves would have their major impact on elderly people. After strong protests, including protests by members of Congress, the proposals were abandoned.

Social Security is a costly program, and the Social Security Trust Fund, which holds the payments employees and employers make, has generally contained large amounts of money. Members of Congress, advocacy groups for the aging, and others protested strongly against any reductions, and the Clinton proposals were abandoned. Social Security is difficult to reduce for several reasons, as any clear analysis would demonstrate. First, its principal advocates are older people, who are effective in influencing elected officials because they can articulate the issues that affect them and are also more likely to vote than other population groups. Older people and their organizations also strongly protect Social Security because, over the past decades, it resolved one of the most critical problems in the United States—the poverty of older adults. Although they are not all wealthy now, before Social Security was improved and stabilized in the 1970s and 1980s, the elderly were the poorest group in the nation. After the reforms that was no longer true. The levels of benefits were increased, and the annual cost of living adjustments kept those benefits from being eroded by inflation. Furthermore, older people often feel financially vulnerable because most of the means available to younger groups to prevent future poverty— such as seeking better-paying work or setting up pension plans for their retirement—are not available to them. They feel trapped because they are subject to public policy decisions that are beyond their own control. A critical analysis makes it clear to most elected officials that threatening Social Security will often literally be self-defeating.

Part of the problem with analyzing policies such as Social Security and social services such as chore services is knowing all of the sources of information available to various groups of people. New presidents, for example, have since the 1960s been from the executive branches of the federal or state governments. Presidents Carter, Reagan, and Clinton had most recently been governors. Presidents Nixon, Ford, and Bush had most recently been vice presidents, although all three also had prior experience in Congress. Those who hear most from constituents about problems with income and concerns about Social Security are members of Congress. That is because, as discussed in chapter 4, members of Congress devote major portions of their time and effort to "constituent services"—to hearing from and trying to resolve problems for their constituents. Executive branch officials such as presidents and governors do not devote much of their time to constituent services. They work, instead, with members of Congress on legislative programs. Therefore, they do not always know the extent of concerns about individual problems such as poverty among the elderly. In many cases representatives of the legislative branch, whether the U.S. Congress or a state legislature, will have much better information on constituent reactions to specific proposals than will executive branch leaders.

The Role of Human Services Workers in Policy Analysis

Human services workers need the ability to analyze policies for a variety of reasons. In order to carry out their professional responsibilities to be aware of and to influence policy, they must be skillful in understanding and analyzing policies. Those who are involved in administration need policy analysis skills in order to implement policies effectively. Skill in social policy analysis is a necessary part of the ability of social policy practitioners, some of whose roles are discussed in chapter 9.

Intentional and Unintentional Consequences

Perhaps the primary overall objective of policy analysis is to develop policies that have the results, or consequences, they are designed for and to avoid results, or consequences, that are not intended. Unintended consequences are the nightmares of policymakers, who may set out to solve a problem such as developing a new catastrophic health insurance program under Medicare, as Congress did in 1988. The costs were to be financed largely from additional taxes on upper-income elderly people. Advocates for the new program appeared to approve of it partly because many older people thought they would be receiving new coverage for nursing home care. When they discovered that their taxes increased and that there was no nursing home care included, the elderly rebelled and demanded that the program be repealed, which Congress did in 1989 (Ginsberg 1990). The unintended consequence was that large groups of older adults protested strongly and demanded repeal of the changes. Congress, which thought it was satisfying the need to hold down the cost increases as well as supporting the preferences of older constituents, discovered that the consequence of the act was to anger those constituents (Ginsberg 1990).

Unintended consequences are always a social policy concern that is just below the surface of policy-making. If the federal government provides health insurance coverage for all citizens, which was being debated as this book went to press, will the policy increase the use of health care so greatly that the costs for everyone will rise prohibitively? If Aid to Families with Dependent Children benefits are increased to a more generous level, will assistance compete with low-wage employment and, in

159

turn, reduce the labor force and the amount of tax revenues? When involuntary commitment procedures for public mental hospitals were made more restrictive, was an unintended consequence the creation of the problem of homelessness?

Those who work with social policies always want to achieve specific objectives. They also try to analyze their policies so that they will know about, and perhaps, be able to avoid, unintended consequences.

Financing

Another overriding issue in analyzing social policy is financing. How much is actually allocated to implementing a policy? How will a carefully developed, idealistic policy be financed, or will it be financed at all? Understanding policy also means understanding the financing of policy. In the public policy component it is important to look not only at the content of legislation or court decisions and administrative orders but also at the financing that goes with them. Everything costs money, even if it is a charitable effort directed by volunteers. Such fundamentals of program operation as postage, telephone costs, and transportation are always required. If all the funds are donated, that is the answer to how the program is financed. But financing is always a factor and is probably the first series of questions one must answer when analyzing policies. Whatever one is examining—the human services that are to result from the policy, the relationship between the extent of the funding and the actual impact it will make, and the priorities of the agency or government that develops the policies—money is at the heart of any analysis.

An example of money driving policy comes from *The Chronicle of Higher Education* (10 Mar. 1993), which reported in its "Marginalia" column that employees of Pennsylvania State University were forbidden to drink soft drink products that compete with Pepsi-Cola because the university had a contract with the parent corporation, Pepsico, which required employees, when they publicly consumed soft drinks, to drink only Pepsi.

FRAMEWORKS FOR ANALYSIS

There are many social work and social science frameworks or models for analyzing social policies. None is universally accepted or used in social work. Most include similar elements, although the emphases differ from model to model. H. A. Burch (1991), D. Chambers (1992), A. W. Dobelstein (1990), D. Gil (1976), N. Gilbert, and H. Specht & P. Terrell (1992), W. J. Heffernan (1992), D. Pierce (1984), P. H. Rossi & H. E. Freeman (1989), D. Stoesz & H. J. Karger (1992), and J. E. Tropman (1987) are among the authors who have developed policy analysis approaches. All of these frameworks, or models, vary, and all are much more complex than the "problem, policy, provision" model proposed by Weissman in 1959.

The models differ in length. Some contain just a few elements, as the specific illustrations in this chapter demonstrate, while others include a larger number of elements. Some focus more heavily on philosophical and value issues while others place more emphasis on finances. Some place more emphasis on quantification than others. All, however, if systematically and carefully applied, should give the analyst a better understanding of the policy that is being analyzed than would be possible without a systematic model.

Deborah Rice (1992) examined a number of those models and summarized them. Similarly, many of the texts on social policy also discuss and summarize other models along with their own. Most of the models follow, to some extent, the general features of the scientific method as E. D. Hirsch, Jr., et al. (1988) describe it: (1) careful observation; (2) deduction of natural laws (in the case of the social sciences and human services, reviewing what knowledge has been developed and what questions have already been answered through, for example, a review of the existing literature); (3) formation of hypotheses or generalizations (in the case of social policy the proposal of specific policy solutions designed to deal with the issues being addressed); and (4) experimental or observational testing of the validy of the hypotheses, or policy solutions. The problem, policy, provision triad (Weissman 1959) is in some ways an abbreviated version of the scientific method.

J. E. Tropman (1987) suggests that there are five phases to the policy cycle:

1. Problem Definition
2. Proposal Development
3. Decision Phase
4. Planning and Program Design
5. Programming and Evaluation

Within each of the phases Tropman (1987) details a number of methods or techniques, several of which are technical methods such as needs assessment, Delphi, flow charting, and lobbying. (Many of these are more applicable to the policy practice component and are discussed in more detail in chap. 9.)

In one way or another the policy analysis models described in this chapter deal with the phases specified by Tropman. The models tend to incorporate the approaches of other models, even though they do so in different frameworks and with different language.

Who Wins, Who Loses

Policy analysis usually involves specific examinations; for example, one of the classic policy analysis questions is "Who benefits, and who loses?" This is similar to a classic political science policy analysis question: "Who gets what, when, and how?" (Lasswell 1958). There is a general, usually correct assumption that every social policy helps some individuals and groups and also costs some individuals and groups. Often these costs can be translated into money. President Clinton, for example, early in his term of office, laid out that proposition clearly (*Los Angeles Times* 1993); he said there were sacrifices needed in order to render the American economy healthy. He said that the sacrifices would be greater among those who had benefited most during the Reagan and Bush administrations. Those were the wealthiest Americans, whose proportion of American income increased dramatically during those years (Ginsberg 1992), as opposed to the least-wealthy and lower-middle-income groups, whose incomes declined or remained steady. His policy would, he suggested, help all wage earners, by reducing the budget deficit and the need to pay for as much interest on the national debt, while it would disproportionately hurt the highest-wage earners. Seldom are matters so clearly stated.

For another example from my experiences in state government, during one exceptionally cold winter the administration learned that many people were being forced to choose between "heating and eating." They could not afford both adequate food purchases and the costs of utilities or heating fuel to stay warm. Energy costs had increased dramatically because of conflicts in the Middle East. Illness and death seemed the potential consequences for many residents. We thus tried to develop a policy that would require the utility companies to provide low-income people with lower-cost service. Utility rates, however, were set in our state—and in all states—by regulatory commissions that allow the electric and gas companies to charge on the basis of their costs. If they gave reduced costs to low-income families, those reductions would be passed on as increases to higher-income families. In effect, we would be imposing a tax on some for the benefit of others.

Fortunately, the federal government developed and has maintained a program for home heating assistance called the Low Income Energy Assistance Program. The funds are appropriated from the regular tax revenues of the government and given to the states on the basis of their weather: states with the coldest climates and the longest winters receive more funds per low-income person than warmer states. Less directly, that program is still one in which people pay taxes that are redistributed to low-income people to help them with their utility costs. The mechanism was not as direct as it would be if the companies would lower the costs to lower-income people, but the principle is the same: *in any policy decision some people benefit, while others pay.* The utility companies also provided means for their customers to make voluntary contributions that would be applied to the utility bills of low-income customers. Those efforts have yielded some assistance for low-income people, but not as much as a government appropriation provides.

Cost-Benefit Analysis

Another technique often used in policy analysis is cost-benefit, or, as it is sometimes called, cost-effectiveness, analysis: Does the cost of the policy, one asks, provide commensurate benefits? One example of applying that concept is in determining eligibility for assistance programs such as Aid to Families with Dependent Children and food stamps. Those who study aid programs know that most of those who are certified as eligible are, in fact, eligible. There are a few fraudulent claims that can be prosecuted through the law enforcement systems. There are also several cases in which people are slightly, almost technically, ineligible because they neglected to report some earnings or a gift or because the value of their property increased and they did not report it. The cost of eliminating *all* of the ineligible applicants—down to the last fraction of a percent—is not viewed as beneficial enough to justify the cost. Eliminating all ineligible clients costs a great deal more than eliminating almost all of them, especially all who only slightly exceed the eligibility guidelines. Another way to express it is to say that such an intense effort is not likely to be cost-effective, because it costs more than it is worth.

163

EXAMPLES OF POLICY ANALYSIS MODELS

As suggested, there are many examples of policy analysis outlines and models. Most require the analyst to answer a series of questions about the policy. The result of answering those questions is an analysis of the policy. The following sections describe some currently used policy analysis models.

It is worthwhile to note that any usable policy analysis framework will include several dimensions. One is the nature of the decision-making process associated with the policy, changes in it, or its replacement. Who are the contending parties? Who has the power to make the decisions? What values are inherent in all sides of the issue? And who is affected, positively or negatively, by the policy? If one takes the single most controversial social policy issue of the 1980s and 1990s, abortion, the issues may be clearly seen. The debate over abortion is, fundamentally, over two value questions: When does life begin, at birth or at the moment a sperm and an ovum unite? And are there justifiable social limits on the rights of a woman over her body and its functions? Those with opposite value positions are arrayed against each other on the issue. The "pro-choice" position is favored by those who believe women have authority over their own bodies and bodily functions as well as by those who want women to be as free as men to make their own plans and live their own lives. On the other side are some who believe abortion is a form of murder (because they believe life begins at conception, not at birth), some aspiring adoptive partents, who believe abortion has reduced the number of children available for adoption, and a variety of others. Analyzing the issue of abortion, and any other issue, requires some effort to investigate the decisions that led to its implementation or to its rejection.

Finances are also always a subject of discussion in any policy analysis model. How much will the policy cost? How will the funds be raised to pay for it? And what else might have to be eliminated to make the policy affordable?

What are the alternative approaches to solving the problem or implementing programs that could be solutions? If government wants to make it possible for more parents, especially mothers, to work outside their homes, should government set up a national day care program? Should government give money to parents to purchase day care from centers or in-home providers? Or should government provide vouchers to parents that can only be used for day care? What, the next question becomes,

164

are other alternatives, and what are the strengths and weaknesses of the alternatives? For example, if government gave money to families, some might simply keep the money and use it as a substitute for employment outside the home. Or they might use the money to pay a relative (like the chore services providers described earlier), who would then care for children rather than working outside the home themselves. Some parents with older children might convince those children to care for themselves— and stay free of trouble—with their new money. A cash approach has many more possibilities than other approaches. Yet cash payments may not be viewed as being in the best interests of the families, children, or society. Setting up a network of day care facilities could assist in educating children, screening them for health problems, and gaining access to their parents for educational and other activities. In fact, Head Start is, in part, a day care program that achieves some of those other advantages.

Those are the kinds of debates in which social policy experts engage. When they do so they also consider the experiences of others in addressing similar problems. They search the literature for comparable examples, communicate with comparable governments to learn how they might have addressed the problems, and otherwise attempt to propose the best alternatives with full knowledge of what has and has not worked in other locales or at other times.

Another persistent question is how the program will be implemented. Some methods are through mailing applications, word of mouth, or a formal public education and outreach effort or by adding resources and the new program to an existing organization.

How will we learn what the policy is achieving? Some form of program evaluation, designed to determine the program's impact, is generally part of any proposal for a program. The evaluative information is used to improve the program or as a basis for cancelling the program in the future.

The Hobart Burch Framework (1991)

The Why's of Social Policy: Perspectives on Policy Preferences (1991) contains Hobart Burch's framework. Burch first asks what the issue under consideration is, or, in other words, what is the problem? What are its boundaries? What are opinions and perceptions about it? What values are related to the problem, and what would be the ideal situation? (Rice 1992).

Second, Burch would inquire about the nature of the situation—key elements such as the socioeconomic, cultural, legal, and political contexts. What is currently being done to address the issue? Who are the key players in this issue and any decisions about it?

Third, Burch would ask what might be done by exploring alternative objectives and means; the alternatives proposed by those opposing the policy alternatives and their merits, strengths, and possible compromises that might satisfy two or more sides. The best policy would then be chosen in terms not only of the desirability of the policy but also its feasibility.

The third phase of the Burch model is comparable to military planning procedures in which commanders develop alternatives and explore their opponents' potential responses to the alternatives. Again, planning, analysis, and action models in many fields follow the general precepts of systematic, scientific inquiry. Social policy analysis is no different.

The Bruce Jansson Approach (1990)

Jansson's primary thrust in social policy is to educate people who are able to practice the discipline, an orientation that is discussed in a later chapter. He also, however, includes extensive discussion of analytic skills in his book *Social Welfare Policy: From Theory to Practice* (1990) and presents a straightforward model that includes three steps: (1) analyzing the presenting problem; (2) finding a policy remedy that will effectively address the problem; and (3) convincing other persons to accept the recommendations. When he explains his three steps he includes the kinds of issues cited by others who present analytic models, such as developing and presenting data to explain the problem and solutions to it, examining alternative policy solutions, and making choices.

Although his emphasis is on practice skills, he offers some important insights into elements of social policy which are often overlooked, especially the nonrational components of the subject (Jansson 1990). Some human services workers are puzzled when they encounter opposition to or strong support for policies that do not appear to be in the interests of those on either side. Jansson devotes a part of his 1990 book to understanding some of the nonrational factors that have an impact on policy; the roles played by emotion, sentiments, prejudices, and power in the development of policy are important in any effective analysis.

166

The Gilbert, Specht & Terrell Model (1992)

Neil Gilbert, Harry Specht, and Paul Terrell were at the University of California, Berkeley, School of Social Welfare, when they developed their policy analysis concepts in their book *Dimensions of Social Welfare Policy*. Actually, the 1992 volume is the third edition of a book that was published in two earlier editions by Gilbert and Specht alone. The model is one of the most widely accepted in social welfare policy analysis. One of the authors' major theses is that there are three approaches to analyzing policy: studying the process of formulating the policy; studying the product, or what is actually done; and studying performance—that is, evaluating the outcomes of implementing the policy.

Their book is primarily an explication of their model, which focuses on the process of policy development or formulation. They present and develop a basic four-part model, with four questions:

What are the bases of social allocation?
What are the types of social provisions to be allocated?
What are the strategies for the delivery of these provisions?
What are the methods of financing these provisions?
(Gilbert, Specht & Terrell 1992, 43)

They attribute their model, in part, to Eveline Burns, who was one of the architects of Social Security and who, for many years before her death, was a leading writer and thinker about policy development. Burns's four questions were narrower because they focused on issues of Social Security, including a variety of financial assistance programs. The authors explain that they wanted to develop an analytic framework that could cover the larger spectrum of the entire social welfare field (1992).

Their four-part framework, which they describe as their dimensions of social welfare policy—the title of their book—also ties their four dimensions to three "axes," which are the range of alternatives that are possible, the values that are part of the alternatives, and the theories behind the alternatives.

Gilbert, Specht, and Terrell (1992) describe their first dimension, the bases of social allocation, as the "who" of social welfare—the same who as in the "who wins" issue described earlier. They also describe the various alternatives, values, and theories that could apply to this who. This "basis" is much more complicated than it seems. For every possible group to be served there are alternative approaches. As pointed out, one of the persistent conflicts in social welfare history and social policy theory is over how one might best help financially disadvantaged individuals. One group of approaches would provide assistance directly to those individuals, with revenues collected in the form of taxes from the nondisadvantaged. Another group of approaches would suggest providing money, tax relief, or other advantages to the affluent, who would, in turn, attempt to earn more by expanding or creating new businesses. Actually, these two approaches are both always being used in the United States to some extent. AFDC is an example of helping disadvantaged individuals directly. Tax reductions and depreciation allowances for businesses are the opposite approaches. The first, as will be recalled, is popularly known as "trickle-up" theory, based on the idea that the disadvantaged will receive their help and spend it so that it will ultimately reach all levels of the economy, including the top, where businesses will use their new earnings to begin new enterprises or expand their existing ones. The second is called "trickle-down" theory, in which top earners use their wealth to expand, thus creating jobs, and ultimately the added wealth trickles down through all levels of the economy.

This example represents all three of the axes that Gilbert, Specht, and Terrell describe. Two alternative approaches exist for examining serving the disadvantaged. First, there is the issue of *values,* such as are revealed by such statements as "People deserve to be helped directly when they are in need" and "People should not be helped directly, but growing employment in a growing economy will provide for them." Second, there are *theories* about how money is distributed in an economy. In fact, both of these approaches, these ways of looking at the problem, have worked and continue to work in different ways at different times, just as both the trickle-up and trickle-down theories have each been correct at times. The differences are probably in degrees rather than absolutes and in what the values of proponents and opponents are.

Gilbert, Specht, and Terrell make a valuable contribution to social policy analysis by defining their axes because they show that, almost always, there are many alternative ways of achieving a social policy objective; because they explain that social policy is not simply a technical concern but one that is affected by values and beliefs; and because they show that theoretical considerations and theories are also part of the process of social policy analysis.

The second element of the framework, the types of social provisions to be allocated, deals with what is actually done. The various ways in which child care could be provided is an example of the types of social provisions that could be applied when serving the who, or parents, in that case. Social provisions are the "what" element of the "who wins" question. Who wins? . . . What is the issue? The what can be financial assistance, day care, mental health counseling, nutrition assistance, housing, family planning, health care, and almost anything else that can be assumed under the social policy rubric. The three axes of alternatives, values, and theories are also applied in analyzing a policy or issue.

Gilbert, Specht, and Terrell's third element, the strategies for delivering the provisions, is the "how" of social policy analysis. The strategies, however, are not programmatic but, rather, administrative in nature. An example might be the ways in which financial assistance has been delivered to low-income people with disabilities. Chapter 2 shows that in early history that group, in many cases, was served by counties through institutional care. When the provision of assistance evolved from assistance in kind, such as housing and food, to assistance in cash, and from "indoor" to "outdoor" relief, the delivery strategy changed too. In the original version of the Social Security Act the economically disadvantaged disabled received assistance through a matching program of federal and state funds which was administered by the states, as chapter 5 describes. Each state had a different payment level, based upon its appropriations. In 1972 the Supplemental Security Income system was established, which provided for national standards and administration by the U.S. Social Security Administration. So, the delivery system has changed from local to state to federal government.

Medical insurance for the low-income population with disabilities, however, has not been handled in the same way. Had the disadvantaged disabled been incorporated into Medicare, which is principally for people sixty-five and older, they would have received medical insurance in the same way and through the same federal agency as Social Security beneficiaries. Yet they were not. Instead, the states are essentially required to cover SSI recipients through their Medicaid programs, which are financed with state and federal funds and administered by the states. To help them meet their nutritional needs food stamps are available to almost all SSI recipients. The food stamp program is another delivery system. The stamps are provided at no cost to the states by the U.S. Department of Agriculture. The states, in turn, provide the stamps to the individuals and families who are eligible for them.

Housing for the disadvantaged disabled population is delivered in a variety of other ways, many of them with some federal financing but, in most cases, with local administration. As can be seen from the example, the delivery systems are varied, even for meeting the basic economic, food, housing, and health needs of a special population. For each delivery mechanism it is necessary to discuss the three axes of alternatives, values, and theories.

The fourth dimension is the financing of the services, or provisions, which is also affected by the three axes. Some of the variations in financing have been discussed already. One might recall that Social Security's social insurance and Medicare are financed by employee and employer contributions, which are held in trust funds. Those who benefit tend to believe that they are fully entitled to what they receive—that they paid for it. Other programs, especially those designed for people who cannot pay for their own, are financed through general tax revenues.

How programs are financed is often the most interesting of the policy analysis discussions. In recent years there have been many artful examples of financing good works by taxing perceived evils. Some suggest that health care for people who are cigarette smokers ought to be financed by cigarette taxes, for example, so that those who cause their problems also pay for treating them. In North Dakota nonprofit organizations are permitted to support their own human services, or to finance those of other organizations, by sponsoring gambling. The net revenues from the gambling are then used to support the services (Conrad 1990). In other cases "luxury taxes" on expensive items such as automobiles, boats, furs, and the like are dedicated to paying for services to the disadvantaged. In other situations the provision of services is paid for through full or partial fees for those services. Community mental health centers, family service programs, day care centers, leisure time and recreational programs, and many others are financed in whole or in part by fees that the recipients of the services pay. Whatever the arrangements, however, it is always important to examine the nature of the financing that is used or planned for the services. Finances are a crucial part of any social policy analysis, if not the most crucial part.

The foregoing brief examples show how alternatives, values, and theories are important in decisions about the financing of social provisions. There are many alternative ways to finance services, and the alternatives chosen are products of the values as well as the theories of those who make the decisions.

Special attention has been given to the Gilbert, Specht, and Terrell (1992) approach because it takes into account so many of the relevant elements that ought to be considered when analyzing policies. It provides a comprehensive approach to analyzing any kind of social policy. It is also a popular model that is widely used in baccalaureate and master's social work education.

Diana M. DiNitto on Policy Analysis

Diana M. DiNitto, the author of another popular text in social welfare policy, *Social Welfare: Politics and Public Policy* (1991), discusses social policy analysis under the rubric of program evaluation. She focuses on the impact of social policies, on learning about the consequences of policies. In her discussion of the process of evaluation she makes the important distinction between understanding what social policy "outputs" (what the provisions are) and social policy "impacts" (what the effects of those policies are on the target population and the larger society). Although DiNitto focuses on government policies and provisions, the principles of program evaluation which she suggests also apply to nongovernmental organizational policies and provisions.

As her model for program evaluation, DiNitto incorporates a model proposed by P. H. Rossi and H. E. Freeman (1989). They suggest that an evaluation deal with several questions:

1. Is the problem correctly conceptualized?
2. What is the extent of the problem and where is the target population?
3. Does the program design fit with the objectives?
4. Is there an underlying coherent rationale?
5. Are there efforts to maximize the chances of success of the provision?
6. What are the real or projected costs?
7. What is the benefit, as related to the costs?
8. Does the service reach the population targeted?
9. Is the program being delivered as it was designed?
10. Is the program reaching its goals?
11. Is something other than the program causing the positive results?
12. How much does it cost and how much does it benefit the recipients?
13. Is this program the most efficient alternative?

Although this model is called program evaluation, it actually provides an outline that is similar to Gilbert, Specht, and Terrell's as a framework

171

for policy analysis. It asks the questions of who, what, and how and deals with financing arrangements. It also deals with cost-benefit issues and unintended consequences, when it asks if the results might not be the product of other forces. The question is an important one because sometimes social problems are resolved even if no programs are developed to assist them. It has been suggested, for example, that the Great Depression of the 1930s was resolved by the economic growth resulting from World War II, not from the New Deal social programs set in place by the federal government.

There are many other examples and a whole school of thought that suggests that the best approaches to solving human problems are to leave those problems and their victims alone while concentrating, instead, on economic improvement because that is the ultimate, lasting solution to human need of all kinds. Such points of view, which have varying degrees of support at different times, must be considered in any realistic policy analysis.

The Donald Chambers Model

Donald Chambers, a professor at the University of Kansas, has developed a social policy analysis scheme that he hopes will preserve "the sanity and dedication of social practitioners who, on behalf of clients, must daily interpret, enforce, advocate, circumvent, or challenge those policies and programs" (1992, 1). He includes the elements for analysis and also the sub-elements that make them up. He provides the alternatives, values, and theories, axes suggested by Gilbert and Specht (1992) as part of his overall outline. The outline was summarized by Deborah Rice (1992), who has used the book to teach undergraduate social work students, as follows:

1. What is the social problem the policy is directed toward resolving? How is the problem defined?
   What are the causes to which the problem is attributed and its most serious consequences?
   What is the ideology that makes the events of concern come to be defined as a problem?
   Who suffers and who actually benefits from the existence of the problem?
2. What are the goals and objectives of the policy?
   —manifest versus latent, abstract versus concrete

—evaluate in terms of clarity, measurability, manipulability, and concern with ends, not means

3. What forms of benefits or services are provided?

—material goods/commodities, expert services, cash, positive discrimination, credits/vouchers, market or wholesale subsidies, power of decisions, and loan guarantees

—evaluate in terms of cost effectiveness, target efficiency, stigmatization potential, and consumer sovereignty

4. What are the entitlement rules?

—prior contribution, means tests, professional discretion, administrative discretion, judicial rule, administrative decision, demonstrating attachment to the work force, and private contract provisions

—evaluate in terms of potential for alienation or stigmatization, potential for off-targeting, potential for raising overwhelming cost or over- or under-utilization, potential for creation of work disincentives, potential for creation or procreational incentives, marital instability, and/or generational dependency

5. What is the administrative/service delivery system that is being utilized?

—centralization/federation, case management, use of indigenous workers, constructing racially oriented agencies, referral agencies, administrative review/appeal procedures, due process rights, and client/citizen empowerment

—evaluate in terms of integration/continuity, accessibility, ability to relate to ethnic and racial diversity, and accountability

6. What are the financing methods?

—prepayments and the insurance principle, publicly regulated private enterprise contracts, voluntary contributions, general revenue appropriations and charges for services

—evaluate in terms of ability to generate year-to-year continuity; to provide security for future benefit payments, to protect against inflation; to protect against recession and depression; to protect against demographic change, control income transfers, hidden rewards for those contributing financing, and allocation of cash flow and other side-effect profits

7. What are the interactions between these characteristics and between this policy and program and others?

—coentitlement, disentitlement, contrary effects, and unintended duplication of benefits or services

—evaluate in terms of any undesirable interactions that may work against any of these criteria

(Summarized from Chambers in Rice 1992, chap. 4)

Chambers's model has the virtue of including almost everything imaginable as benchmarks for policy analysis. He has adapted his outline to cover many of the current social policies in the United States. For example, some of the work experience and training programs developed by the federal government and implemented by the states provide special incentives for employers. One finds a place to discuss that phenomenon in the Chambers model. Instead of leaving the discussion of financing of provisions open-ended, Chambers lists some of the alternative ways in which financing might occur. For the newcomer to policy analysis and for students the Chambers model is useful because it presumes little prior knowledge and provides a place for the analyst to examine the policy. Of course, experienced policy analysts may find the Chambers outline less useful, because of its detail.

K. McInnis-Dittrich offers another model of policy analysis. She uses the letters of the word analysis as the eight elements in her model. The system she uses is:

Approach—a brief description of the methods used in the current or proposed policy.

Need—what need does the policy attempt to address?

Assessment—what are the program's or policy's strengths and weaknesses?

Logic—does the proposed or current policy logically address the connection between the need and a means of solving the problem?

Your reaction—from your professional experiences does the policy seem effective?

Support—what is the financial support for the program?

Innovation—what provisions have been made for changing the program if necessary?

Social justice—does the program address the important issue of social justice as expressed by society and the social work profession?

(McInnis-Dittrich 1994, 133)

Another approach to analyzing social policy has been developed by D. Iatridis (1994). He analyzes social policy from an international perspective and also discusses some of the capitalist and socialist contrasts in the development and consequences of social policy.

ISSUES ANALYSIS

In addition to models of policy analysis there are books published annually on current social problems and on more comprehensive issues in social policy. There are books on child care, health services, crime and delinquency, race relations, and any number of other topics. These do not provide a general framework but, instead, analyze a specific issue in a detailed manner. One current and well-written example is D. Stoesz and H. J. Karger's *Reconstructing the American Welfare State* (1992). The authors propose a totally new way of organizing and delivering American social services. On specific subjects such works provide detailed and helpful analyses of current issues or problems.

POLICY ANALYSIS MODELS—A SUMMARY

Only a few of the policy analysis models that have been developed and published are included here. There are many others, and more are being created. They are important because it is important for social workers to be able to analyze social policies realistically and effectively. Because social policies are the heart of the practice of the human service professions, understanding what those policies are and developing the capacity to think about and suggest alternatives to them is a requirement for human services professionals.

Any one of the models presented here will help human services professionals develop a sophisticated understanding of a given policy. Mastering one or more of them will help the human services professional achieve an even more sophisticated understanding. Then, when encountering a new policy, program, or problem, the professional will be able to examine it and think through its merits, possibilities, and deficits.

Policy analysis methods are critical to the well-informed professional because policies are the essential building blocks for resolving human needs and solving social problems. Without the capacity to critique policies or proposals for policies objectively and systematically, however, human services professionals may be encouraged to pursue approaches to problems that may not achieve the desired goals, may cost too much, or may conflict with strongly held public values. There are times when complex human problems such as substance abuse are under discussion. Invariably, simplistic policies will be proposed—lock up all of the users, give life sentences to all "pushers," legalize illegal drugs, expand treatment

175

facilities. The sophisticated human services professional is able to evaluate all of these as well as think through alternatives that may be more comprehensive and more effective. The professional who wants to influence policy decision makers must be able to dispassionately convince them of the value of a specific policy. Doing so requires the capacity to analyze and communicate about those policies in persuasive ways.

CONCLUSION

This chapter has presented information on the policy analysis process. It has suggested some of the elements that may be included in policy analysis. The analytical component is only one of the six necessary for a thorough understanding of social policy.

Social policy analysis is a dynamic tool that can be applied and reapplied to any social problem, policy, or provision. As such, it may be the most useful of the skills that one may learn from this book or from the study of social policy.

DISCUSSION QUESTIONS

1. Select a current social problem, policy, or program, and analyze it with one of the models presented in this chapter. Answer all of the questions listed in the model to the extent possible with the information about the item to be analyzed which is available to you. If you want more detailed information on the model, consult the source, which is listed in the references.
2. Some social policy specialists suggest that if one were to learn only one of the components of social policy that it should be policy analysis. Do you agree or disagree? Justify your answer.
3. Discuss the roles that alternatives, values, and theories play in the analysis of social policy. What are some examples of each, relative to a specific problem, policy, or program?
4. I. Weissman (1959) proposed a three-part model for understanding policy. Do you agree or disagree with the assumption that the current models of policy analysis, such as those discussed in this chapter, are really just expanded versions of Weissman's model? Justify your answer.

REFERENCES

Barker, R. L. (1991). *The social work dictionary,* 2d ed. Silver Spring, MD: NASW Press.

Boehm, W. (1959). *Objectives of the social work curriculum of the future.* New York: Council on Social Work Education.

Burch, H. A. (1991). *The why's of social policy: Perspectives on policy preferences.* New York: Praeger.

Chambers, D. (1992). *Social policy and social programs: A method for the practical public policy analyst,* 2d ed. New York: Macmillan.

The Chronicle of Higher Education. (1993, 10 Mar.) Marginalia. *39* (27), A4.

Conrad, K. L. (1990). Charitable gambling in North Dakota. In Ginsberg, L., et al. (Eds.). *Encyclopedia of Social Work: 1990 Supplement,* 18th ed., 94–96. Silver Spring, MD: NASW Press.

DiNitto, D. M. (1991). *Social welfare: Politics and public policy,* 3d ed. Englewood Cliffs, NJ: Prentice-Hall.

Dobelstein, A. W. (1990). *Social welfare: Policy and analysis.* Chicago: Nelson-Hall.

Gil, D. (1976). A general framework for social policy analysis. In J. Tropman, M. Dluhy, & W. Vasey (Eds.). *Strategic perspectives on social policy.* Elmsford, NY: Pergamon Press.

Gilbert, N., Specht, H., & Terrell, P. (1992). *Dimensions of social welfare policy,* 3d ed. Englewood Cliffs, NJ: Prentice-Hall.

Ginsberg, L. (1990). Introduction. In Minahan, A., et al. (Eds.). *Encyclopedia of Social Work: 1990 Supplement,* 18th ed., 1–11. Silver Spring, MD: NASW Press.

Green, C. (1993, 9 Feb.) Increase in benefits to stay put. *Columbia State* (SC), 1A.

Hamilton, G. (1940). *Theory and practice of social work.* New York: Columbia University Press.

Heffernan, W. J. (1992). *Social welfare policy: A research and action strategy.* New York: Longman.

Hirsch, E. D., Jr., Kett, J. F., & Trefil, J. (1988). *The dictionary of cultural literacy: What every American needs to know.* Boston: Houghton-Mifflin.

Iatridis, D. (1994). *Social policy: Institutional context of social development and human services.* Belmont, CA: Wadsworth.

Jansson, B. S. (1990). *Social welfare policy: From theory to practice.* Belmont, CA: Wadsworth.

Lasswell, H. D. (1958). *Politics: Who get what, when, how.* New York: Meridian.

Los Angeles Times. (1993, 7 Feb.) Economic sales pitch under way. *Columbia State* (SC), 3A.

McInnis-Dittrich, K. (1994). *Integrating social welfare policy and social work practice.* Belmont, CA: Wadsworth.

Meyer, C. H. (1987). Direct practice in social work: Overview. In Minahan, A., et al. (Eds.). *Encyclopedia of Social Work,* 18th ed., 409–22. Silver Spring, MD: NASW Press.

Pierce, D. (1984). *Policy for the social work practitioner.* New York: Longman.

Rice, D. (1992). The analytic approach to social welfare policy education. Unpublished paper for Social Work 841, Fall semester 1992, College of Social Work, University of South Carolina.

Rossi, P. H., & Freeman, H. E. (1989). *Evaluation: A systematic approach,* 4th ed. Newbury Park, CA: Sage.

Stoesz, D., & Karger, H. J. Foreword by Midgley, J. O. (1992). *Reconstructing the American welfare state.* Lanham, MD: Rowman & Littlefield.

Tropman, J. E. (1987). Policy analysis: Methods and techniques. In Minahan, A., et al. (Eds.). *Encyclopedia of Social Work,* 18th ed., 268–83. Silver Spring, MD: NASW Press.

Weissman, I. (1959). *Social welfare policy and services in social work education.* New York: Council on Social Work Education.

Chapter 9

PRACTICING SOCIAL POLICY

Thus far this book has focused on the ways in which human services workers can best understand social policy. The five components described here for comprehending social policy—the ways in which it is developed, its impact, and its outcomes in the forms of social provisions or programs—are historical, social problems, public policy, descriptive, and analytical. Yet there is a sixth component that is of growing importance in the human services field. That component is the practice of social policy—the actual involvement in making and implementing social policy.

For many human services workers as well as for those who write and teach about social policy, the discipline is something that one does rather than something that one simply studies. In 1991 N. Wyers wrote about "policy-practice" in social work. He called policy practice a "nebulous concept" (242) but said it was essentially the combining of the practice of social work with social policy.

Although the literature on the human services worker as a practitioner of social policy is relatively new, in fact, for the whole history of modern welfare, human services workers have been policy practitioners. A. J. Kahn (1993) is one of several social policy scholars who argues for the importance of preparing social workers for work in the practice of social policy.

THE TASKS OF SOCIAL POLICY

Practicing social policy includes a number of tasks, the first of which is the development, or simply the writing of, social policies. The preparation of statements of policy which can be turned into rules and regulations and, ultimately, social provisions or programs is the primary job of many human services workers. Creating a policy that can be studied and acted upon by a legislative or executive branch of government is a complex task. The language must be specific, and the rules and regulations must be concrete.

A task that is related to the preparation of policies is the analysis of policy alternatives, which is discussed in chapter 8. Understanding and allowing for the consequences of policies, both intended and unintended ones, calculating the costs of the policies, estimating the numbers of people who will be affected by the policy, and examining other analytical elements are part of the job of the policy writer.

In many cases the policy specialist develops policy statements, or other documents, that are then used by executive branch agents or legislative bodies to create official social policies. For example, if a state government wanted to develop a policy for dealing with the homeless, one of the first steps toward solving it, after the identification of the problem, would be the preparation of some kind of policy statement, or plan. Perhaps the plan would include provisions for housing and feeding homeless people. Perhaps it would provide for cash assistance to the homeless so they could purchase their own food and shelter. Perhaps the policy would even be punitive, demanding imprisonment of those who did not have permanent residences. In any case, revenue sources would have to be identified, and a budget would have to be prepared to deal with the problem of homelessness.

In most cases a policy of that magnitude would be undertaken by a legislative body, such as a state legislature, for passage as a law or statute. In some cases, however, an executive branch agency might be able to promulgate a policy to deal with homelessness as part of its general powers. In still other cases a court may order the executive branch of government to provide assistance to the homeless. The policy for doing so would be prepared by personnel in the executive branch.

PERSONNEL INVOLVED IN POLICY DEVELOPMENT

Although human services workers may often lead the way in developing social policies, they are not the only participants in the process. In many cases, attorneys (especially those with experience in drafting legislation), accountants, and other kinds of professionals collaborate on policy development. It often takes the knowledge and skills of several different disciplines to develop policies that are of major consequence.

There are thousands of human services workers throughout the United States who are engaged full-time in the development of policy. Some work for executive branch agencies. They spend their time preparing policy statements and plans to be proposed to higher-level executive branch officials, such as governors, or to state legislative committees that have requested policy ideas for solving designed specific human problems.

180

Many of the human services workers who deal with such policies are not full-time policy specialists. They may also play roles as administrators of progams. The staff members of an adult social services office in a state department of social services, for example, might be assigned the job of preparing the policy on homelessness described earlier.

Preparing Legislation

As suggested, many executive branch human services workers develop legislative proposals to carry out specific social policies. They often do so at the request of legislative bodies such as committees on human services or social welfare. For example, a member of a legislative body, such as a state representative or senator, might wish to pass a policy into law which would resolve the problem of homelessness in his or her state. That legislator would very likely ask the state department of social services or a comparable organization to prepare a piece of legislation to accomplish that goal. A human services worker with policy responsibilities in that department would likely be assigned the task of drafting the legislation. Lawmakers often have access to human services workers who are employees of legislative bodies to carry out the same kinds of responsibilities.

Drafting a bill that can become a law is a complicated and technical task. Human services workers are generally well acquainted with elements of bill drafting. One of the most important technical tasks is identifying the portions of the existing state code, or laws, which need to be modified to include the new legislation. That might mean creating a new section of the law, or it might simply mean an amendment is needed for an existing law.

In addition, a specific budget note, or fiscal note, usually must accompany the legislation. Preparing such information often requires expert knowledge. Most often attorneys must handle the legal aspects of a new piece of legislation, and accountants or other financial specialists must deal with the fiscal information. The experts in human services often prepare the substantive parts of the legislation; that is, they define the program—the ways in which it will be operated, the ways it will be paid for—and otherwise write the portions of the legislation which describe its administration and implementation. Many human services workers also become experts on the legal and financial aspects of the law, either through their educations or because of long experience in dealing with social programs.

181

In many places in the United States legislatures employ human services workers full-time to work on social policy. Their task is to prepare legislation on social policy issues and to evaluate existing social policies, keep track of social problem indicators and otherwise serve as experts on social poilcy for the legislative body. Social workers, teachers, counselors, and many other human services professionals are full-time employees of legislative bodies who regularly carry out these kinds of responsibilities.

TOOLS FOR POLICY PRACTITIONERS

One of the primary tools of the policy practitioner is the development of factual information about the nature and extent of social problems. In order to be effective in understanding problems and in developing solutions for them, policy planners must conduct research or be aware of and use the research conducted by others on specific social problems and solutions.

Legislative bodies, executive branch officials, and other decision makers in the policy-making process want to know the facts about problems and solutions before they make decisions. Therefore, policy practitioners are regular students of public documents, government statistical reports, and other sources of facts about human beings and issues affecting their lives. A major employer in the practice of social policy is "think tanks" and other policy study groups and institutions. Some of the most prominent are the Brookings Institution, the Institute for Policy Studies, the American Heritage Foundation, the American Enterprise Institute, the Center for Budget and Policy Priorities, and the National Center for Policy Analysis. There are hundreds of these around the nation, many of which receive funds from foundations and most of which are tax-exempt because they are engaged in study rather than in lobbying or politics. These groups are often important sources of information about social policies; executive and legislative branches call upon them for their data and their ideas.

Influencing Legislation

Another significant task in the practice of social policy is influencing legislation, or, as it is often called in the United States, lobbying (which is also discussed in chap. 4). The job of the lobbyist is to work for the pas-

182

sage of legislation that is favorable to the organization that person is representing. Most of the national social welfare organizations have legislative representatives, many of them in Washington, whose job is to influence the U.S. Congress, and others in the states whose role is to influence state legislation. Such familiar organizations as the National Association of Social Workers, the American Public Welfare Association, the Child Welfare League of America, and similar groups have Washington representatives or legislative specialists who are, in fact, lobbyists. J. Figueira-McDonough (1993) points out that several social work scholars have proposed that all social workers be educated in lobbying and has also written about ways in which lobbying itself might be taught in social work curricula. In fact, many social workers and other human services workers are employed as lobbyists for voluntary and governmental organizations.

Some Observations about Lobbying

As discussed in chapter 4, lobbying is a normal, perhaps necessary, part of public policy-making in the United States. For some lobbying has a reputation as a sort of sinister practice involving people who pursue special interests in not quite legitimate ways. Some people believe that lobbyists use bribery and other kinds of inappropriate influences to win their organization's objectives.

Although it is true that lobbying is always about the pursuit of specialized interests, the use of inappropriate lobbying techniques or bribery is unusual. It is not well understood in American life that special interests include a range of concerns and that not all of them are selfish. In fact, all lobbyists pursue their objectives from some sort of idealistic point of view. Most organizations sincerely believe in their purposes and pursue their legislative objectives hoping the result will be beneficial to the people they represent. The National Rifle Association, whose activities many in the social services community would consider in negative terms, believes it is pursuing an important social goal by making it possible for citizens to purchase and own weapons for personal defense, sports, and hunting, with a minimum of governmental interference. The defense industry, too, believes in its efforts to protect the American people from foreign enemies. The tobacco industry believes that its lobbying preserves the rights of tobacco users as well as the economic well-being of tobacco farmers and tobacco product manufacturers. So, all lobbyists, including those who pursue social welfare goals, view themselves as pursuing worthy goals on behalf of citizens.

Most Americans are members of organizations that lobby, although they may not know it. Churches, the American Automobile Association, conservation groups, professional and trade associations, and most other large national organizations lobby. Being able to join organizations and help them finance their lobbying is a basic right, having to do with free speech and freedom of association.

Methods of Lobbying. The methods and techniques used by lobbyists are not as self-serving or pecuniary as is often supposed. Many times the primary task of the lobbyist is to draft or analyze legislation so that lawmakers can best introduce it or to understand legislation that has been proposed by others. Much of the legislation that is ultimately passed in the United States, both in Congress and state legislatures, is originally drafted by lobbyists. The lobbyists for the American Association of Retired Persons (AARP), for example, propose specific changes in Social Security which would benefit older adults. That legislation is received by members of Congress who are interested in Social Security legislation and who, in turn, incorporate the AARP ideas into bills that are introduced into Congress. Often the member of Congress or a committee of Congress will modify the bill that has been drafted by the lobbyist, but, in some cases, the bill is introduced, acted upon, and becomes law without many changes at all.

In other circumstances, lobbyists testify before legislative committees on the impact of a given policy proposal or law. Often, because of his or her deep involvement in the specific area, the lobbyist has more detailed information on the consequences of a piece of legisalation than do the members of Congress or others who must act on the legislation.

In other cases lobbyists mobilize support for or opposition to a piece of legislation which involves their organization's interests. They do so by asking their members to telephone, telegraph, and write to their representatives in Congress or the state legislatures opposing legislation that could be detrimental to their organization's interests or in support of legislation that pursues those interests.

Lobbyists use other methods, including those that win support from legislators, such as inviting legislators for meals and receptions, helping to obtain campaign support for legislators who are facing reelection campaigns, and inviting legislators to speak at organizational conferences, which may help them gain votes and which may also earn them honoraria. Many groups also sponsor receptions and banquets to which legislators are invited. These are methods commonly used by lobbyists, including those who represent social welfare organizations.

184

Special interest groups for which lobbyists work are not always private organizations, and not all lobbyists are representatives of nonprofit associations of people with legislative concerns. Although they are not usually called lobbyists, the executive branch agencies also have employees who carry out extensive lobbying activities. Every department of government at the federal or state level has an interest in the activities of legislatures. In fact, their interests may be greater in some cases than those of any voluntary association or organization. Federal executive branch agencies have official designated legislative liaisons who are, in many ways, lobbyists. Their full-time job is to answer questions from legislative bodies, testify before legislative committees, and pursue the legislative objectives of their agencies. Many state government executive branch agencies have similar personnel with similar responsibilities. The programs, budgets, even the survival of executive branch agencies depend, in large measure, on the ability of the agency to influence its legislative body. Therefore, most agencies actively press for their points of view and their programs.

It is important to point out, parenthetically, that the use of the general term *lobbyist* and the legal definition of a lobbyist may differ. Most legislatures do not define executive branch personnel as lobbyists and do not require them to register as such, which they do require of private organizational lobbyists.

As suggested, most of the lobbying in the United States is carried on by voluntary associations representing specific interests or activities. There are public policies dealing with how extensive lobbying activities may be. There are also public policies dealing with the tax status of organizations that lobby. Whether or not an organization lobbies has some impact on its tax-exempt status. For example, a tax-exempt voluntary national human services organization is limited in the amount of its resources it may use for lobbying purposes.

Many organizations do not lobby directly but, instead, organize specialized subsidiary groups that have lobbying as a primary purpose. In the same way organizations that lobby often cannot make contributions to political candidates. Corporations cannot make political contributions either. Therefore, there are many political action committees (PACs) which have the solicitation and distribution of political contributions as their primary purpose. Such organizations collect money from the members of the specialized group. They have boards of directors which determine how the contributions they collect are distributed to candidates. PACs are important in influencing elections and, in fact, in the legislative process. Legislative and executive branch members who receive funds from PACs are assumed to be more likely than others to support legislation favored by the organizations or industries that have supported them financially.

Lobbying the Executive Branch. Not all lobbying is carried on in the legislative branch of government. In fact, some observers think that the most effective kind of lobbying takes place within the executive branch, instead. The executive branch has great influence over the legislation that is ultimately passed by legislative bodies, their primary influence being in the kinds of legislation they propose to legislative bodies. Much of the legislation that is ultimately passed by these bodies originates in the executive branch. Therefore, the priorities and specific policies of the executive branch greatly influence what is ultimately passed. Lobbyists who want to have an impact on legislation often start by attempting to influence the executive branch proposals that are made to legislatures. The weight of the opinion of the executive branch agency has great significance for any legislative body, as does the work of the executive branch lobbyists, who are often consulted by the legislative bodies and their committees.

Persuading the executive branch agency to propose or support the legislative priorities of an interest group is often the most useful expenditure of that group's time and resources. If the group can persuade the commissioner or director or any chief executive officer, or any others with the ability to influence the organization's policy, to support the organization's priorities, they may accomplish what they want much more readily than if they tried to influence the legislature directly. Such lobbying activities are not always difficult; in many cases the interest group's and the executive branch agency's priorities coincide. It is also not unusual for a lobbying group to prepare legislation for an executive branch agency to modify and introduce as its own contribution to solving a social problem.

IMPLEMENTING LEGISLATION

Often the most important element of the practice of social policy is the implementation of policies by executive branch agencies. Again, there are thousands of human services workers around the country whose job it is to translate legislation into operational rules and regulations for the executive branch agencies that employ them.

Legislation is often not extensively detailed or concrete and, therefore, cannot easily be used to implement a policy or carry out a program. The legislation may be broad in scope and only suggestive of specific activities in which executive agencies will engage, though this is not always true. Some legislation is highly specific and detailed and, therefore, is easier to implement.

For the most part, legislation, to be implemented, needs at least some fine-tuning and often much hard work, and this requires policy specialists in executive branch agencies. Assume, for example, that a legislative body has passed a statute that deals with the requirement to provide services such as food and shelter to the homeless. How will the program be operated? If voluntary organizations are to receive contracts from the government to provide such services, what organizations are eligible? How will they be paid? Who will handle their payments? What kinds of statistics will they keep, and what forms will they use for keeping these statistics? What health and safety standards will shelters be required to maintain if they are to receive public funds for caring for the homeless? These are only some of the issues that would arise out of the passage of such legislation.

As B. S. Jansson (1990, 380) says, "Enacted policies are merely paper directives, that is, abstract guidelines and objectives that reflect the preferences of the framers of policies, who have often balanced value, political, and analytic considerations when constructing them."

Rules and Regulations

In many cases state legislatures require specific procedures for the development of the rules and regulations that implement the statutes they have passed. In the federal government that is also true, and there is a special procedure used by the federal government to develop such rules and regulations.

The Federal Register. For federal social policies executive agencies must print their rules and regulations in the *Federal Register,* a document published by the government daily which includes the rules and regulations for all federal government agencies on all subjects. When the executive branch agency makes the rules and regulations that implement legislation and when it changes its own policies, it is required to publish those changes as proposed modifications in the *Federal Register.* Usually, the rules or regulations are outlined in detail. A comment period is also

187

announced. Those who want to comment on the proposed rules or regulations are invited to make written remarks to a specific address within a specified time frame, usually a matter of several months. The agency then collects and analyzes these remarks. The analyses are published later in the *Federal Register,* along with an announcement that the agency has made some final rules or regulations on the policy. These are typically the rules and regulations that were first announced, with, in some cases, modifications based upon the comments that have been received.

All sorts of groups and individuals make comments on rules and regulations. Industries, interest groups, corporations, state government officials, and any other group or individual with an interest in the proposed rules can do so. The agency analyzes the comments and reports on the number and kinds of them it has received (again, this is in a later edition of the *Federal Register,* when the rules are made final).

Human services workers who are practitioners of social policy in the federal government play a large role in proposing rules and receiving comments on them following their publication in the *Federal Register.* Their first task is to translate effectively legislation into operational rules and regulations that conform to the intentions of Congress. Doing so often requires practitioners to study the *Congressional Record,* a daily journal of everything that is said in Congress, to examine minutes of committee meetings and committee hearings, and to pay particular attention to the debate on the bill and the points of view of those who support the legislation. Again, the rules and regulations that are developed must follow the intentions of Congress. If they do not, they can lose a court challenge in which the courts might decide that the executive branch agency's rules and regulations do not fulfill Congress's objectives in passing the legislation. Being accurate about the intentions of Congress requires research into the congressional debates, committee hearings, and speeches made by those who proposed and support the legislation.

Of course, effective practitioners of social policy must also write rules and regulations that reflect the wishes of their bosses—the governor or president, secretary, or commissioner. There is usually some latitude in the way legislation is written which allows it to be interpreted in ways that will satisfy executive branch officials as well as support the intentions of the legislative body.

As suggested, many state governments have procedures for executive rule making and legislative implementation that are similar to those used by the federal government. Some states publish comprehensive documents like the *Federal Register;* others require some kind of publication of rules and regulations before they are made final; others require public hearings on rules and regulations. Yet others use a special kind of legislative committee to monitor and approve or disapprove of executive branch rules and regulations. Such committees receive the rules and examine them before they become final. After the rules and regulations are approved by the legislative committee they become law for the state.

It is perhaps obvious that much of the lobbying that takes place occurs at the time rules and regulations are made. Lobbying to have legislation passed is one matter. Making sure that the executive branch implements the law in the way one's organization wants it to be implemented is yet another. The latter is equally as important, in many cases, as the former. Some would suggest that it is not so much a matter of what the law says as what the implementing agency says the law says.

In addition to writing the rules and regulations and to carrying them through the necessary processes, it is also a function of human services professionals who are practicing policy to conduct public hearings and comment periods, to tabulate, and analyze comments, and to write about the results of those comments for later publication.

To sum up, the tasks of the social policy practitioner include writing proposed policies, lobbying for the passage of those policies by legislative bodies or the implementation of them by executive branch agencies, preparing rules and regulations to implement social policies, conducting public comment periods, including public hearings, and writing about the results of those public comment periods. In addition, the policy practitioner who works for an association, organization, or state government may also lead constituents in their comments on proposed policies. Thus, policy practitioners function at every level of the policy process.

POLICY INTERPRETATION

There is another role in which policy practitioners function, and that is as interpreters of policies that already exist. Most large human services organizations, especially those that are connected with government, employ full-time units that answer policy questions for workers in the field. In programs such as AFDC and Medicaid, for example, which have very complicated rules that may not clearly cover every possible situation, policy experts are available to answer questions from workers about the applicability of certain policies. How much of the incomes of all the family members has to be considered as part of the resources available to a family applying for AFDC? How does one determine the actual value of a collection of guns, which might be considered a resource in calculating AFDC eligibility? What are the employment requirements for a mother with a child who is chronically ill and whose family is receiving AFDC? Questions such as these are asked and answered every day in public social services agencies and in large voluntary agencies as well. Many human services professionals practice their professions as policy experts.

Policy units in large public agencies also analyze and evaluate legislation as it develops. Typically, during a legislative session, or even between sessions, when bills are being proposed for introduction, the policy unit of the department analyzes how much the bill will cost, what impact it will have on other services, and how it might be implemented by the agency. It also makes suggestions about the reactions of the agency to the legislation, sometimes going so far as to "oppose" or "support" bills, an action that does not fit most agencies, in which the chief executive officer is appointed by the governor. By definition, the agency supports the governor's program, whatever that program happens to be, even if the staff or the leadership of the agency might generally support or oppose the legislation. In other situations, in which the agency is controlled by a commission and is not directly under gubernatorial authority, the agency may be freer to take specific policy positions on legislation.

CONCLUSION

This chapter has shown the ways in which social policy is more than a single subject of study. It is a whole field of human services practice—what some human services workers do as their primary employment.

Policy practice will likely continue to expand as a field because of the growing importance of policy in the creation and delivery of human services. The practice roles for human services workers in policy range from simple tasks of explaining to coworkers what policy means to drafting new policies. It is likely that in the future increasing portions of those employed in the areas of social services and human services will be policy practitioners.

DISCUSSION QUESTIONS

1. Visit a library and look at a proposed human services policy in a current issue of the *Federal Register*. Note some of the proposed regulations and summarize them in a three-page essay.

2. Describe three roles of the policy practitioner. Are these roles totally different than or do they seem to have some connection with the historic roles of social workers described in chapter 4?

3. What are some of the roles that policy practice plays in the public policy component of social policy? Review chapter 2 in answering this question.

4. Visit a government agency—either state or federal—and look at some of its policy manuals. Describe them in a two- or three-page essay. What are their characteristics? Do they show how they were developed? Would you make any observations about their clarity?

REFERENCES

Figueira-McDonough, J. (1993, Mar.) Policy-practice: The neglected side of social work intervention. *Social Work 38* (2), 179–88.

Kahn, A. J. (1993). *Issues in American social policy: The substantive and research challenges for social work doctoral education.* Paper presented at Group for the Advance of Doctoral Education Annual Conference, St. Louis, Missouri, October 15, 1993.

Jansson, B. S. (1990). *Social welfare policy: From theory to practice.* Belmont, CA: Wadsworth.

Wyers, N. (1991, Fall). Policy-practice in social work: Models and issues. *Journal of Social Work Education 27* (3), 241–50.

Tropman, J. E. (1987). Policy analysis: Methods and techniques. In Minahan, A., et al. (Eds.). (1987). *Encyclopedia of social work,* 18th ed., 268–83. Silver Spring, MD: NASW Press.

Appendix

AN ANNOTATED BIBLIOGRAPHY OF SOCIAL POLICY JOURNALS IN HUMAN SERVICES PROFESSIONS

Compiled by David P. Fauri and Barbara J. Ettner

MULTIDISCIPLINARY JOURNALS OF SOCIAL POLICY

American Behavioral Scientist (ABS)

Sage Publications
2455 Teller Road
Newbury Park, CA 91320

A multidisciplinary journal of social science, *ABS* is published six times annually and contains scholarly articles on broad areas of concern to social science professionals. Selected issues are devoted to topics of interest to social workers and to policy analysts and researchers interested in social work theory, program planning, and practice.

Daedalus

Norton's Woods
136 Irving Street
Cambridge, MA 02138

Published quarterly as the proceedings of the American Academy of Arts and Sciences, each issue focuses on a single topic with essays from various disciplines on a common theme. Some issues are devoted to health, family, mental health, or social policy topics, which are examined from different perspectives.

Evaluation and Program Planning

Pergamon Press
395 Saw Mill River Road
Elmsford, NY 10523

Each journal issue contains articles of general interest and on special topics and book reviews dealing with broad social policy concerns. This is a highly policy practice-oriented journal that provides added substance to policy analysis in the social arena.

Evaluation Review

Sage Publications
2111 West Hillcrest Drive
Newbury Park, CA 91320

This journal of applied social research, which is directed toward researchers, planners, and policymakers, reports the findings of evaluation studies in such fields as child development, health, education, income security, manpower, mental health, and criminal justice. There is an emphasis on the application of evaluation results to policy and planning.

Journal of the American Institute of Planners

1776 Massachusetts Avenue, NW
Washington, DC 20036

Published quarterly by the American Institute of Planners. Encourages articles that represent significant contributions to knowledge about planning or urbanism. Included are articles on social policy and planning. Useful for information on urban problems such as housing policies.

Journal of Social Issues

Plenum Publishing Corporation
233 Spring Street
New York, NY 10013

This is the journal of the Society for the Psychological Study of Social Issues of the American Psychological Association. Its primary audiences are psychologists and social scientists who are concerned about the impact of important social issues. It seeks to publish scientific findings regarding theory and practice about human problems of individuals, communities, groups, and nations. Quarterly issues often focus on a particular problem, such as child care policy research, in varied contexts.

Journal of Social Policy

Pitt Building
Trumptington Street
Cambridge CB21RP
England
or
40 West 20th Street
New York, NY 10011-4211

This international journal of the Social Administration Association is published quarterly. Included are scholarly papers that analyze any aspect of social policy and administration. The policy-oriented articles discuss social problems in England and the rest of the world. Each issue includes a section of twelve to twenty book reviews on social policy.

Journal of Social Service Research

Haworth Press
10 Alice Street
Binghamton, NY 13904-1580

This quarterly publication contains articles on clinical research in the behavioral and social sciences and empirical policy studies, particularly from the international social policy perspective. The articles in the *Journal of Social Service Research* are characterized by careful methodological design and rigorous data analysis.

Policy Review

214 Massachusetts Avenue, NE
Washington, DC 20002

This is a quarterly publication of the Heritage Foundation. Articles in each issue cover a wide range of social policy topics. The authors have diverse viewpoints that do not necessarily reflect the conservative philosophies of the Heritage Foundation. A major goal of the journal is to expand discussion and debate on contemporary social policy issues.

Policy Sciences

Institute of Policy Sciences and Public Affairs
Duke University
4875 Duke Station
Durham, NC 27706

This international journal devoted to the improvement of policy-making focuses on an integrated, interdisciplinary, analytical approach to policy, with contributors from many disciplines. Emphasis is on the process of policy development and analysis.

Policy Studies Journal

Department of Public Administration
University of Kansas
Lawrence, KS 66045

This is a quarterly publication of the Policy Studies Organization, the Institute for Public Policy and Business Research, the University of Kansas, and the Maxwell School of Citizenship and Public Affairs, Syracuse University. Contributors come from the fields of economics, public administration, social welfare, and other areas. A wide range of public policy topics are included, and articles demonstrate application of political and social sciences to important public policy problems. Emphasis is on formal policy design and analysis.

Policy Studies Review

University of Illinois
361 Lincoln Hall
702 South Wright Street
Urbana, IL 61801

This is a journal of the Policy Studies Organization and the Morrison Institute for Public Policy, Arizona State University. The journal is devoted to the substance (the nature of public policy, its causes and effects) and procedures (methods of arriving at societal decisions that maximize benefits, reduce costs) of policy studies. Articles on social policy issues such as health, education, welfare, and unemployment are included.

Prevention in Human Services

Haworth Press
10 Alice Street
Binghamton, NY 13904

The editors of *Prevention in Human Services,* a biannual publication, are committed to producing a multidisciplinary journal with articles and special issues on aspects of prevention programming for various populations (elderly, children, mentally ill, etc.). This journal overlaps with other specialized areas such as mental health, health, families, and gerontology, and it is the successor to *Community Mental Health Review.* It stresses the preventative aspects of policies and programs in various disciplines.

Public Administration Review

1120 G Street, NW
Washington, DC 20005

This journal is published by the American Society for Public Administration. It is dedicated to improved management in public service. The articles are addressed to government administrators, teachers, researchers, consultants, students, and civic leaders. Some are related to management issues, but many articles address public policy issues. The topics tend to be general, as the contributors are encouraged to communicate with readers who have varied interests and specializations.

195

Public Interest

National Affairs
10 East 53d Street
New York, NY 10022

In an effort to seek solutions to social problems of our time, this journal publishes articles on a wide variety of social issues. Contributors are from various disciplines such as political science, law, sociology, and health. Social policy issues such as poverty, aging, education, and crime are included.

Social Forces

University of North Carolina Press
Box 2288
Chapel Hill, NC 27514

An international journal of social research associated with the Southern Sociological Society, the journal publishes research on social problems. The contributors are primarily sociologists who present research studies on broad social issues with policy implications.

Social Policy

33 West 42d Street
New York, NY 10036

This journal, which advocates fundamental social change, publishes articles on issues in the human service areas of health, education, welfare, and community development. Emphasis is given to major institutional change and issues involving equality and discrimination.

Social Thought

Catholic Charities USA
1319 F Street, NW
Washington, DC 20004

Publication of *Social Thought* is cosponsored by the School of Social Service of the Catholic University of America and Catholic Charities USA. It offers a multidisciplined perspective on issues and problems in social welfare and social work practice, with particular emphasis on the development of a society in which the principles of social justice and charity are incorporated. Included are articles that integrate social work theory, policy, and practice with ethical, philosophical, and theological principles.

196

JOURNALS OF POLICY ANALYSIS AND POLITICS

Evaluation and Program Planning

Pergamon Press
395 Saw Mill River Road
Elmsford, NY 10523

The primary goals of this journal are to improve evaluation and planning practice and to add to the knowledge base of this profession. The journal contains articles concerning planning efforts in organizational, public health, mental health, social service, corrections, education, and substance abuse settings. Fiscal, legal, and ethical perspectives are presented on various policy problems.

Journal of Policy Analysis and Management (*JPAM*)

Graduate School of Public Policy
University of California at Berkeley
2607 Hearst Avenue
Berkeley, CA 94720

JPAM's major purpose is to promote communication regarding social policy issues among public policy analysts and public administrators. Areas of interest and journal topics are diverse, and the editors strive to include articles that would be of interest to a diverse group of professionals, academics, and students in the policy sciences and management sciences.

Journal of Policy Modeling

Elsevier Science Publishing Company
655 Avenue of the Americas
New York, NY 10010

The *Journal of Policy Modeling* is published five times each year by the Society for Policy Modeling. Its major goal is to provide a forum for debate concerning international policy issues. The fundamental theoretical framework of the journal is that methodological understanding and development of policy modeling techniques will lead to a better understanding of socioeconomic environments. Understanding and sharing ideas are seen by the editors as being necessary for solving social problems, and the subject matter reflects this view.

Law and Policy Quarterly

Baldy Center for Law and Social Policy
511 O'Brian Hall
Buffalo, NY 14260

This journal publishes research papers that analyze the role of legislative process in public policy. Theoretical and empirical works are presented and topics include

197

social welfare, criminal justice, economic analysis, and government regulation. Particular attention is given to the relevance of legal issues in the policy process and use of appropriate methodology to address issues.

Policy and Politics

School for Advanced Urban Studies
Rodney Lodge
Grange Road
Bristol, BS84EA
England

Policy and Politics is a quarterly journal that provides an overview of contemporary policy issues in Europe and the United Kingdom. *Policy and Politics* presents broadly ranging articles on social, housing, education, health, transportation, and environmental policies. Particular themes of interest to the journal editors are theories, implementation, and effectiveness.

Public Productivity and Management Review

Tennessee State University
Box 231
Nashville, TN 37209-1561

This journal is devoted to publishing articles on administrative, technical, legal, economic, and social factors that influence productivity in public and private sectors. Its publication is cosponsored by the Section on Management Science and Policy Analysis of the American Society for Public Administration and the Center for Public Productivity. The underlying theme of the journal is that improved productivity enhances policy-making and policy-implementing processes.

SOCIAL WORK/SOCIAL WELFARE JOURNALS

AFFILIA Journal of Women and Social Work

Sage Publications
2455 Teller Road
Newbury Park, CA 91320

This is a quarterly journal publishing diverse forms of writing related to women and social welfare. Writing styles range from poetic to analytical, and topics are equally far-reaching along a broad social issues continuum.

198

Administration in Social Work

Haworth Press
10 Alice Street
Binghamton, NY 13904

This quarterly journal of human services management is written for executives and middle managers in social service-providing organizations. The journal focuses on theory, research, and practice, with special attention to the relationship between social administration and social policy planning. Included are articles that show administration as the link between social policy planning and social service delivery. Special issues address specific policy and practice topics.

Journal of Social Work Education

1600 Duke Street
Alexandria, VA 22314

Published three times a year by the Council on Social Work Education, the journal is concerned with education in the field of social work knowledge and social welfare. It serves as a forum for creative exchange on trends, developments, innovations, and problems relevant to social work professional education at the undergraduate, master's, and doctoral levels. The journal includes articles related to the teaching of social policy and policy practice, with emphasis on the educational response to social policy issues and social policy as part of the social work curriculum.

Journal of Sociology and Social Welfare (JSSW)

School of Social Work
Western Michigan University
Kalamazoo, MI 49008

JSSW is a journal devoted to publishing articles that bridge the gap between theory and practice in social work. The articles included in the journal deal with diverse areas including social welfare institutions, policies, and problems.

Public Welfare

1125 15th Street, NW
Washington, DC 20005

Published quarterly by the American Public Welfare Association, this journal covers every aspect of the public welfare and related fields, with articles directed toward welfare practitioners. Included are reports of significant work in the field, national policy issues, and social legislation.

Social Service Review

969 East 60th Street
Chicago, IL 60637

Edited by the faculty of the School of Social Service Administration of the University of Chicago, this quarterly journal is written for social workers and those in other disciplines concerned with social welfare issues. Included are research-based articles on social welfare research, practice, policy, and history.

Social Work

750 First Street, NE
Washington, DC 20002

This official publication of the National Association of Social Workers is published six times each year. The purpose is to improve practice and extend knowledge in social work and social welfare. Articles on practice, research, social problems, and the social work profession are included. While only a few articles present true policy issues and there is little on policy methodology, policy issues presented are directly related to social work and are of particular interest to the social work professional.

JOURNALS ADDRESSING SPECIALIZED AREAS OF INTEREST

Child Abuse

Child Abuse and Neglect

Pergamon Press
660 White Plains Road
Tarrytown, NY 10591-5154

The journal concerns itself with all issues relating to child maltreatment on all levels from family to society. The articles are descriptive and evaluative of child welfare topics that have important implications for policy analysts and program planners.

Child Abuse and Neglect: The International Journal

Pergamon Press
395 Saw Mill River Road
Elmsford, NY 10523

The journal provides an international, multidisciplinary forum on diverse topics concerning child abuse and neglect. The editors are especially interested in publishing articles that deal with treatment and prevention and with articles describing factors that facilitate or negate family cohesiveness. Articles are contributed from diverse fields of law, medicine, psychology, nursing, education, anthropology, and social work.

Child and Youth Services

Haworth Press
10 Alice Street
Binghamton, NY 13904-1580

This biannual publication contains articles on diverse topics concerning child welfare and service delivery to children and youths. Relevant policy implications concerning youth issues are treated in depth in selected articles.

Child Welfare

67 Irving Place
New York, NY 10003

The Child Welfare League of America publishes articles that extend knowledge in child-family welfare and related services. Topics include any aspect of administration, supervision, casework, group work, community organization, teaching, research, and issues of social policy that bear on the welfare of children and their families. It is a good source on child welfare policy.

Children and Youth Services Review

61 West 34th Avenue
Eugene, OR 974405

An international multidisciplinary quarterly review of the welfare of young people, this journal is concerned with a multidisciplinary approach to improve the quality and effectiveness of services to children and youth. The emphasis is on the problems of children and youth and the service programs designed to address these problems. Policy issues are confined to those affecting this segment of the population.

Families in Society: The Journal of Contemporary Human Services

Families in Society
11700 West Lake Park Drive
Milwaukee, WI 53224

This publication, a continuation of *Social Casework,* is dedicated to presenting practice and issue-related articles for human service professionals. Subject matter of this journal includes public policy issues as well as family theory, practice, and management. The journal contains sections with viewpoints, essays, questions and answers, letters and comments, feature articles, research, special reports, and book reviews.

Family Relations

Family and Child Studies Center
Miami University
Oxford, OH 45056

This journal of applied family and child studies is directed toward practitioners serving the family field through education, counseling, and community services. There is an emphasis on innovative methods and the application of research and theory to practice and policy.

Journal of Family Issues

Sage Publications
2455 Teller Road
Newbury Park, CA 91320

This quarterly journal concerns theory, research, and practice regarding marriage and family life. Two issues each year are devoted to topics of current interest, and two issues are devoted to articles, commentary, and advocacy pieces concerning family matters in contemporary society. The journal editors seek to serve those who work with and who study families.

Journal of Marriage and the Family

Department of Sociology
University of Nebraska–Lincoln
Lincoln, NE 68588-0367

Published as a quarterly journal of the National Council on Family Relations, it seeks to reach persons working in family research, teaching, and social welfare. There is an emphasis on promoting family welfare and influencing family policy.

Gerontology

Gerontologist

Gerontological Society of America
1275 K Street, NW, Suite 350
Washington, DC 20005-4006

A bimonthly publication of the Gerontological Society of America targeted at practitioners, this journal draws on all areas of gerontology, including articles with a multidisciplinary focus, which pertain to practice, policy, and applied research. Included are editorials that highlight policy implications of articles in the current issue. The journal seeks to enhance the understanding of human aging.

Journal of Applied Gerontology

Sage Publications
2111 West Hillcrest Drive
Newbury Park, CA 91320

This journal contains articles on diverse issues related to aging and the field of gerontology. Long-term care, daily living, senior centers, and mental health services are some of its primary topics. Articles on research, theory, and practice are also published in this journal.

Journal of Gerontology

1275 K Street, NW
Suite 300
Washington, DC 20005-4006

Published bimonthly by the Gerontological Society of America, targeted to present research results, this journal promotes exchange among the various disciplines concerned with the study of aging and fosters the use of gerontological research in forming public policy. The content of the journal is divided into four sections: medical science, psychological sciences, social sciences, and biological sciences.

Health Policy

AIDS and Public Policy Journal

University Publishing Group
107 East Church Street
Frederick, MD 21701

This journal publishes original articles, case studies, and commentaries on legal, health, and social policy issues concerning AIDS. The articles come from diverse disciplines and intellectual perspectives and deal with theory, research, and practice.

AIDS Policy and Law
AIDS Weekly

These two entries are newsletters that contain brief articles concerning AIDS legislation, regulation, litigation, and epidemiology. They are included here because they contain information that may be of assistance to policy analysts in various disciplines, even though the articles do not meet the scholarly standards of other academic journals included in this annotated index.

American Journal of Public Health

1015 15th Street, NW
Washington, DC 20005

Published monthly, this is the official journal of the American Public Health Association, which was organized to protect and promote personal and environmental health by exercising leadership in the development and dissemination of health policy. All disciplines and specialties in public health are represented. Many of the articles are research studies of public health problems which may have policy implications. The journal also makes position statements on health policy issues.

Health and Social Work

750 First Street, NE
Washington, DC 20002

This quarterly journal of the National Association of Social Workers is committed to improving social work practice and extending knowledge in the field of health. Articles deal with all aspects of health which are of professional concern to social workers. Included are articles on practice, policy and planning, legislative issues, and research. This journal is a good resource for information on social work involvement in health policy.

Social Work in Health Care

Haworth Press
10 Alice Street
Binghamton, NY 13904

This quarterly journal of medical and psychiatric social work is directed to social workers in all areas of health care. There is a focus on articles that reflect a commitment to the humanization of health care in practice and policy.

Journal of Health Politics, Policy and Law

Duke University Press
6697 College Station
Durham, NC 27708

Sponsored by Duke University, the journal publishes papers from scholars, policy-makers, and practitioners from any discipline concerned with health. All areas of health policy are addressed, but there is some emphasis on the economic perspective.

204

New England Journal of Medicine

10 Shattuck Street
Boston, MA 02115-6094

Published weekly, this medical journal is addressed primarily to physicians but is a good source for health policy issues closely watched by the media. Included are abstracts of articles which can be cut out and filed under key words.

Social Science and Medicine

Address for North America:
Pergamon Press
Maxwell House, Fairview Park
Elmsford, NY 10523

This international journal, which is published twenty-four times a year, focuses on the interrelationship between medicine and the social sciences. Included are articles on anthropology, economics, education, psychology, social work, and sociology which relate directly to mental and physical health practice and policy.

Mental Health Policy

Administration and Policy in Mental Health

Human Sciences Press
233 Spring Street
New York, NY 10013-1578

Addressed primarily to administrators in mental health and human service programs, the journal publishes articles on organizational relationships, planning, policy, and administration. The journal publishes case reports and original articles on all aspects of these topics.

Community Mental Health Journal

Human Sciences Press
233 Spring Street
New York, NY 10013-1578

This official publication of the National Council of Community Mental Health Centers, Inc. is devoted to the broad fields of community mental health theory, practice, research, and policy. It is a multidisciplinary journal, which includes contributions from psychology, the social sciences, and medicine.

Hospital and Community Psychiatry

1700 18th Street, NW
Washington, DC 20005

Articles are directed toward staff members of facilities and agencies concerned with the care of the mentally disabled. A publication of the American Psychiatric Association, the journal seeks to improve care and treatment, to promote research and professional education in psychiatric and allied fields, and to advance the standards of psychiatric services and facilities.

Justice Policy

Crime and Delinquency

Sage Publications
2111 West Hillcrest Drive
Newbury Park, CA 91320

Published quarterly in cooperation with the National Council on Crime and Delinquency, this policy-oriented journal is directed toward professionals in the criminal justice field. Included are articles that fall into the following criminal justice areas: the social, political, and economic context; the victim and the offender; the criminal justice response; the setting of sanctions; and the implementation of sanctions.

Journal of Criminal Justice

P.O. Box 1563
Ann Arbor, MI 48106

Published bimonthly, this international journal is directed toward practitioners and academicians in the criminal justice area. The articles are related to crime and the criminal justice system, with some emphasis on policy implications.

Journal of Criminal Law and Criminology

357 East Chicago Avenue
Chicago, IL 60611

The journal publishes articles and book reviews of interest to justice policy analysts and practitioners. A legalistic approach is presented which is useful for the study of social policy in this important area.

Juvenile and Family Court Journal

University of Nevada
P.O. Box 8970
Reno, NE 89507

Published quarterly by the National Council of Juvenile and Family Court Judges, this journal includes articles on the juvenile justice system, juvenile and family courts, and the treatment and control of juvenile delinquency.

Futures Policy

Futures

Butterworth-Heinemann Ltd.
Linacre House
Jordan Hill
Oxford OX2 8DP
England

This is a multidisciplinary journal concerned with forecasting and policy-making on the future of the earth and its inhabitants. Issues dealt with in the journal include economics, technology, politics, and the environment. Long-term policy-making issues are of particular interest to these editors.

Future Survey

World Future Society
4916 St. Elmo Avenue
Bethesda, MD 20814-6089

This monthly publication of the World Future Society contains abstracts from books, articles, and reports concerning policy issues and the future. Works in areas of economics, education, scientific technology, health, communities, the environment, and politics are abstracted in this publication. Discussing the impact of world change on policy development and trends is the major focus of *Future Survey.*

Futurist

World Future Society
4916 St. Elmo Avenue
Bethesda, MD 20814-6089

This journal, a publication of the World Future Society, is their organization's communication medium containing articles concerned with future developments on this planet. Society, economics, technology, and politics are discussed from the particular perspective of the future. Implications of change in all these areas are debated and described.

INDEX